Spiritual Path,
Sacred Place

Spiritual Path,

Sacred Place

Myth, Ritual, and Meaning in Architecture

THOMAS BARRIE

SHAMBHALA

Boston & London

1996

SHAMBHALA PUBLICATIONS, INC.
Horticultural Hall
300 Massachusetts Avenue
Boston, Massachusetts 02115

9 8 7 6 5 4 3 2 1
First Edition
Printed in the United States of America
⊗ This edition is printed on acid-free paper that meets
the American National Standards Institute Z39.48 Standard.
Distributed in the United States by Random House, Inc.,
and in Canada by Random House of Canada Ltd

Library of Congress Cataloging-in-Publication Data

Barrie, Thomas.
    Spiritual path, sacred place: myth, ritual, and meaning
in sacred architecture / by Thomas Barrie.
        p.   cm.
    ISBN 1-57062-005-9 (alk. paper)
    1. Church architecture.   I. Title.
NA4600.B37   1996   95-35552
726'.5—dc20   CIP

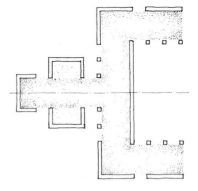

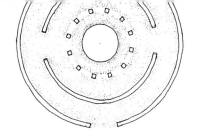

Acknowledgments   ix

CHAPTER *1*
Departure   1

CHAPTER *2*
Symbols, Structures, and Rituals
Symbols and Forms   11
Archetypes, Structures, and Patterns   16
The Hero's Journey   20
Pilgrimage as Spiritual Journey   27

CHAPTER *3*
Elements and Experience
The Path and Place in Architectural Theory   37
Elements and Space   40
Perception and Experience   47

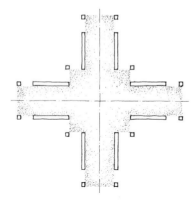

CHAPTER *4*

■ *The Sacred Path and Place*

Place and Meaning	51
Sources and Expressions of the Myth	54
A Place Apart	56
Where the Gods Have Been—the Place of Creation	60
Center of the World, Axis Mundi, Primordial Mound	61
Image of the Cosmos, Celestial City	64
Sacred Geometry	67
Setting for Ritual	73

CHAPTER *5*

■ *Many Paths, Many Places*

The Axial Path	79
The Split Path	103
The Radial Path	111
The Grid Path	116
The Circumambulating Path	118
The Segmented Path	125

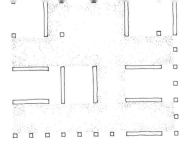

CHAPTER *6*

■
A Journey to Selected Sites

The Temple of Amun-Re　　149
The Sacred Way and Temple of Apollo　　166
Koto-in Zen Temple, Daitoku-ji Monastery　　180
The Cathedral of Sainte-Madeleine　　213
The Brion-Vega Cemetery　　232

CHAPTER *7*

■
Arrival　251

Notes　261
Bibliography　273
Illustration Credits　277
Index　279

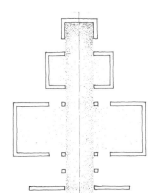

Acknowledgments

This book is in part a celebration of all the men and women throughout the ages who have walked on, meditated upon, and made manifest in architectural form, the spiritual path—and to the gods and religious ideals that were its goal.

Many people have contributed to the genesis and development of this book. Family, friends, colleagues, and my students have all helped me to define and explore the phenomena of the spiritual path and place in sacred architecture. The book is the result of many conversations, acts of kindness, challenges, and influences, and to all I offer my sincere thanks. I would also like to especially acknowledge the people who have contributed in particularly direct or intimate ways.

First of all I want to thank my parents, Carl and Eleanor Barrie, for offering me their open, thoughtful, and inquisitive view of the world. I also recognize the lasting influence of my grandmother Elizabeth Angel Colwell and her belief in the essential value of knowledge.

I am grateful for the friendship and encouragement of Nader Ardalan, who in conversation over lunch one day mentioned that in contemporary American culture there is not a well-traveled path of spiritual inquiry. I never forgot this observation and, consequently, I am thankful to those with whom I have walked along the way. I would like to thank Geoffrey Borwick for our many conversations over the years concerning religion, philosophy, architecture, and "life in general" which have been instrumental in clarifying my thoughts. I would also like to thank Professor Jaan Holt from Virginia Tech who led me to the threshold of the spiritual in architecture, all those with whom I worked at Oasis Studio in Boston, Professor Arnoldo Hax for his friendship and advice, Soren Ekstrom for his inner guidance, and my brother Jeff and Mark Chason, with whom I first experienced the "joys of the road." This book is also in memory of Lisa Woodams, who first showed me the life and meaning of mythology and iconography.

Many have assisted me in my research and in the preparation of the manuscript. This book is based in part on a master of philosophy research degree in architectural history theory from the University of Manchester, England. I would like to thank my advisors, Professor Roger Stonehouse and Mike Maidens, for the generous amount of time they devoted to my research and dissertation, their invaluable advice, and the meaningful conversations the work afforded us. I would also like to thank Professor Masami Kobayashi from Kyoto University for all the assistance he provided during my time in Kyoto, and Hiro Kobayashi for his help as guide and interpreter. Dr. Sheri Wendelken from the Department of Fine Arts at Harvard University provided essentia᷄ ᷄cism of my Japanese research at a time when I neeᵤ the most. Elizabeth Buckley and Shelly Payette McGarry provided resources at critical times during the completion of my dissertation.

I would like to thank Peter Turner of Shambhala Publications for our work together from the early stages of the book to its completion. Norman Crowe of the University of Notre Dame provided a comprehensive review of the final manuscript. Dr. Rochelle Martin from Lawrence Technological University also read the final manuscript and helped me to clarify my points, and Professor Rudolf Arnheim took time from his busy schedule to read portions of the final manuscript and provide expert criticism. My teaching assistant Eric Anderson was most helpful during the latter portions of research and writing. A staff development grant from Lawrence Technological University assisted in the production of the book, and I offer my thanks to Dean Neville Clouten, my colleagues, and my students for their support.

Lastly, I dedicate this book to my son, Ian, and to my wife, Lisa, whose expertise, consistent editing and criticism, patience, and support made it possible.

Spiritual Path,
Sacred Place

CHAPTER 1

▪ *Departure*

This book is about sacred architecture. It is a comparative study of how sacred space is formed and entered, documented by architectural examples from many different religions, locations, and historical settings. Moreover, it intends to establish correspondences between the religious and cultural setting and the architecture, arguing that sacred architecture often symbolizes the spiritual path and its goal. The Way, the spiritual path, the sacred journey—these are all terms that describe the process of spiritual development; but they not only describe a psychological setting, they often suggest a physical one as well. Much has been written about spiritual paths in terms of spiritual practice, but rarely about their physical setting. The book argues that sacred architecture often provided a detailed "symbol posted" way to spiritual transformation. To this end chapter 6 includes an in-depth analysis of the entry sequences and articulated places in selected examples of ancient and modern architecture.

I define sacred architecture as places built to symbolize the meanings and accommodate the rituals of the particular belief system of its time. In other words, it is limited to structures intended for communal religious uses. Often, the terms *sacred architecture* and *sacred geometry* are applied to a wide range of historical examples, regardless of their use and function (though it should be noted that the distinction between the sacred and the secular was not as clearly defined previous to

This shrine had been built by a former governor of the province with stately columns, painted beams and an impressive stone approach, and the morning sun shining directly on the vermillion fencing was almost dazzlingly bright. I was deeply impressed by the fact that the divine power of the gods had penetrated even to the extreme north of our country, and I bowed in humble reverence before the altar.

—**Matsuo Basho,** The Narrow Road to the Deep North

our modern age). I believe this perspective is too open-ended and risks applying personal or modern values to ancient models. Therefore, all of the examples given are architectural sites that directly served religious rituals and, based on available historical and literary information, include descriptions of their use.

It is imperative in any historical study to avoid either condemning or idealizing the past based on our modern perspective. Studies of the past often err in one of these ways, due in part to our modern conceit that "our time" is distinguished and separated from the past. Architectural history has certainly been prone to a patronizing attitude toward its precedents, viewing the architecture from other times or cultures with condescension. For example, the nineteenth-century architectural historian Bannister Fletcher dismissed "monoliths, dolmens, (and) tumuli" as having "little architectural value" and characterized non-Western architecture as "nonhistorical" and "scarcely as interesting from an architect's point of view as those of Europe." This attitude, though not so stridently stated, still can be found implied by historians today. We tend to summarize the past from a "godlike" vantage point and rarely arrive at the mystery and essence of what each example was.

Conversely, it is often equally tempting to idealize the past and its architecture while dismissing the contemporary architectural milieu. Thus we find a contemporary author labeling current architecture "eclectic and uninteresting," and stating that architecture is in a "terminal state of decline."[1] Viewing ancient architecture as "better" than contemporary architecture in terms of spiritual content, or as the pinnacle on a steady decline to the present age, is to resort to generalizations and characterizations just as blind as the modernist obverse view. We need to see architecture plainly and dispassionately as a reflection of the times in which it was built. In truth, all ages are cyclical, with peaks and troughs. It may very well be that our time will be seen as confused and unfocused in terms of spiritual values and meaning in architecture; aspects of our dominant Western culture seem to confirm this. But it is important to strive for perspective and to avoid a romantic view of the past, because it is certainly likely that most eras, like our own, were a mélange of positive and negative forces, of the secular and the sacred, the banal and the evocative. Moreover, though it is difficult to describe our era in spiritual terms, it is not devoid of spiritual values.

Another form of our modern conceit is the perception that contemporary men and women are far removed from our primitive ancestors, though in fact it has not been that many generations since our ancient past. And, as Carl Jung argues,

> The psyche is not only of today. It reaches right back to prehistoric ages. Has man really changed in ten thousand years? Have stags changed their antlers in this short lapse of time? Of course the hairy man of the Ice Ages has become unrecognizable when you try to discover him among the persons whom you meet on Fifth Avenue. But you will be amazed when you have talked to such moderns for a hundred hours about their intimate life. You will then read the mouldy parchments as if they were the most recent thrillers. You will find the secrets of the modern consulting room curiously expressed in abbreviated mediaeval Latin or by intricate Byzantine hand.[2]

Our bodies are virtually the same as our preliterate ancestors, and much of our social behavior originates from our primitive past. Similarly, our psyches are a result of the legacy of the preceding generations, a thread of interconnections woven back into the fabric of time. We are the same species that painted the walls of our subterranean chapels in France and Spain with images of our animal gods, grunted with exertion as we dragged sarsen megaliths across the Salisbury Plain, and knelt in adoration and reverence before the relics of a saint. As Mircea Eliade so eloquently stated regarding our common humanity, "Do what he will, he is an inheritor. He cannot utterly abolish his past, since he is himself the product of his past."[3] In part, our mythological and spiritual life erupts in what Eliade describes as the "crypto-religious behavior" of modern humans. Architecture, as in other areas of our culture, practices ancient rites, though often unconsciously. For example, there are "groundbreaking" ceremonies for new buildings, a ritual that symbolically sacralizes the building site. There are also "topping-off" ceremonies when the building superstructure is completed, often by means of attaching a sprig of pine to the tallest point of the building, thus symbolizing rebirth and regeneration.

Eliade also argues that there is a general "desacralization" of our contemporary culture, a point with which few would argue. This is apparent in the pervasive degradation of symbolic content in our daily lives and the structures within which they are enacted. We are a society of hero worshipers, but rarely do we get to play the hero ourselves. Architecture, as a powerful symbolic environment and the setting of our lives, can provide meaningful models in this regard. The examples given may offer some alternatives to our often myopic and spiritually impoverished time. We need to establish some perspective from our narrow, contemporary belief systems. Perhaps ancient cultures and their architecture, as well as notable modern and contemporary examples, can provide for this. We may never fully understand the distant past and its beliefs, rituals, and architecture. We have in fact lost our "memory," a phenomenon that Eliade describes as the "second fall" of humanity.[4] However, as products of our past, we can still understand some of these forgotten concepts. Sacred architecture provides a threshold to this understanding.

Much of the world's surviving ancient architecture is religious in nature. I believe there are two reasons for this phenomenon: first, prior to our modern age there was little separation between the spiritual and the secular, religion and daily existence being essentially inseparable; second, sacred architecture was typically the result of communal efforts that marshaled the human resources of a particular society and directed them to a common goal. The architecture as a symbol of the continuity of the belief systems of a society needed to symbolize permanence and, consequently, was constructed from more durable materials on a scale exceeding typical residential architecture.[5]

Religion, mythology, and ritual are fundamental elements of human consciousness and society and have long served as a means to explain the world and humans' place within it. The creation of belief systems essentially provided answers to questions of existence and thus offered a degree of security in an otherwise insecure world. Architecture is a fundamental act that has served similar purposes. It is essentially shelter but also provides for symbolic needs. Architecture can express meanings associated with human existence at its deepest, most fundamental level; this is especially evident in the path and place in sacred architecture.

This book argues that meaning in sacred architecture occurs at essentially three levels. First, the sites are an overt representation of aspects of the religion, expressed either pictorially or symbolically, as in the use of stained glass, fresco, and sculpture in Christian churches. For example, at the Scrovegni Chapel in Padua, Giotto used the interior of the building virtually as a canvas to depict scenes from the life of Christ.

Second, meaning is interpreted at a deeper, abstract level within the composition of the form. This interpretation can occur at the unconscious level of the mind. For instance, themes of trial and redemption, found throughout the Bible, also find expression in the architectural symbolism of the medieval cathedral.

Lastly, religious beliefs are also symbolized and enacted by rituals and ceremonies, and there is often a close correspondence between the rituals and architectural form. This correspondence is not just at a pragmatic facilitating level, but also at the deeper symbolic level, because both the ritual and the architecture are concretizations or enactments of the same existential need that has given cause for the particular myth. In other words, the architecture, in addition to directly symbolizing the belief system, in essence acts as a stage that accommodates and facilitates the enactment of the myth through ritual. The myth is embodied in the form of the architecture, the act of the ritual, and their interplay.

The following chapters provide an analysis of entry sequences and articulated places in selected examples of both ancient and modern sacred architecture. The various means of entry in sacred architecture and the sequence of spaces within their structures are documented. The intention is to establish correspondences between the religious and cultural setting and the architecture, and to suggest that sacred architecture typically symbolizes the spiritual path and its goal. The range of examples and the depth of discussion make the case that religious architecture is fundamentally "built myth" that both symbolizes a culture's belief systems and accommodates and facilitates the enactment of shared rituals.

Myth, according to Joseph Campbell, is the "spontaneous eruption of the psyche." Architecture as built myth is similarly linked to the psyche and its need for spiritual orientation, wholeness, and transcendence. Much of what our ancestors built was perhaps not rational or intentional, at least in the context of our current understanding of these terms. Their great monuments and humble dwellings were more "spontaneous eruptions" of their spiritual and physical needs. They need to be understood in this context.

This book in part utilizes a typological and morphological approach applied to a broad range of religious sites. The examples are analyzed according to their space-making and constructional elements, and their spatial characteristics and ordering. Aspects of the path and place are examined fundamentally in terms of their physical and symbolic characteristics, and are placed in the context of their cultural and religious settings. The terms *path* and *place* correspond to definitions formulated by, among others, Kevin Lynch and Christian Norberg-Schulz, whose writings form part of the book's analytical approach. The range of the various forms of path and place are illustrated in chapters 4 and 5.

A premise of the book is that architecture not only can be classified typologically, but is in itself comprised of fundamental elements. These elements are basic constructive and space-forming components such as walls, columns, beams, arches, and domes, as well as types of organization and means of articulation. Functions and use may change with time, as well as aspects of symbolism and meaning, but the architectural form and space, and the elements of which it is formed, remain. They are both timeless and fundamental.

I also briefly outline the phenomenology of how humans react to their physical environment. Though there are many theories about human perception, this book focuses on those aspects that relate to spatial sequence. Consequently, it also addresses the kinesthetic experience of passage through an architectural setting, the texture of surfaces in the context of the physical act of ambulation. The role that our bodies play in meaningfully interacting with our environment should not be underestimated.

The spiritual path and place is a recurring theme in world religions, mythology, and sacred architecture. From the Via Dolorosa in Jerusalem to the labyrinth of King Minos, heroic trials and quests are found throughout religious and mythological traditions. For example, there is the universal practice of pilgrimage. Christianity, Hinduism, Islam, Buddhism, and Taoism all practice pilgrimage as an integral part of their faiths, which I discuss in chapter 2. Moreover, in mythology there are many renditions of heroic and spiritual journeys, from Greek mythology to Japanese folktales. The path and place in the examples given are discussed according to the correspondence between this aspect of sacred architecture and the religion it serves. Architecture, it should be noted, is not the only goal of pilgrimages; there are natural sacred sites such as the Ganges River in India or Mount Tai-shen in China. However, architecture as deliberately created by humans is the most symbolic and is able to express the beliefs of a particular culture. Books on pilgrimage describe journeys *to* the sacred site, but rarely the journey *at* the sacred architecture. The section on pilgrimage in chapter 2 focuses on the latter aspect.

Chapter 2 also discusses paradigms in religions that appear, in numerous interpretations, pan-culturally and transhistorically. Writers such as Eliade and Campbell have described repeating themes in religion and mythology, making the case for what Campbell described as the "universal myth"; one such theme is the spiritual pilgrimage or "hero's journey." Their premise is that world religions, though exhibiting a multitude of interpretations and varieties, share certain fundamentals. Like Campbell and Eliade, I use the terms *myth, mythology, religion,* and *belief systems* interchangeably.

Lastly, the conclusion discusses themes and elements common to all the sites and suggests that there are architectural elements and patterns of a pan-historical and transcultural nature. I argue that these, being analogous to Jungian archetypes and "universal" mythology, provide collective architectural frameworks. The search for common themes in sacred architecture is not one that has been comprehensively explored in architecture. However, certain other disciplines have identified unifying archetypes, and these will be discussed with the intention of establishing parallel approaches. For example, in addition to Joseph Campbell's work on the universal myth, I will examine Jungian psychology in terms of archetypes.

It is my premise that similar to the universal myth, sacred architecture is comprised of paradigmatic elements and patterns. As a direct result of shared belief systems, it evidences particular architectural archetypes. The book documents paradigms present in sacred architecture that are expressed in numerous interpretations through the path and place.

The process necessarily entails isolating the particular parts that comprise the whole. However, even though one can categorize the components, they do not exist in isolation; it is only in combination, in the totality of the composition, that their meaning can be expressed. Otherwise, the elements and patterns may become frozen and stale, losing their meaning through isolation from the whole and their social and cultural context. Also, I do not believe that these identified elements, once separated, can be prescriptively applied in the architectural design process. Only in combination, in a particular time and setting, do they have power. Therefore, the sacred place is described and analyzed in its totality, as a result of its underlying belief system and the combination of its constituent parts.

My approach is holistic and integrative. I am concerned with the interrelationships and organizations of the architecture, as well as the separate elements of which it is comprised. The book is also homologic in spirit and strives to discover common sources for the various manifestations of architectural form and organizations.

This is not a history of sacred architecture, nor of the path and place in architecture. The examples are limited in number but were chosen to reflect a range of religions, regions, and historical periods. Each is analyzed in depth, yet much remains to be researched and documented. As an architect, I have concentrated on the architectural qualities of the sites; the belief systems and symbolism are covered in less detail. A subsequent study might take just one example and cover all of its aspects more thoroughly.

Establishing the historical time frame for the analysis of the sites is difficult. Because this study seeks connections between belief and form, it has been necessary to sift through the strata of belief in each particular culture and attempt to understand the sites in their original social, cultural, and religious settings. However, I also believe that an important part of understanding the sites is the present experience of them. In fact, all of the examples I examine in depth in chapter 6 are to varying degrees reasonably intact, and their use is adequately documented. Consequently, I examine them both in terms of the time of their creation and how I experienced them during my fieldwork.

In describing ancient sacred sites one cannot know with any certainty the meaning they held for their creators and users; one can arrive at reasonable hypotheses perhaps through the combination of understanding surviving writings and records and by comparison between similar examples. Assumptions will need to be made concerning the experience of the architecture at the time that it was built and limitations accepted as to our ability to understand the religion and myths of that time. There is also the danger of interpreting ancient beliefs by translating them into contemporary values and terminology. Moreover, there are obvious risks in a study that not only intends to analyze the fundamental raison d'être of the architecture, but also seeks to establish connections between a number of sites from widely varying time periods. Nevertheless, I make what I believe to be the reasonable assumption that certain aspects of the myths the architecture symbolizes in all ages are still powerful and meaningful. In other words, the myths that we invent to give our lives meaning have aspects that are fundamentally timeless and universal, and therefore so is the architecture of the sacred path and place.

CHAPTER 2

▪ *Symbols, Structures, and Rituals*

Symbols and Forms

When humans build, whether a simple dwelling or a vast sacred complex, we do so for a number of identifiable and meaningful reasons. The raison d'être for a culture's architecture ranges from the practical to the metaphysical, and only together can the multitude of reasons for its construction and use be completely explained. However, this book will focus on the symbolic and ritualistic role of architecture, and the relationship between form and meaning.

I have suggested that sacred architecture is in many examples "built myth." Myths are particularly potent symbolic vehicles because of their ability to weave symbols into a narrative. Similarly, sacred architecture is often a narrative of symbolic images and spaces. In particular, certain architectural settings symbolize the spiritual journey.

The use of symbols is an activity unique to human beings, and ever since our ancestors first learned to communicate, symbols have played an important role in the distinctly human need to define our place in the world. Most commonly, symbols have been used to express what otherwise might have been inexpressible religious and mythological themes. A symbol, according to Jung, possesses specific connotations in addition to its conventional and obvious meaning. It implies something vague, unknown, or hidden from us. . . . Thus a word or an image is symbolic when it implies something more than its obvious and immediate meaning. It has a wider "unconscious" aspect that is never precisely defined or fully explained. Nor can one hope to define or explain it. As the mind explores the symbol, it is led to ideas that lie beyond the grasp of reason. . . . Because there are innumerable things beyond the range of human understanding, we constantly use symbolic terms to represent concepts that we can't define or fully comprehend. This is one reason why all religions employ symbolic language or images.[1]

Because the ordinary range of means of communication is inadequate to explain religious and mythological themes, humans needed to invent symbols for this purpose. Religion and ritual depend significantly on shared symbols for their effect and meaning. Similarly, the experience of sacred architecture is powerful and meaningful because it utilizes a shared symbolic language and facilitates the enactment of shared rituals.

One reason humans need symbols is because of the split between our conscious and unconscious mind, a process that first began with human self-awareness and progressed to what might be described as the profound separation present in our modern age. The widening gap between our inner and outer self, the process of erecting boundaries, is partly a result of our rational, scientific, technological age.[2] Throughout their use symbols have acted as a bridge between the psychic layers of the unconscious and conscious mind.[3] Joseph Henderson calls them "symbols of transcendence" and states that they "provide the means by which the contents of the unconscious can enter the conscious mind."[4] Because humans are (apparently) alone in being able to question their existence, the need for symbols to serve as bridges to "answers" remains undiminished. Additionally, this "bridge" often takes the form of dreams. Through symbolic language the dream joins one's unconscious with the conscious mind, though its message is typically in cipher. Like dreams, a symbolic language, including that found in architecture, needs to be decoded.

As stated in the introduction, we have not radically changed physiologically from our early ancestors. In fact, not many generations separate our time from theirs.[5] Our need for symbols remains, and we are still deeply affected and influenced by them, though our use of symbolic language is perhaps dramatically different from our predecessors. Indeed, the modern age is defined in part by a breakdown in the ability of symbols to communicate deep meanings. Rollo May has stated that our technological age has replaced symbols with "tools and techniques," symbolic language with "facts," and has impoverished our lives accordingly.[6] Symbols, May states, are seen merely as "temporary concessions to our ignorance in matters which we should soon be able to describe in clear, rational terms."[7] And yet, according to Jung, symbols that are consciously perceived simultaneously resonate with the collective unconscious and are therefore timeless and universal. Even though culturally and technologically we are very different from our distant ancestors, our psychic needs are remarkably similar.

Symbols need to be distinguished from signs, a task that is particularly difficult for the modern mind with its penchant for facts. Paul Tillich makes the distinction between symbol and sign by stating that the former possesses "innate power"; it "has a power inherent within it that distinguishes it from the mere sign which is impotent in itself."[8] Symbols serve to lead one to a deeper meaning that cannot be adequately communicated otherwise. They arise from a deep psychic source and characteristically occur spontaneously. The sign is limited to the surface of the conscious mind. Jung states that "a sign is always less than the concept it represents, while a symbol always stands for something more than its obvious and immediate meaning," and that "insofar as a symbol is a living thing, it is the expression of a thing not to be characterized in any other or better way. The symbol is alive only insofar as it is pregnant with meaning."[9]

There are collective and individual symbols, the former typically being religious. Tillich states that a symbol needs to possess "perceptibility," or the attribute of rendering the invisible visible and thus objective. Tillich also discusses the requirement for "acceptability" of a symbol. Its need may arise from the individual, but ultimately it is a "social act." In other words, for a symbol to have meaning, its power and significance must be shared by many.

While symbols arise from the common need to express the inexpressible, like mythology, they take a multitude of forms. For example, the unconscious contents of the psyche often reveal themselves in the narrative of dreams. The contents of dreams typically contain elements that are both specific to the dreamer and relate to shared or archetypal components. In the Epic of Gilgamesh, the hero travels to the cedar forest of Humbaba and dreams of struggle and assistance in a battle with a wild bull. It both portends the future and resonates with the shared theme of heroic trial. "I seized hold of a wild bull in the wilderness," he tells his companion Enkidu. "It bellowed and beat up the dust till the whole sky was dark, my arm was seized and my tongue bitten. I fell back on my knee; then someone refreshed me with water from his water skin." To which his friend replies, "That wild bull which you saw is Shamash the Protector; in our moment of peril he will take our hands. The one who gave you water from his water skin, that is your own god who cares for your good name, your Lugulbanda. United with him, together we will accomplish a work the fame of which will never die."[10] Dreams commonly utilize collective figures because they are illustrating common and repeating human conditions, not just the individual's specific dilemma. For example, dreams that occur during the onset of middle age often feature tutelary figures that symbolize guides to the next stage of life.

Like dreams, myths and folktales arise from the depths of the psyche and translate both personal and shared themes into objective symbolic form. Ancient humans experienced a world saturated with portentous messages and needed to invent mythology to decipher them.[11] Myths from around the world share common themes but also display a remarkable diversity. Through them life's struggles and lessons are symbolically expressed. For example, in Grimm's fairy tales we find the archetypal theme of growing up and leaving childhood in

"The Frog King," where the golden ball that is dropped by a young girl into the depths of a well begins a series of events that result in her leaving her father and home with the transformed prince. "He told her how he had been bewitched by a wicked old witch, and that no one had the power to release him from the well, but the little princess, and to-morrow they would travel back to his kingdom together." I will return to the subject of myth in greater depth later in this chapter when we discuss the myth of the "hero's journey."

Certain natural objects traditionally have served symbolic functions, from sacred rocks to sacred mountains. In the Old Testament story of Jacob, he wakes from his dream to venerate the stone that was his pillow as a sacred object. "So Jacob rose early in the morning, and he took the stone which he had put under his head and set it up for a pillar and poured oil on top of it" (Gen. 28.18). Analogously, the Shinto faith commonly assigns animistic attributes to natural objects including rocks, such as the "married rocks" at Futami-ga-ura, near Ise. Here, two rocks rise up off the Japanese coastline, one larger than the other, and each year they are ritually joined by a symbolic rope as if in marriage. Indeed, the choice of natural objects and phenomena as symbols seems limitless: thunder attributed to Zeus, the sea to Poseidon in Greek mythology; the sun represented by Amaterasu, the moon by Tsukiyumi in the Japanese cosmology. Rivers, valleys, mountains, forests, oceans, animals; each culture offers its own interpretation of the symbolic power of these natural objects. Handmade objects as well have traditionally assumed symbolic content. The standing stones at Carnak in Brittany and at Stonehenge in England were imbued with symbolic content, as have other constructions, from boats to dwellings. Similarly, geometric forms have served symbolic functions; circles, triangles, and squares are assigned different functions pan-culturally. In the East there is the geometry of the mandala and its symbolism of spiritual journey toward psychic wholeness.[12]

The arts, of course, have consistently served as vehicles laden with symbolic content. The history of art and religion, an inseparable relationship since prehistoric times, provides a compendium of the symbols that were powerful and meaningful to our ancestors.[13] Probably the most well-known example of early two-dimensional art is found in the cave paintings in Spain and France which date from the last Ice Age. Here scenes of hunting symbolize, in part, themes of sacrifice and fertility, something that is found in many hunting cultures throughout the world. Indeed, animal symbolism is a convention that is found not only in traditional hunting societies, but in religions such as Christianity which depicts Saint Luke as an ox, Saint Mark as a lion, and Saint John as an eagle. Christianity, throughout its long and rich history, has utilized two- and three-dimensional art to depict symbolic themes. Around the world, humans have painted and carved, striving to represent and make objective the divine. Paintings and sculpture that depict the Buddha figure in its many incarnations, relief panels from Assyrian palaces, Minoan frescoes at Knossos, the sculptural frieze of the Parthenon, the tympana of Romanesque churches—all utilize artistic media to communicate symbolic themes.

It is in architecture, however, that we find the most potent and meaningful use of symbolism, because here the symbol is not only representational, but spatial and temporal as well. Architecture utilizes means of expression common with art; there are two-dimensional elements that appear on the surfaces of walls, as in Egyptian examples, as well as three-dimensional sculpture epitomized by Hindu Temples or the west front of Christian cathedrals. The totality of the architectural experience, however, is a powerful synthesis of the various media used to communicate symbolic themes. In essence, it is the symbol, transformed into myth and represented by architectural plan, geometry, surface, form, and space. Moreover, it is not a static experience, such as the viewing of art, nor a passive one such as listening to the retelling of a folktale, but a dynamic experience in which the participant, moving through the architecture, apprehends its messages both spatially and temporally. It is the inexpressible expressed three-dimensionally and experienced totally.

Archetypes, Structures, and Patterns

Carl Jung's "archetypes of the collective unconscious," Claude Lévi-Strauss's "structural anthropology," Joseph Campbell's "Universal mythic themes"—these explorations in psychology, anthropology, mythology, and comparative religion seek to reveal shared elements and patterns within their own discipline. One of the purposes of this book is to pose questions of a homologic nature, to ask if perhaps there is a common source of structures and patterns in architecture as evidenced by particular examples of sacred architecture. The approach that I take is holistic and integrative; focusing on relationships as opposed to separate entities. Moreover, I examine the dialectical interrelationship between structure, space, and form. I examine the explorations of this type from other disciplines, though it is beyond the scope of this book to comprehensively outline the various methodologies. By focusing on the particular aspect of paradigms, however, parallels between other disciplines and the field of architecture will be established.

Jungian psychology is perhaps the consummate example of a rigorous approach toward discovering shared themes. What Jung calls "archetypes of the collective unconscious" he defines as certain shared elements of the human psyche. First, Jung makes the distinction between the "personal unconscious" and the "collective unconscious." The former is "limited to the state of repressed or forgotten contents" and is called "the shadow"; the latter is at a deeper level and is named the "collective unconscious." Jung states that,

> I have chosen the term "collective" because this part of the unconscious is not individual but universal; in contrast to the personal psyche, it has contents and modes of behavior that are more or less the same everywhere and in all individuals. It is, in other words, identical in all men and thus constitutes a common psychic substrate of a supra personal nature which is present in every one of us.[14]

Jung states that the collective unconscious is composed of archetypes and argues that these shared components are present in each individual's psychic makeup. In other words, all humans share a psychic "strata," defined as an archetype, that transcends the specifics of each individual and culture. Jung describes the phenomena of myth and fairy tale as an "expression of the archetypes."[15] According to Jung, the psyche, most of which lies in the realm of the unconscious, expresses itself through mythology. Just as the psyche contains certain archetypal elements, mythology, as a product of the psyche, comprises certain shared values. Jung's conceptual model of "universals" and "archetypes" is particularly relevant to religion and mythology and its associated architecture, a point to which I will turn later.

The Swiss linguist Ferdinand de Saussure researched the dialectic between *langue* and *parole*, or language and speech. The former is the structure or rules of language; the latter, individual use and interpretation. Each language has a specific structure comprised of vocabulary and its various relationships, but within this, there is tremendous freedom for one to communicate the most personal, profound, and emotional concepts. Claude Lévi-Strauss, who was greatly influenced by Saussure and was a key figure in the development of structuralist theory, studied the mythology of cultures around the world. His theory was that there was an "astounding similarity between myths collected in widely different regions" around the world. Additionally, their underlying structure was consistent, something that could be proved by diagraming the myths by means analogous to an orchestra score.[16] The repetitive nature of myths, Lévi-Strauss said, was "to render the structure of the myth apparent."[17] Lévi-Strauss saw the examination of patterns to be the primary task toward understanding the unknown. "If there is meaning to be found in mythology," he argues, "it cannot reside in the isolated elements which enter into the composition of the myth, but only in the way those elements are combined."[18] Similarly, if we consider architecture to be, at least in part, mysterious and possessing meaning, particularly the architecture from ancient cultures, then a similar method of pattern recognition is appropriate.

Similar to Jung, Joseph Campbell described myths as "spontaneous productions of the psyche, and each one bears within it, undamaged, the germ power of its source."[19] He also researched similarities between the world's mythology, which he termed "universal mythic themes," in which repeating mythic themes appear pan-culturally but find unique expression in each particular culture. The myth, according to Campbell, "will always be the one shape-shifting yet marvelously constant story that we find, together with a challengingly persistent suggestion of more remaining to be experienced than will ever be known or told."[20]

Two architectural theoreticians stand out as adopting similar methodology in the context of theories of architecture and design: the Dutch architect Herman Hertzberger, and British-born Christopher Alexander. Hertzberger, well schooled in structuralist theory, compares *langue* and *parole* analogously to architecture as "structure" and "interpretation." He offers as an illustrative example the game of chess, where there are a strict set of rules but limitless possibilities, and states that "chess is an outstanding example of how a fixed set of rules does not restrict freedom but rather creates freedom."[21] Hertzberger also describes structure as a "generative spine," which he illustrates by means of the analogy of "warp" and "weft" in the weaving of fabric. Similar to the warp, which creates the overall ordering of the fabric while allowing limitless variety of texture, pattern, and color in the weft, an overall ordering of the architecture can accommodate a rich variety of spaces and experiences.

Christopher Alexander talks about "generative rules," patterns that order and synthesize the elements of an architectural composition. Analogous to biology and linguistics, Alexander's "pattern language" is able to inform the designer regarding the appropriate ordering and form of buildings and cities. Through use of the "pattern language," the building "almost 'makes itself,' just as a sentence seems to when we speak."[22] It is an "egoless" process, which in part is why it has been challenged and resisted by many architects. I will return to Hertzberger and Alexander and their important theories in the conclusion.

I have established that the psyche is the source of mythological and religious expression and that it is partly composed of certain shared archetypes. I have also stated that an essential quality of sacred architecture is that it is "built myth" that symbolizes cultural beliefs and facilitates the enactment of shared rituals. If we accept that there are common elements that religion and mythology comprise, and that architecture is a spatial and temporal symbolization of myth and religion, then the question as to whether there are shared architectural patterns in architecture is valid. This interrelationship could be diagramed as

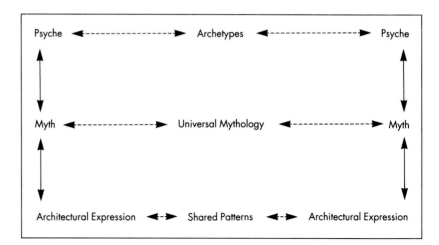

Fig. 1. Architecture as built myth.

in figure 1. For example, I argue that there is a corollary between the myth of the "hero's journey"[23] and the path and place in sacred architecture. In other words, referring to the above diagram, the myth of the hero redeemer arises from the psyche, and from this an architectural setting is created to symbolize the spiritual quest. Consequently, the path and place in sacred architecture, in its many forms from a wide range of historical settings, suggests an archetypal pattern in architecture. It is this relationship that will be addressed in the following chapters. However, before we turn to the path and place specifically and to particular examples, we will look at the myth of the hero's journey, or spiritual quest, and its many manifestations, including that of religious pilgrimage and its architectural implications.

The Hero's Journey

The hero's journey, according to Joseph Campbell, appears in two versions: a physical trial or the spiritual quest.[24] In the first, the hero is challenged to fight a battle, save the life of another, or obtain a precious object. The Arthurian legends are myths of this type and typically involve journeys to fight battles of honor, or heroic quests such as for the Holy Grail. The second type of myth involves a spiritual journey in which the heroes, through circumstances sometimes beyond their control, are called to begin their quest. The hero departs, passes through a number of trials, attains the goal or destination, and returns spiritually transformed.

The distinction between these two myths, though not always exact, is useful for our purposes because the spiritual quest more clearly suggests architectural expression. Campbell describes the spiritual quest as a process in which the familiar is abandoned and the unknown entered, either willingly or not. He defines the hero simply as one who gives his life over to something bigger than himself,[25] and similar to Jung, argues that mythology, and in particular the hero figure, expresses the psyche's drive for spiritual fulfillment.[26] The myth of the spiritual quest is characterized by the dual process of retreat from and then return to the world. According to Campbell, the pilgrim retreats "from the world scene of secondary effects to those causal zones of the psyche where the difficulties really exist. . . . His second solemn task and deed therefore . . . is to return then to us, transfigured, and to teach the lesson he has learned of life renewed."[27]

The hero's journey is characterized by the sequence of "separation, initiation, and return,"[28] in which the pilgrim experiences a rite of passage and emerges, in most cases, spiritually transformed. According to Eliade, in traditional societies if a man or woman is to become "complete," they must be born a second time. "Access to spiritual life always entails death to the profane condition, followed by a new birth."[29] One's childlike self dies and one returns an adult. Initiatory rites typically perform the function of a rite of passage from one mode of being to another. Common rites of passage are marriage, childbirth, and death and have traditionally had their attendant rituals. Initiates to religious orders typically go through similar rituals. In Christianity, baptism symbolizes a second birth and acceptance of Jesus—being "born again." In many faiths, submitting to the spiritual life includes taking a new name and changing one's physical appearance and ways of dressing.

Puberty rites are common initiation rituals, and in some examples there is obstetric symbolism of death and rebirth. Certain circumcision rites eloquently illustrate this process, where the young men are removed from their mothers, taken to "a place of men" to endure a painful trial, and return no longer boys but men.[30] Eliade documents numerous examples of primitive puberty rites in which the initiate's trials mirror the process of birth.[31] In this case, the symbolic journey is one of traversing through darkness toward light, from constriction to openness, a theme that has direct architectural implications.

The act of separation suggests physical as well as psychological distance. The journey is generally divided into four segments: the finding of the path, trials along the path, the attainment of the spiritual place, and the return. The finding of the path and the journey of trials appear in the myths, religious texts, and folktales of cultures around the globe and throughout history. Christianity has many examples of this type of myth. In the Gospel of Saint John, Jesus says, "I am the way, and the truth, and the life; no one comes to the father, but by me" (John 14.6). The Old Testament contains numerous examples of spiritual quests: Moses who must ascend to the summit of Mount Sinai to receive the Ten Commandments from God, Jonah who descends into the belly of the whale and emerges transformed, and the Israelites who must journey from Egypt to the Promised Land. The Gospels in the New Testament describe the event of Calvary and the trials that Jesus must endure on the way to his crucifixion.[32] In the Koran we find written, "Do you think that you shall enter the Garden of Bliss without such trials as came to those who passed before you?"[33]

In Buddhism there is the myth of the Buddha's first spiritual awakening, the story of "The Four Passing Sights" as told in the legend of the Buddha Shakyamuni. The young Buddha, the son of the king of a northern India principality, is married to a beautiful woman. Shortly after his birth, the king had been told by the sage Asita that his son will become either a great ruler or a religious man. Desiring that his son succeed him as ruler, the king decides that he will live a sumptuous and untroubled life so as to not be tempted by the world outside the palace. He therefore surrounds his son with sensual delights, a

Fig. 2. The spiritual and physical trials Jesus endured on the way to his crucifixion can be seen as a potent example of what Joseph Campbell calls the hero's journey. *Christ Bearing the Cross*, after Giovanni Bellini (ca. 1505).

magnificent palace, and ten thousand alluring courtesans who see to his every wish.

> This palace was as brilliant as that of Shiva on Mount Kailasa. Soft music came from the gold-edged tambourines that the women tapped with their fingertips, and they danced as beautifully as the choicest heavenly nymphs. They entertained him with soft words, tremulous calls, wanton swayings, sweet laughter, butterfly kisses, and seductive glances. Thus he became a captive of these women who were well versed in the subject of sensuous enjoyment and indefatigable in sexual pleasure.

The prince, however, becomes dissatisfied with his life and wishes to see what lies beyond his palace. Thus began the four journeys that transform his life. In the first journey, even though the king had taken the precaution to clear the road of all undesirable sights, the prince sees an old man for the first time. Upon asking his charioteer what this means, old age and its inevitability is explained. Troubled and confused, he asks to return to the palace. During the next two journeys similar occurrences happen: a man with a diseased body is seen, then a rotting corpse, which prompts the prince to exclaim, "This is the end that has been fixed for all, and yet the world forgets its fears and takes no heed!" On the fourth journey, a mendicant monk appears, an example of one who has abandoned the world of sense desires. Shortly thereafter, the prince decides to leave his family and home—"I want to depart from here today and win the deathless state!"—and thus begins his spiritual journey.[34]

There are numerous examples of the spiritual journey from cultures around the world. It appears in the form of the vision quests and the sacred quest for peyote in the Native American tribes of the Southwest.[35] The Plains Indian Black Elk tells compelling stories of spiritual quests and visions, the boon that this shaman figure brings back to his people. In the following, he describes one such journey and its preparations:

After a long winter of waiting, it was my first duty to go out lamenting. So after the first rain storm I began to get ready.

When going out to lament it is necessary to choose a wise old medicine man, who is quiet and generous, to help. He must fill and offer the pipe to the Six Powers and to the four-leggeds and the wings of the air, and he must go along to watch. There was a good and wise old medicine man by the name of Few Tails, who was glad to help me. First he told me to fast four days; I could have only water during that time. Then, after he had offered the pipe, I had to purify myself in the sweat lodge, which we made with willow boughs set in the ground and bent down to make a round top. Over this we tied a bison robe. In the middle we put hot stones, and when I was in there, Few Tails poured water on the stones. I sang to the spirits while I was there being purified. Then the old man rubbed me all over with the sacred sage. He then braided my hair, and I was naked except that I had a bison robe to wrap around me while lamenting in the night, for although the days were warm, the night were cold yet. All I carried was the sacred pipe.

They journey to a high bluff, where they consecrate the ground with sage, mark its center with a "flowering stick," and place offerings at the four cardinal points. Now alone, Black Elk prays to the four corners of the world and spends a sleepless night "lamenting."

Few Tails told me what I was to do so that the spirits would hear me and make clear my next duty. I was to stand in the middle, crying and praying for understanding. Then I was to advance from the center to the quarter of the west and mourn there a while. Then I was to back up to the center, and from there approach the quarter of the north, wailing and praying there, and so on around the circle. This I had to do all night long.

Visions appear to him during his long vigil. The following morning his guide returns, and they return to the village. There he purifies himself again and then tells his visions to the tribe's wise men. They decipher the messages and tell him what he must do next to help his people.[36]

An early heroic quest is that told in the Sumerian legend of Gilgamesh. His friend Enkidu, because he has eaten the Bull of Heaven, sickens and dies. Afterwards the hero grieves and meditates on the phenomenon of death.

> When I die, shall I not be like unto Enkidu?
> Sorrow has entered my heart
> I am afraid of death and roam over the desert . . .
> (Him the fate of mankind has overtaken)
> Six days and seven nights I wept over him
> Until the worm fell on his face.
> How can I be quiet?
> My friend, whom I loved, has turned to clay.[37]

The hero then departs on a quest to the underworld in search of immortality. Indeed, death and a journey to the underworld are a common mythological theme. Greek mythology contains many examples of this type of myth: the story of Psyche and Cupid, in which Venus sets Psyche the task of journeying to the underworld to fill a box with some of Proserpine's beauty; the tale of the twelfth labor of Hercules; the myth of Orpheus and Eurydice; and most eloquently, the journey of Aeneas to find his father. The Japanese myth of Izanagi and Izanami recounts the perils of a journey of this type and serves to explain the phenomenon of death.

Often the mythic quest is in the form of the folktale. The Japanese folktale "Sankichi's Gift" is a story about a young sumo wrestler who is indentured to a harsh feudal lord. As punishment for his lack of subservience, the youth, Daihachi, is commanded to drag a cart full of rice, payment for land tax, to a distant lord's castle. This is how his journey begins, ending with a pilgrimage to a mountaintop shrine.

> The path led up and up, winding through endless groves of mountain shrubs, some bright with flowers. The day grew darker, and its dwindling light lent everything an eerie, brooding strangeness that made

> Daihachi conscious of his solitude and what he now looked on as his small strength. . . . At last he saw the carved roofs of the shrine, with its lacquered vermilion and gilded eaves spread outward like protecting hands beneath the darkening sky.[38]

Daihachi goes through a series of trials and is rewarded by Sankichi, the guardian deity of the shrine. Spiritual quests are also found in Japanese religious writings, such as the reflections of spiritual journeys written by Basho, a seventeenth-century Zen Buddhist monk and haiku poet, entitled *The Narrow Road to the Deep North*. In all stories of this type there is typically an event of transformation, a journey from one consciousness to another.

An essential component of the hero's journey is the attainment of the spiritual place. In "Sankichi's Gift" the shrine must be attained. Jesus needs to go to the desert alone to suffer the three temptations of the devil and complete his spiritual journey (Luke 4.1–13). A similar event happens in the life of the Buddha, who sits beneath the Bo Tree vowing not to get up until he has reached enlightenment. It was Muhammad whose spiritual path led him to the cave on Mount Hira.

The final component is the return of the hero who, having passed through his trials and attained spiritual transformation, brings the boon of his knowledge to the people. Moses descends from the mountain to deliver the Ten Commandments; Jesus returns from his forty days of temptation; the Buddha emerges from his meditations under the Bo Tree to begin his ministry.

The myth of the hero's journey displays a remarkable consistency in structure and content throughout the world's folktales and religious texts. Campbell states, "Essentially, it might be said there is but one archetypal mythic hero whose life has been replicated in many lands by many many people."[39] For example, Dionysus, Osiris, and Jesus are parallel figures that symbolize death and resurrection. Jesus was "the true vine" and God, "the vine dresser." "Every branch that does not bear fruit he prunes, that he may bear more fruit" (John 15.1–2). Dionysus died in the autumn, was torn to pieces, but was reborn. His resurrection was analogous to the withering of the grapevine—the plant associated with his cult—and its rebirth in the spring. Osiris is murdered by Seth, his body cut up and scattered, but he is gathered up and resurrected. Similarly, there are many parallels between the life and ministry of the spiritual figures of Jesus and Buddha.[40] This is of particular interest in the case of the sacred path and place as I examine architectural examples from all of these faiths and cultures (as well as other religions) and seek corollaries between them.

The hero's quest is a journey from the known to the unknown. For Gilgamesh to answer his question "Shall I not be like unto Enkidu?" he must leave the familiar and take a symbolic journey to the underworld. Campbell has stated that "ritual is the enactment of the myth." Often initiatory rituals are a mimesis of the original hero's deed. In *The Imitation of Christ*, Thomas à Kempis's fifteenth-century work, Gerhard Groote intones, "Deny thyself, take up thy cross and follow Jesus." Or in the *Rigveda* one reads, "Yama is the one who first discovered the way; this trodden path is not to be taken away from us; on that way that our forefathers travelled when they left us, or that way the later born follow each his trail."[41] The ritual enactment of the myth symbolizes a return to the beginning of time when the hero first performed his deed and returned with his boon for humankind. The spiritual quest, such as is found in the act of pilgrimage, often symbolizes the original spiritual trials and journey of the deity to apotheosis.

Pilgrimage as Spiritual Journey

The rite of pilgrimage, analogous to the spiritual journey, is found in all the world's major religions. Moreover, the characteristics that define the act of pilgrimage are strikingly consistent among all the faiths. Christian pilgrimage and pilgrimage sites are well known, as is the Islamic requirement for the hajj to Mecca. What is less well known, perhaps, is that in Judaism, Buddhism, Taoism, and Hinduism pilgrimage is an integral component of the religion; for example, there are over one hundred and fifty important Hindu pilgrimage sites. Only Protestantism rejected pilgrimage during the Reformation, as part of its challenge to papal authority, the veneration of relics, and the cult of the Virgin Mary. However, Christian pilgrimage is still active today, dominated by healing sites such as Fatima, Lourdes, Grough Patrick, and Knock. The phenomenon of pilgrimage is found in ancient religions as well, including Egypt, but it wasn't until around the fifth century BCE that its religious nature became more fully defined. In Greece, the oracle of the Temple of Apollo at Delphi was an important destination, a site that is discussed in depth in chapter 5. Greek pilgrimage also included journeys to temples sacred to Asklepios, the god of healing.[42]

The act of pilgrimage has always centered on the individual. The journey often involved large groups of pilgrims, often for reasons of security, but the essential act was an individual one, a spiritual quest as a test or affirmation of one's faith. It was, and still is, both an outer and an inner journey, a physical journey to distant locations, that leads the pilgrim to a deeper spiritual understanding. Often, pilgrimage involved long, sometimes dangerous journeys, of which preparation and trial were a part. The goal, the sacred place—be it an oracle, or holy person, a healing site, or a reliquary—through its architecture, often created a microcosm of the pilgrimage. An internalized world was created in which the pilgrim's journey is reenacted in the architectural setting— the spiritual path and place.

Most religious pilgrimage, similar to the hero's journey, shares the following characteristics: spiritual preparation for the journey; separating from one's society and everyday life; trials and rituals along the pilgrim's way; arrival at the sacred place; and the return in a changed state. Richard Barber cites anthropological studies that suggest pilgrimage replaced initiation rites of traditional societies, of which preparation, separation, and return in a changed state are an essential part.[43] The Islamic hajj places particular importance on preparation prior to undertaking the pilgrimage. Called *ihram*, it involves the trimming of hair, beard, and nails for men; specific clothing for men and women; codes of behavior, such as mutual respect and refraining from sexual activity; and special prayers, all of which need to be completed before the pilgrim passes the sacred boundaries of Mecca. Historically, all of the faiths prescribed certain codes of dress associated with pilgrimage.

Medieval Christian pilgrims wore long tunics, broad-brimmed hats, pouches for possessions and money, and carried a walking staff, all of which were sometimes blessed before the journey began. Similarly, Japanese, Chinese, and Hindu pilgrims dressed in certain ways, for example, in the saffron robes of the latter. Often upon their return the pilgrims would display an ornament testifying to the completion of their journey. Pilgrims returning from Santiago de Compostela wore scallop shells,[44] and those returning from Ise in Japan brought with them a small piece of the previously dismantled sacred shrine. The ritualized codes of appearance, dress, and behavior served to establish the pilgrim as separate from society and ordinary existence, an intermediary zone characteristic of initiatory rites, which has direct corollaries with the myth of the hero's journey.

The act of separation is perhaps one of the most significant components of the pilgrim's journey. Similar to ancient initiation rites, the pilgrim is separated from society and placed in a "marginal state."[45] This intermediary zone acts as a bridge between the pilgrim's old life and the hoped-for healing cure or spiritual transformation; it is both a physical path and an emotional state. This is similar to Joseph Campbell's definition of the hero's journey as being comprised of the triad of separation, initiation, and return.

Physical and spiritual trials and specific rituals in part define the act of pilgrimage. Practices range from crawling on one's hands and knees to the sacred spot, to extreme acts of self-mortification. Along the route to Compostela, pilgrims circumambulated columns set for that purpose and could be observed displaying self-inflicted brands of crosses, or bearing "iron manacles, fetters, chains, hobbles, shackles, traps, bars, yokes, helmets, scythes and diverse instruments of penance."[46] At Roc Amadour in France, pilgrims would bind themselves in chains and crawl up the 126 steps to the Chapel of Our Lady on their knees.[47] In Tibet, pilgrims circumambulate the sacred Mount Kailas, some fully prostrating themselves every few steps for the entire thirty-two-mile journey, an act of both trial and spiritual merit.[48] At the Kataragama cult site in Sri Lanka, devotees are attached to a central pole by means of hooks and cords, and similar acts of self-mortification are practiced by pilgrims in India, as well as appearing in many ancient initiation rites.[49]

After the journey there is the arrival at the sacred place, the goal of all pilgrimage, both physically and symbolically. In Christianity it might be the crypt underneath the choir of the cathedral that contained the relics of a saint, which were possessed with prayer-granting powers. In Mecca it is the Great Mosque and the Kaaba, the sacred black stone. Even on arrival within the sacred precinct, the sacred place was not easily accessible, and the pilgrim's journey continued with gateways, thresholds, and paths that had to be passed before the inner sanctum was attained. At some Gothic cathedrals, labyrinth patterns were set into the floor of the nave through which penitents would crawl on their hands and knees, a miniaturized journey to the sacred place. The one at Chartres is a 660-foot circumambulation said to re-create the pilgrimage to Jerusalem. Others were found at Amiens, Saint Quentin, and Reims.[50] The labyrinth, in fact, is a recurring theme in pilgrimage and the spiritual quest, to which we will return in chapter 4.

In some cases the "holy of holies" is attainable only to the initiated, the priesthood, as we shall observe at the Temple of Amun-Re at Karnak; or it is unobtainable to all, as in the central stupa at Borobudur in Java. Rites performed within the sacred place often mirror the pilgrim's journey. Christians walk along the ambulatory of the cathedral and pray at the stations of the cross, and Hindus circumambulate certain temples, typically in a specific direction.[51] At the Great Stupa at Sanchi in India, Buddhist pilgrims pass through its gateway, ascend steps at the base of the reliquary dome, and circumambulate clockwise around its circumference. The rock-cut temples at Ajanta are another pilgrimage site. Here the pilgrims approach these sacred carved caves up steep, narrow paths and then enter into their damp gloom. With the cave wall on their left and the stone colonnade on their right, they circumambulate in a clockwise direction, spinning around the "cosmic egg" of the enclosed stupa.[52] These are acts that mark the place as a sacred center, an *axis mundi*, and as Eliade states, the pilgrimage path

Fig. 3. View of a *stupa* surrounded by colonnaded ambulatory, Ajanta, India. After entering this rock-cut temple, pilgrims circumambulate its sacred center inside the colonnade.

is "a road of life . . . a peregrination to the center of the world."[53] Observances at the sacred site precede the eventual return and reintegration into society. For some, though, the journey is a trip of no return. Suicides are associated with particular Chinese mountain sites, and there are mythical stories of monks, both Japanese and Celtic, who set sail for paradise located beyond the horizon, never to return. For most, however, the return is an integral part of the journey, though its importance varies among religions. In early pilgrimages in the East, the boon to be returned was often in the form of religious texts as well as beneficent talismans collected along the way. In all faiths, though, the common theme is of spiritual transformation and increased status within the society. One rejoins the family, the village, as a new person, spiritually reborn by the trials and knowledge of the pilgrim's way.

The reasons for pilgrimage are varied and individual, and there are many interpretations in different religions, but they can be limited to the following: for physical or spiritual healing; for special requests or thanks to patron saints; for penance; as part of seasonal festivals; as simply an escape from everyday life in a religious setting; and lastly, as a test of faith and for spiritual development.

A common reason for pilgrimage is to visit a place of healing, a practice that dates from ancient religions such as the Greek cult of Asklepios. It is still popular today, especially in Christianity which, more than other religions, has traditionally emphasized miracles and cures.[54] The relics of Christian saints—first unearthed from the Roman catacombs and later recovered from the Holy Land as part of the plunder of the Crusades—were distributed to reliquaries throughout Europe. Included were such items as the umbilical cord and foreskin of Jesus, said to have been packed in oil by an angel, as well as the more common bones, partial or otherwise, of the many Christian saints. At first, perhaps they were simply objects of veneration; later they began to possess miraculous curative powers.[55] It has been suggested that the rise of reliquary cults was not only because of their documented ability to duplicate New Testament cures, but because they replaced pagan shrines that had formerly served this same purpose. The veneration of relics was not limited to Christianity. India has many sites associated with parts of the Buddha's body (such as Sanchi), and the arm of Muhammad is said to have been in the mosque at Cordoba at one time.

Next to Jerusalem, the cathedral of Saint James at Santiago de Compostela was the most important of Christian pilgrimage sites, due to the presence of the relics of Saint James and a network of pilgrimage roads that were established during the Middle Ages.[56] This is attributable in part to the rise to power of the Benedictine monasteries that spread across Europe from their enter at Cluny. There were four major routes from northern France to Santiago de Compostela along which many of the great Romanesque churches were located. After crossing the Pyrennes, at the famous Puente-la Reina, the four routes became a single road that continued its arduous and often dangerous way to its goal in northwest Gallicia. The first sight of the Cathedral produced the cry of *Montjoie!*, and the pilgrims continued to the *Porta Coeli*, or "heaven's door." Inside the "pilgrim's causeway" they traveled east to the statue of Saint James, where still today pilgrims approach and embrace it from behind.

Most contemporary pilgrimages in Europe center around healing sites dedicated to the Virgin Mary, a cult that first appeared in the fourteenth century. There are also sites associated with other patron saints. Traditionally, these are places where a pilgrim might journey to give thanks for a prayer already granted, such as sites associated with patron saints of sailors. Often a votive offering is left, found commonly today in the form of photographs, as well as the contemporary practice of lighting a candle as a form of offering. There are also pilgrimage sites dedicated to a multitude of requests and prayers, both important and mundane. Japanese Shinto shrines, for example, are typically dedicated to requests regarding success in business, marriage, or fertility. Many Hindu pilgrimages center around similar requests, though a deeper spiritual aspect is rarely missing.[57] Jews traveling to Jerusalem place their prayers written on pieces of paper in cracks of the Western Wall.[58] The shared ritual of journey to where god is present for either petition or thanks is found in many faiths and is interpreted in a multitude of ways.

Rome provided the setting for another type of pilgrimage, for those seeking either absolution or indulgences from the Pope. Rome had many sites important to the history of Christianity, from Saint Peter's Cathedral to the catacombs. However, it was also the capital of the Christian world, and thus, more often many traveled there to see church officials rather than visit religious sites. During the Middle Ages, pilgrimage to Rome was often imposed as a punishment for crimes, or self-elected for the purpose of expiating past sins. Indulgences, first appearing in the twelfth century, provided another impetus for travel to Rome. In medieval belief, unredeemed sinners went to hell; the redeemed, however, suffered in purgatory for an amount of time commensurate with their sins. The purchase of indulgences, however, initially in the form of visiting a prescribed number of churches in Rome, later by giving money, could lessen or eliminate the time spent in purgatory. The eventual abuse of this system was one of the chief complaints of Protestant reformers.[59] Similarly, there were jubilee years that centered around the granting of indulgences. They now appear every twenty-five years and include a processional celebration and the pope's ritual opening of a door to Saint Peter's that is kept closed at all other times.

Seasonal festivals were often an impetus for a pilgrimage. The Torah required Jewish men to make a thrice-yearly pilgrimage "before the Lord God," as described in Exodus 23.17. Four yearly festivals were associated with a pilgrimage to Jerusalem: Passover, the Sukkoth, Shabuoth, and Hanukkah. Not merely a celebratory festival, the gatherings were in essence a gathering of the tribes of Israel, scattered after the destruction of the Temple of Jerusalem, at times expelled from the city itself. Now all that remains of the Temple of Jerusalem, first built by King Solomon in 957 BCE and twice destroyed, is the Western Wall, the penultimate Jewish pilgrimage destination.

India is a culture filled with festivals. One of the most important is the Kumbha Mela, held at Allahabad every twelve years; in 1989 it attracted over fifteen million participants. A diverse gathering of Hindus, it centers around a ritual bathing in the Ganges.[60] The yearly Islamic pilgrimage to Mecca, however, provides one of the more compelling examples of seasonal pilgrimage, though otherwise it does not fit the description of a festival. Islam is the only religion that requires its believers to make a pilgrimage, the once-in-a-lifetime hajj to Mecca which attracts over two million pilgrims a year.[61] Upon arrival at the Great Mosque of Mecca, the pilgrims enter through the Gate of Peace into the courtyard that contains in essence a second mosque, within which is the Kaaba. The Kaaba is said to date from "before time" and to be located in the "navel of the world," the place associated with primordial creation, and Adam is said to have dwelt there after his expulsion from paradise.[62] God then created the world around it in concentric circles, symbolized today by the ritual circumambulation of the Kaaba. Though the Kaaba is the apogee of the hajj, pilgrims also visit other sites associated with the faith, including Medina, the city in which Muhammad lived after escaping persecution in Mecca, and the Mount of Mercy at Arafat.

Other pilgrimages can be described more as simply an escape from one's ordinary life, a pleasure trip of sorts. Japan is often cited as a culture that embraces this variety of pilgrimage. However, along with prayerful journeys, most pilgrimages result from an individual's need to escape from normal existence as a means of testing one's faith and for spiritual development. The destinations of this type of pilgrimage are often places identified with the life of the god. For example, Jerusalem is also a holy site for Muslims, in particular the Dome of the Rock, where Muhammad ascended to heaven on his white steed, named al-Buraq, or in another version by scaling a holy ladder. Jerusalem is also sacred to Christians, as are other sites in the holy land associated with the life of Jesus. Pilgrimage to the Holy Land was first described by the Pilgrim of Bordeaux, who noted distances and places, set during the post-Constantine age when pilgrimage to Jerusalem first became established.[63] During the Middle Ages, pilgrimage to the Holy Land became the penultimate Christian devotion, and the Crusades were in part waged to maintain access to the holy sites. The principal site in Jerusalem is the Church of the Holy Sepulchre, the scene of Jesus' crucifixion and entombment, though there were many sites associated with his birth, early life, and ministry.

Early Buddhist pilgrimage sites were located in India and were centered around the life of Buddha: Kapilovasta, the site of Buddha's birth; Bodh Gaya, the site of his enlightenment; Sarnath, the place where Buddha first preached; and Kushinagara, the site of his death. There are also Buddhist reliquaries containing parts of Buddha's body. King Ashoka, who promulgated the early Buddhist faith, is said to have taken the relics from the original ten stupas that contained them and distributed them to eighty-four thousand sites.[64] Chinese monks were the first to make pilgrimages to Buddhist sites in India for the purpose of veneration, spiritual devotion and to collect Buddhist texts.[65] In China there was a guidebook for Buddhist pilgrims called the *Guide for Obtaining Audience at the Four Famous Mountains;* many Buddhist pilgrimage destinations were centered on sacred mountains, such as Mount Kailas in Tibet. Taoist sites were also typically sacred mountains, the most famous of which is Tai-shen with its Holy Street and approach stairs composed of seven thousand steps.

Hinduism has perhaps more sites associated with pilgrimage than the other major faiths. Some of the Hindu sites are associated with the myth of Sati and Shiva and their unrequited love, which resulted in Sati's suicide. In his despair, Shiva whirled Sati's body through the air until it fell to pieces across the land; the places where the pieces landed became holy.[66] Many pilgrimages in India involve journeys to sacred rivers. Benares is cited as the most important of Hindu sites, as well as being sacred to Buddhists and Jains. It is a place for ritual bathing in the Ganges, and for the immolation of corpses and the deposition of their ashes in the sacred waters. In addition to the Ganges, the most important Hindu site in Benares is the golden temple of Vishwanath, built in 1777.[67] Like other faiths, Hinduism also had pilgrim guides, versions appearing in ancient texts such as the *Mahabharata* and the later *Puranas.*

In all the pilgrimages associated with devotion to the faith and spiritual development, there were instructions for proper preparation and codes of behavior during the journey. Whereas the European examples such as Picaud's *Pilgrim's Guide* were more worldly in their approach, in the East spiritual matters were emphasized. A Japanese guide stated that "a hasty journey with a heart full of business does not lead to piety. One is only brought to shame by it. Without other intention or thought, calmly and without haste, with 'Namu Daishi Honejo Kongo' (a pilgrim prayer) upon one's lips—that is how to make a true pilgrimage."[68]

Religious devotion and spiritual development, however, might be said to be the foundation of all religious pilgrimage. The preparation, act of journey, and attainment of the spiritual place all put the pilgrim outside of everyday life, in an intermediary zone where contact with god was possible. This act not only celebrated the deity and the pilgrim's faith, but also mirrored the god's own spiritual journey. In this way, as we discuss later, the pilgrim performed a mimesis of the god, the archetypal hero's journey common to the world's religions and mythology. The sacred place itself, through its architecture, created at a smaller scale the pilgrim's way, symbolizing this essential religious act, and accommodating the enactment of shared rituals.

CHAPTER 3

▪ *Elements and Experience*

The Path and Place in Architectural Theory

Architectural theoreticians have described and characterized the path and the place, but for the most part in secular terms. For them, it principally possesses formal qualities, related to the forming and entering of architectural space, or orientation and movement within an urban setting. Because I will be talking about the sites not only in terms of their symbolism but formally as well, following is a discussion of the spatial and architectural elements of the path and place as analyzed by particular theoreticians.

Kevin Lynch, in his seminal analysis of urban environments, *The Image of the City*, established the terms *path*, *edge*, *district*, *node*, and *landmark* as principal components of the urban landscape and important characteristics in analyzing movement and orientation within a city. He cited the importance of "clarity and legibility" in the urban environment and suggested that there are typical components humans respond to in a consistent manner that are necessary to orient themselves in space. Lynch states that "structuring and identifying the environment" is an essential activity and need for all "mobile animals." Many of the senses are involved in this activity; sight is the most dominant in humans, but we also utilize hearing, touch, smell, and other means as well. Disorientation, the feeling of being lost, is for the most part, extremely disturbing to humans. Therefore, the urban environment needs a modicum of "identity," "structure," and "meaning" to be legible, successful, and enjoyable. In other words, "an environmental image" needs to have an identity distinct from other forms, the structure of which is discernable and meaningful to the observer. Moreover, a "legible" environment, according to Lynch, establishes a sense of place and emotional security and "can furnish the raw material for the symbols and collective memories of group communication . . .[and] heightens the potential depth and intensity of human experience."

According to Lynch, a *path* needs to have a distinct identity, with a clear sense of directionality and continuity that includes both origins and destinations. Often, paths comprise a "time series"—a sequence of events along the path—and *landmarks* and *nodes* that give identity to each section. A path should reinforce "motion awareness" and offer a degree of "visual scope" to enhance the observer's sense of passage, distance, rhythm, and time.

Edges provide either separation or a joining together of the discreet parts of the environment and are essential to the identification of particular parts of the perceived schemata. City walls or water edges perform this role, as well as the more subtle elements that comprise path or district edges. *Nodes* are defined by Lynch as "strategic foci" that need to have a perceptible "clarity of joint"; the Piazza San Marco in Venice is a particularly successful example. *Landmarks*, such as the Duomo in Florence, are defined as "point references considered to be external to the observer" and serve to establish dominance over their surroundings. *Districts* are defined by enclosure, based on "some common identifying character" and need to possess "singularity" and "form simplicity" to be successful.[1]

J. G. Davies states that "most buildings belong to either the category of a path or that of a place, the one suggesting journey and movement, the other a centre and stillness. . . . Between these two main categories there are structures that combine features of both: such are paths that lead to and include places, the latter acting as foci or nodes." It is interesting to note the similarity of Lynch's criteria for path and place and those offered by Davies. The latter states, "For a path to be identifiable, it must have strong edges; continuity; directionality; recognizable landmarks; a sharp terminal; and end-from-end distinction." Davies goes on to define a place as "a readily comprehensible shape" that possesses a discernable and "concentrated" form with "pronounced borders." The place needs to be "limited in size," "capable of being experienced as an inside in contrast to the surrounding exterior; largely non-directional" and to provide a "focus for gathering."[2]

Kent Bloomer and Charles Moore, among others, also discuss the path and place. They use the terms "place, path, pattern, and edge" and call them "architectural building blocks in the existential space that surrounds us." The authors suggest that a place must be distinguishable as a separate entity and that paths can take a variety of configurations.[3]

Christian Norberg-Schulz quotes the following statement of Dagoburt Frey regarding the path and place: "All architecture is a structuring of space by means of a goal or path." Norberg-Schulz also references Lynch and lists his own terms regarding path and place: "directions or paths," "centres or places," and "areas or domains"; these roughly correspond to Lynch's terms of path, node, and domain. Together they form "the basic schemata of orientation." He states that a path is characterized as a linear progression but is also experienced as having "a character of its own," and goes on to cite the following path types: a singular/axial path, a double path, and circular paths. Moreover, paths represent the willful leaving of one place and a journey to another and therefore represent "a basic property of human existence and are "one of the great original symbols." Additionally, according to Norberg-Schulz, a place always clearly delimits the inside from the outside, and that human concepts of place are related to ancient beliefs that certain places demarcate a sacred center.[4] He cites the cosmogonic implications the path and place have held for ancient societies; the center or place representing the center of the world and the path leading away from this; "the way is always directed from the known to the unknown."[5]

I believe, like the above theoreticians, that the path and place are characterized by specific elements and patterns.[6] It is my premise that architecture, and particularly sacred architecture, often involves a dynamic between both the path and the place. It is possible to examine them separately, but they can only be fully understood in their interplay, as an integrated whole. It is clear that the path and place are not only a fundamental ordering device in the built environment but are imbued with symbolic content as well. A legible path sequence not only orients one physiologically, but psychologically and spiritually as well. Traditionally it has symbolized a going forth from the known to the unknown, the content of which is still present today. Meaningful modern architecture successfully manipulates and elaborates on this archetypal theme.

The architect Aldo van Eyck said that "man is both centre bound and horizon bound," which suggests the fundamental nature of the path and place. My approach is that the path and place are fundamental elements of architectural composition. I have chosen the examples because of their interrelationship with myth and belief. As I have stated earlier, myths have served to provide answers to fundamental questions of existence. The path and place, by symbolizing the myth and facilitating the enactment of ritual, fills the same need. By examining sacred sites in the context of the path and place, my goal is to document the interrelationship of religious beliefs and architectural forms in sacred architecture.

Elements and Space

The specific examples cited are in part examined and analyzed *volumetrically* and *elementally*. In other words, the focus is on the quality and experience of the architectural space as it relates to the constructive and space-forming elements of which it is comprised. I also argue that architectural form and organization is comprised of discrete identifiable elements and spatial forms. There is consistent evidence that architectural space and form are based on underlying orders that allow for a variety of form and interpretation. Analogous to Jungian archetypes and universal mythology, these elements and patterns offer limitless architectural interpretations. Underlying structures in architecture were referred to as "order" by Louis Kahn, as "the multiplicity of living patterns" by Christopher Alexander, and as the "basic pattern-forming processes that, operating within strict limits, create limitless varieties of shapes and harmonies" by György Doczi.[7] Similarly, Herman Hertzberger describes architectural elements and patterns as "an innate ability of all men in the most diverse cultures to arrive at ever different interpretations of essentially the same arch-forms."[8] I identify elements and patterns that comprise the basic constituents of the form and composition of the sacred path and place. I also demonstrate that, through a limited number of organizations that appear pan-culturally and transhistorically, the path and place assume a limitless variety of forms while accommodating a wide range of symbolic functions.

In regard to architectural elements, Francis D. K. Ching describes architectural design in terms of learning "vocabulary," and that, analogous to writing, it is a process of progressing from the alphabet to words and vocabulary. Rules of grammar and syntax must be learned before sentences can be constructed; principles of composition, before essays or novels can be written. Once the basic vocabulary is learned, however, a limitless range of possibilities is available. Ching describes his book *Architecture: Space, Form and Order* as a "morphological study of the essential elements of form and space." These elements are the "critical means of architecture," which "comprise the timeless and fundamental vocabulary of the architectural designer." Through typological and morphological means, Ching argues that there are identifiable fundamental elements that comprise architecture. For example, he identifies a number of primary elements such as the point, line, plane, and enclosure; primary shapes such as the triangle, circle, and square, and primary forms such as platonic solids.[9]

Thomas Thiis-Evensen uses a literary analogy as well, stating that "there is a common language of form which we can immediately understand, regardless of individual or culture." The *floor*, the *wall* and the *roof* are the primary architectural "archetypes" according to the author, and within these major categories are "themes" or "motifs . . . that remain the same regardless of time, place or function."[10] Similarly,

Pierre von Meiss is concerned with "fundamental principles of form and order" that are "independent of style and period."

The above theoreticians are a representative sample of those concerned with what I term an "elemental approach" toward analyzing and creating architecture. It should be noted that there are many theoreticians who offer contrary views and cite the plethora of styles, influences, and periods of architecture as evidence to support their arguments. Our current pluralistic age seems to lend support to this point of view. Additionally, proponents of the argument for "universals" in architecture are commonly seen as romantics in search of an architectural Rosetta Stone, who would deny individual creativity and expression. I also share a degree of caution in regard to theories that veer in this direction. Additionally, shared elements and organizations in architecture, though they may be reduced to component parts, can only be fully understood when viewed as a result of a combination of elements, spatial form and experience, and specific historical and cultural settings.

Elements and organizations, though not a complete description of architectural form and composition in and of themselves, can be isolated—a necessary process in analyzing a particular example. For example, there are constructive and space-forming elements such as walls and columns that perform the role of support and vertical enclosure; and beams, arches, vaults, domes, and other structural forms that span and enclose in the horizontal dimension (fig. 4). There are constructive systems such as ones that utilize massive construction, and those that use the frame, which might also be called cavity and structure.[11] Degree of enclosure is accomplished in these two systems either by "carved" openings (or the "subtraction" of mass) or by infill components (or the "adding" of material).[12]

The relationship of the elements or the organization is often revealed through geometry and proportion (fig. 5). There are also organizations based on plan typology, a subject that Ching and others have comprehensively covered. These types include symmetrical and bisymmetrical plans; linear and axial organizations; radial and centralized

Fig. 4. Space-forming elements, such as walls and columns, and structural forms, such as beams, arches, and vaults, can be isolated as examples of the fundamental elements of architectural form and composition. Choir, Whitby Abbey, Yorkshire, England (early thirteenth century).

Fig. 5. Geometry and proportion often order the relationship of the architectural elements. Abbey Church of Pontigny, France (Cistercian).

plans; and plans that are a result of a repeating module, sometimes referred to as cluster plans. There are also grid organizations, free plans, and fragmented organizations.

The path itself can be described in terms of typology, with two major types appearing: the linear path and the segmented path. There are numerous interpretations of the linear path—axial paths, split paths, radial paths, grid paths, and circumambulating paths—as well as many interpretations of the segmented path. These path typologies are not limited to sacred architecture but define basic organizations in secular architecture as well. However, the particular interpretation and symbolization of these types in sacred architecture are the principal focus of this book. Each of these types of path and their relationship to religious beliefs and ritual is illustrated in chapter 5.

Humans primarily respond to their environment visually and spatially. The spatial emphasis of humans is due in part to the nature of our eyes, which are precise instruments that enable us to rapidly perceive space. Our eyes are located in the front of our heads, giving us stereoscopic vision, and our eyes have separate mechanisms to gather light, identify an object, focus on it precisely, and locate it in space.[13] Though sight was the last of our senses to evolve, it is the most complex, and we rely principally on our vision to apprehend and judge our world. In fact, nearly 70 percent of the body's sense receptors are located in the eyes.[14] In *The Hidden Dimension* Edward Hall explored space and perception. He argues that humans are spatially predisposed, citing as evidence that 20 percent of the words in the *Pocket Oxford Dictionary* refer to space.[15]

Because architecture is principally perceived and experienced volumetrically, spatial sequence will be addressed in depth in many examples. A volumetric approach to understanding and creating architecture was promulgated by the modern architect Bruno Zevi, who scolded most architectural critics for emphasizing the "box" and not its "contents." Zevi states that architectural space can never be accurately represented, and to be fully understood it needs to be experienced, and that "the history of architecture is primarily the history of spatial conceptions. Judgement of architecture is fundamentally judgement of the internal space of buildings."[16] Similarly, another modern theoretician, Sigfried Giedion, reduces the entire history of architecture to "three space conceptions": "architecture as space radiating volumes," "architecture as interior space," and "architecture as both volume and interior space."[17]

As some of the examples demonstrate, there are distinctions between Occidental and Asian conceptions of space. In the West, space is seen typically as the area between objects and as the negative of physical objects; in Asia, space is an entity in itself, and in Japan it is called *ma*.[18] As we will see, the Japanese create architectural space in ways similar to that of the West, but their perception of space occupies a broader context, one of which is its perception as a positive entity in the physical environment. Overall, I will stress a space-positive view of architecture, where, to quote Steen Eiler Rasmussen, "The architect can work with the empty space—the cavity—between the solids, and consider the forming of that space as the real meaning of architecture."[19]

I use the term *space* to describe a wide range of degrees of enclosure. Principally, however, space will either be defined as *inscribed* or *circumscribed*. *Inscribed* space is not fully enclosed but is implied by edges on one or more sides, including but not limited to building edifices, walls, columns, rails, a change in level, or even plantings. *Circumscribed* space is completely or almost completely enclosed and corresponds to the traditional architectural definition of space.[20] Just as there are numerous plan organizations, there are consequently a variety of spatial organizations that often are related to the plan, such as centralized spaces or geometric spaces. Additionally, there are characteristics and relationships specific to space itself; spaces that are paths or places, singular spaces and ones that are comprised of a number of spaces, spaces within spaces, and spaces that form edges and thresholds either vertically or horizontally. The following examples establish corollaries between the form and organization of the space and the functions it served.

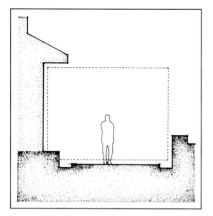

Fig. 6. Inscribed space.

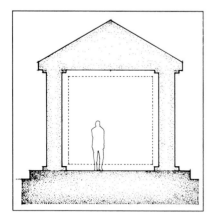

Fig. 7. Circumscribed space.

Perception and Experience

As Rasmussen states, "It is not enough to *see* architecture; you must experience it."[21] And it is important to note that architectural form and space is not apprehended by sight only. The smell of materials, inhabitants, food, surroundings; the feel and texture of materials and surfaces, the sound of echoes and footsteps, all are part of the complete architectural experience. In other words architecture is experienced as a synthesis of many stimuli and is only fully understood in its totality. However, though most of our senses act in concert in experiencing our environment, the principal means through which we experience architecture is through sight and movement. Movement, spatial sequence, and time create the fourth dimension of our perceptual realm, and are an essential component of the experience of architecture.[22] Indeed, outside of vision, though it is not one of the five senses, the movement through space is the most important means through which we assimilate architectural experience.[23] Goethe wrote that "one would think that architecture as a fine art works solely for the eyes. Instead, it should work primarily for the sense of mechanical motion in the human body—something to which scant attention is paid."[24] We view space dynamically, or in terms of movement through it, as opposed to statically. The ease or difficulty of walking along the path and its surface and texture, the scale and distance of the entrance, the shifting views as we move along the route, inclines and steps, all form part of the experience of approaching and passing through architecture (fig. 8). Additionally, our peripheral field of vision is an important component of judging how fast we are moving through a space. For example, narrow corridors or colonnades make us feel like we are traveling faster. Also, the rhythm of flanking elements that comprise the space either reinforce or complement our movement through it. Successful and meaningful paths and places make use of the cadence of space-forming elements such as planes or columns; their rhythm is manipulated in a manner not dissimilar to musical composition. A pause in the cadence

Fig. 8. The physical experience of traversing a steep set of stairs underlines this sequence of approach. The Church of Santa Maria in Aracoeli, Rome (1348).

of the composition, either in music or architecture, produces a reaction of tension and anticipation.[25] Additionally, we first experience our environment psychologically, and our reactions are based on both individual and social criteria. In other words, we psychologically ascend a stair or duck through a low opening before we physically do so. Part of our reactions also have to do with our natural empathy with the environment.[26] Just as we might experience freedom when we view a grand landscape painting or feel grief when we look at a tragic painting, so do uplifting or subdued spaces affect us. Similarly, we feel the strain and weight of squat, short columns and feel the lightness of the thin ribbed arch.[27]

Sight is the primary means through which we structure, interpret, and understand our environment. Our predisposition to experience our environment visually is a result of generations of evolution based on survival skills. Consequently, we have developed the ability to take in and respond to stimuli in a very rapid and at times unconscious manner. Rudolf Arnheim states that to arrive at a "coherent structure" from a "cluster of percepts," the mind selects "regular, symmetrical, (and) stable" forms, as a type of perceptual shorthand.[28] Rasmussen makes a similar case when he discusses the act of "re-creation" from a partial image, which is a process of perceiving the basic form and filling in the details later.[29] This concept is particularly relevant to architecture, which nearly always is perceived in segments and fragments as one moves through or around it.

One of the principal ways we visually measure and judge our environment is through comparison, a process that occurs in two steps.[30] First, we place ourselves in relation to the space, determining the size, proportion, and interrelationship of its constituent elements, and their relationship to ourselves. This in essence sets up a base measure. When we then move from the first space to the next, we compare what we know with what we don't know, measuring the objects in the second space, based on the measure of the first. Moreover, we are visually predisposed to choose the familiar over the unfamiliar. This might be compared to Jean Piaget's concept of "adaption," which is comprised of "assimilation and accommodation," experiencing the environment and then placing it in a familiar context.[31] We are constantly comparing the known with the unknown, placing the unfamiliar in a familiar context. Hall has observed that humans "alter perception as a result of learning,"[32] and Rasmussen describes the process of recognizing the familiar and disregarding the rest as part of our perceptual process.[33] As I discuss later, the manipulation of various scale changes in the built environment, based on the act of comparison, is an effective medium for the creation of a variety of spatial experiences.

The form of the environment can also affect one's conception of time; psychological time as opposed to chronological time, and a varied and rich spatial environment can have the effect of making the experience seem longer than it actually is. This manipulation of experience works at a very basic psychological level. For example, we may recall times in our lives when we have moved to a new city or started at a new school, and the first few months felt like years. Conversely, subsequent weeks or months seemed to pass much more quickly. Similarly, when we are young, time seems to pass very slowly, whereas when we are older, the years tend to blur together.[34] It all has to do with how we take in information in our environment. When we are in a situation where everything is new and we are responding to a lot of stimuli, then time seems to pass slowly. When an environment is familiar, it becomes a more seamless blur, and time appears to go by more quickly. J. B. Priestley cites a famous experiment in time perception that was performed in 1962, when a French speleologist set out to spend two weeks in the darkness of a cave, unable to tell what time or day it was. He emerged after one week, convinced that it had been two, a result perhaps due to the lack of stimulation in his subterranean environment.[35] Priestley, however, cites contrary examples, and it is likely that the experience of time varies with each individual, and because of its relative, personal nature, it is difficult to state definitively the degree of time manipulation. An example is the experience of time passing excruciatingly slowly when one is in a particularly dull or uncomfortable place. Perhaps this phenomenon is also used in sacred paths and places, the monotonous rhythm of columns or repeating spaces, the fear of approaching sacred ground contributing to the effect of the expansion of time.

Literature and the theater often make use of the manipulation of time to further the desired message and experience, either speeding, slowing, or the interplay of each in the narrative. The broad sweep of time in Tolstoy's *War and Peace*, the slowing almost to a standstill of action in Joyce's *Portrait of the Artist as a Young Man* or Sterne's *Tristram Shandy*, or the freezing of the moment epitomized by the Japanese haiku poem. Shakespeare, it is said, deliberately speeded up the action at the end of his plays to counteract the flagging attention of the audience.[36] Analogously, architecture can be seen as a narrative of spaces and events, an unfolding story, that similarly manipulates one's sense of time.

The experience and meaning of sacred sites is often related to its visual, spatial, and temporal composition. As I have noted, our experience can be manipulated through a variety of means and devices. Sacred architecture has always utilized the sensual apprehension of architecture to communicate particular meanings, and there is a range of perceptual reactions that result from a rich spatial environment as particularly evidenced by the sequence of the path and place.

CHAPTER 4

▪ *The Sacred Path and Place*

Place and Meaning

One's identity is contingent on the sense of belonging to a place. The creation of place and entry is a fundamental human activity, enacted by all humans, beginning with the archetypal children's game of creating "houses" for themselves under tables, in boxes, or out of found materials. This activity has a strong psychological component, which is particularly apparent in archaic societies whose self-definition and sense of well-being were often intimately connected to specific places. The following words of a Native American eloquently describe this attitude:

> You ask us to think what place we like next best to this place, where we always lived. You see the graveyard out there? There are our fathers and grandfathers. You see that Eagle-nest mountain and that Rabbit-hole mountain? When God made them, He gave us this place. We have always been here. We do not care for any other place. . . . We have always lived here. We would rather die here. Our fathers did. We cannot leave them. Our children were born here—How can we go away? If you give us the best place in the world, it is not so good for us as this. . . . This is our home. . . . We cannot live anywhere else. We were born here and our fathers are buried here. . . . We want this place and not any other. . . .[1]

A meaningful place needs to possess an environmental identity that gives its inhabitants a sense of belonging and connection. Often this manifests itself in the belief that it is at the center of the world, beyond which lies the undifferentiated unknown. A sense of community based on shared values is typically connected with a specific place, and thus religion and mythology are often deeply rooted in the definition of meaningful places.

Place, in an architectural context, is also imbued with meaning. The physical enclosure creates the context for the experience, and the meanings communicated by the elements that form the space help us to identify with the place. The meaning is significant because it is produced by, and represents, shared beliefs of a particular place and time, though the specific experience may have differed from person to person. Architecture has traditionally aided in establishing a sense of meaningful place and articulating people's beliefs. According to Norberg-Schulz, meaningful architectural space has typically enabled human beings to "gain an existential foothold" in the world and "can be defined as a concretization of man's existential space."[2]

People have consistently structured their environment as a means of establishing their "place" in the world. In this context, the structure, organization, and articulation of these places has served to reflect their belief systems. Consequently, architecture served as a legible place that expressed and communicated values associated with human existence. Over time, especially at sacred sites where stages of construction stretched over generations, there was a dialectic established between the creation and expression of the architecture. Thus the sequence of a temple's construction over hundreds of years was often a consistent variation on a few fundamental themes.

All of the above serves in part as a definition of the sacred place, an architectural setting where "place plus meaning" are powerfully synthesized. As we shall observe, the sacred place has a multitude of origins, uses, and forms. In spite of this diversity, however, it generally conforms to consistent, identifiable themes. The sacred place is a place apart, separated from the profane world. It communicates shared symbolic meanings and provides a place where God or gods are worshiped and rituals enacted. Examples range from a simple clearing in the forest to a complex architectural setting.

According to Eliade the sacred place was an interruption of the infinite and formless immensity that surrounded it; "an irruption of the sacred that results in detaching a territory from the surrounding cosmic milieu and making it qualitatively different." It was a place differentiated from the surrounding profane space where often gods had appeared as revealed by a "sacred hierophany." The sacred was not created by humans but was typically revealed to them; its presence stretches back to primordial time. However, in the absence of revelation, the manifestation of the sacred often was evoked through specific ceremonies.[3]

The break in "homogeneous space" established a fixed point and thus a center—a place of orientation. The place was often seen as the "navel of the world" or the place of primordial creation that took place *in illo tempore*. It often marked an *axis mundi*, a place where the three regions of the world—heaven, earth, and the underworld—were joined. Consequently, it was a place where communication with God was possible, as we find in the dream of Jacob at Bethel, where there is a ladder ascending to heaven and the voice of the Lord offers prophecies. "How awesome is this place!" says Jacob upon awakening. "This is none other than the house of God and this is the gate of heaven" (Gen. 18.17). The "holy rood" that Jesus was crucified on is an ancient symbol of the tree of life that grows at the center of the world. This is the Tree of Life that is found in the Garden of Eden planted "in the midst of the garden" (Gen. 2.9).

The act of settling in a place was often mythologized as the creation of the world, and there were numerous rituals that served to take possession of a place. For example, in classical Greece a new city was consecrated by carrying the fire from the sacred hearth in Athens and kindling it in its own *prytaneion*.[4] There was also the act of Spanish and Portuguese conquistadores claiming the New World in the name of Jesus Christ by planting a cross on the land, thus sacralizing it.[5] The creation of a sacred place has principally provided the existential means for people to establish a center and thus define their place in the world.

This belief in the "founding of the world" for God's "chosen people" presupposes a sense of grave responsibility for the world. The tribe, clan, or society's actions regarding their environment were typically imbued with a sense of destiny and apocryphal consequences, as we read in a statement by the Hopi Nation in 1970:

> We the true and traditional religious leaders, recognized as such by the Hopi People, maintain full authority over all the land and life contained within the Western Hemisphere. We are granted our stewardship by virtue of our instruction as to the meaning of Nature, Peace, and Harmony as spoken to our People by Him, known to us as Massau'u, the Great Spirit, who long ago provided for us the sacred stone tablets which we preserve to this day.[6]

The sacred place also depicted the "image of the cosmos" and symbolized the ideal "Celestial City." It was an "earthly reproduction of a transcendent model."[7] Sacred geometry was often utilized for this reason and, in turn, served to reveal the divine sources in its manifestation. Lastly, the sacred place was never an impassive backdrop; its form was never disassociated from its use and content. It was a dynamic place, often charged with emotional energy and experienced spatially and temporally as its users moved through its spaces or entered its sacred enclosures.

Sources and Expressions of the Myth

Myths commonly served the purpose of explanation; the mysteries of existence were concretized by the story. The hero figure became the personification of each individual's quest for a meaningful existence; the world was explained and one's place within it established. The shared enactment of the ritual transformed one's personal struggles into the suprapersonal realm where they were explained and joined with others who had gone before them.[8] The architecture of the spiritual path and place also concretized existential questions and concepts. The built form symbolized the rite of passage and spiritual transformation.

The path to the sacred place, today as in the past, often re-creates the pilgrim's journey and its three components of preparation, separation, and return. Typically, there is a clear delineation of entry, a place of decision as to whether to start the journey or not. This threshold also establishes what may be the first of many points of separation between the sacred and the profane, and generally involves some kind of ritualistic shedding of the outside world, as in ablution. The entrance gains access to the path or to an entire enclosed sacred precinct. Typically following the entrance, there is a sequence of defined spaces, places, or events along the path that grow increasingly more sacred, often including a number of choices. A spatial sequence provides a symbolic narrative as one travels along it and increasingly anticipates the arrival at and attainment of the sacred place.

The sacred place shares similar qualities, such as a clearly defined entry or threshold to the inner sanctum, which performs functions similar to the entrance to the path. The sacred place itself is a clearly defined enclosure that has precise boundaries and is separated from the outside profane world. Typically, there is a delineation or hierarchy of space to accommodate specific rituals, and a form and language that has symbolic content. The result is the concretization of the myth of the spiritual or hero's journey in which the architecture symbolizes and accommodates the enactment of a pilgrimage. In the case of the solitary pilgrim, the trials of the passage are enacted as one proceeds along the path. Often however, the performance of the journey is reserved for the initiated, and thus the priests or nobility become actors, performing the cosmic journey for society. The journey through the increasingly sacred spaces therefore symbolizes "every-man's" journey while also institutionalizing the position of the priests and nobles.

We have seen in our discussion of mythology how the psychological archetype of passage and transformation has been translated into what Joseph Campbell calls the "universal myth." Through numerous examples and cultures, the spiritual journey of passage and transformation was told through the myth, which was often translated into the symbolic physical form of the sacred place. Let us now turn to a closer examination of the different origins and symbolisms of the sacred path and place.

A Place Apart

The sacred place took many forms, as it still does today, but was characterized by the marking of a sacred area and a clear separation from the secular world, principally established by enclosure. This enclosure, in its numerous forms, established the boundaries of the sacred place so as not only to mark and consecrate the ground but to protect the uninitiated from entering. "The sacred," Eliade points out, "is always dangerous to anyone who comes into contact with it unprepared, without having gone through the 'gestures of approach' that every religious act demands."[9] Thus when God appears before Moses in the form of the burning bush, he commands, "Do not come near; put off your shoes from your feet, for the place on which you are standing is holy ground" (Exod. 3.5). Later, after the Israelites escape from Egypt and make their way to Mount Sinai, God instructs Moses to "set bounds around the mountain, and consecrate it" (Exod. 19.23) and that the penalty for crossing this sacred border is death.

The demarcating of the sacred ground was typically accomplished architecturally by the form and geometry of the sacred place and by surrounding it by an enclosure wall. At Giza, for example, the pyramid of Cheops, though clearly distinguished from its surroundings by its scale and geometry, was surrounded by a temenos and entered only by means of the mortuary temple. We will observe the act of architecturally articulating the sacred ground in the examples to follow, though the separation was in some instances produced by environmental elements such as water and topography. For example, the medieval monastery of Mont-Saint-Michel is located on a rocky island off the coast of Normandy and is separated from the mainland at high tide. Similarly, Lindisfarne Priory located on Holy Island off the Northumbrian coast in England is similarly cut off from the mainland at high tide.[10]

At Zen Buddhist temples, the principal subtemple building is typically surrounded by gardens. The stone, moss, and shrubbery gardens are designed to symbolize the ocean, and the temple building is reached by a bridgelike threshold space called a *gen-kan*. The monastery Couvent de Ste-Marie-de-la-Tourette (1957–1960) designed by Le Corbusier utilizes an analogous bridgelike device. Set on the side of a steep slope in the hills outside of Lyon, the rectangular mass of the building hovers on *pilotis* and appears to be moored to the land by the single bridge that serves as the main entrance. Similarly, Eero Saarinen's chapel at MIT in Cambridge, Massachusetts, which was completed in 1955, is principally a concrete and masonry cylinder surrounded by a circular pool of water (fig. 9). A rectangular enclosure, which serves as an entrance and support space, bridges over the sur-

Fig. 9. A view of the main approach and entrance to the chapel at the Massachusetts Institute of Technology, Cambridge, Mass., Eero Saarinen (1955). The cylindrical chapel on the right is surrounded by a reflecting pool-moat and reached by the bridge-like building on the left.

57

rounding water to reach the sanctuary. The enclosure of the sanctuary is a double-shell construction with the pure cylinder form on the outside and undulating masonry walls on the inside. It hovers over the water, raised up on concrete-and-brick piers and arches, and admits light into the space that is reflected off the surface of the water. Its siting and means of entry is reminiscent of the archetypal separation of the sacred from the profane by means of a natural element.

A definitive separation of the sacred place from the secular world has typically been found at mountainous locations. For example, the mountaintop location of the Acropolis in Athens provided both a defensive site and a sanctuary for the goddess Athena. Christian monasteries were often built in mountainous locations, such as those on the mountainous peninsula of Mount Athos in Greece, and Saint Catherine's, located on the slopes of Mount Sinai. Early Zen Buddhist monasteries and Taoist temples were located in mountainous sites in China. Jains hold mountain locations as holy; their temple city on Mount Girnar is perhaps the most striking. In Tibetan Buddhism there is the Potala in Lhasa, the traditional spiritual seat of the Dalai Lama, which is located in a remote mountainous site in Tibet.

At the sacred place itself, in most cases, the separation and enclosure are further delineated by an opening or entry threshold, and an entry path. The threshold acts as a transitional zone between the outside and the inside; it both separates and joins these two opposing zones. Often the threshold is a clearly defined exterior space, as found at Sant 'Andrea in Mantua, or the exterior porch of Filippo Brunelleschi's Pazzi Chapel in Florence. There are many examples of a threshold "room" of this type in mosques such as the Masjid-i-shah in Isfahan and the El-Aqsa Mosque in Jerusalem (fig. 10). Transitional spaces of this type not only establish a boundary, but symbolize passage from one mode of existence to another. That is why bridges and narrow gates are common mythological themes concerning spiritual transformation. There are many rituals associated with the crossing of the threshold, the taking off of shoes; rites of purification and sacrifice; even places of judgment.[11]

To reach the threshold and sacred place, often there is a path and entry sequence. The path that leads to the place can take many forms, from an axial, linear progression, to a labyrinthine maze, and typically involves a series of spaces or events, each becoming increasingly more sacred. This sequence acts as a market of the sacred ground, as protection for the uninitiated, and as a trial to be endured for those seeking the divine. Walking along the path and the attainment of the sacred place repeats the sacred act enacted by the god *in illo tempore* or mythological time.[12] According to Campbell, "The one who enters the temple compound and proceeds to the sanctuary is imitating the deed of the original hero. . . . The way is arduous and fraught with peril because it is, in fact, a rite for passing from the profane to the sacred."[13] The path is rarely easy but is experienced as a trial, either physically or psychologically. In some cases, narrow and lengthy stairs form the final portion of the path. We find this at the ascent to the Buddhist rock-

Fig. 10. A threshold space created by an exterior colonnade. El-Aqsa Mosque, Jerusalem (1033).

Fig. 11. Guardian figures often flank the entrance to the sacred place as in the lion figures at the west front entrance of the Basilica of San Zeno, Verona (twelfth century).

cut temples at Ajanta, the three thousand "Steps of Repentance" at Mount Sinai, and the seven thousand steps of Mount Tai-shen in China. However, the process if often contradictory, being simultaneously easy and hard, clear and obscured, close and distant.[14]

The pilgrim's route along the path underlines the gravity of the journey being undertaken and gives opportunities for the initiate to turn back. Often the paths and entrances to temples are guarded by colossal deities. In the Epic of Gilgamesh, "scorpion people . . . whose radiance is terrifying and whose look is death" guard the threshold to the land of immortality, which is at a pass of the mountain of Mashu.[15] At the Upper Nile site of Abu Simbal in Egypt, the colossal Pharaonic guardian deities mark the threshold to the inner sanctum beyond. Doorways are often marked by guardian deities. Caryatids atop beasts guarded the entrance to the ancient Syrian temple at Tell Halaf, and at the Mesoamerican temple of Chichén Itzá, giant stone serpents continue to guard the entrance to its colossal stairway. At the Romanesque basilica of San Zeno in Verona, which dates from the early twelfth century CE, two guardian beasts flank the elaborately carved west front doors (fig. 11). Similarly, the guardian figure of Christ in Judgment is commonly depicted on the west front-entrance tympanums of medieval churches as found at the Judgment Portal of Strasbourg Cathedral, the Last Judgment of Bourges Cathedral, and at Vézelay.

Where the Gods Have Been—the Place of Creation

In addition to being characterized as a place apart, separated from the profane world, and reached by a path and threshold, the sacred place also had other symbolic aspects. For example, in some cases the sacred place represented where the gods had been, a place where scenes of religious significance had taken place. The marking of the sacred place repeated this act of divinity. As has been previously mentioned, the sacred place was never chosen, but was discovered.[16] Thus, in the Japanese Shinto faith, forest clearings marked by a holy straw rope denote a place where a local *kami*, or deity, had been present.[17] According to Eliade, the sacred place often was believed to be a place where it was possible to come in contact with the gods; "however diverse and variously elaborated these sacred spaces may be, they all present one trait in common: there is always a clearly marked space which makes it possible (though under varied forms) to communicate with the sacred."[18]

In one of the holy texts of Hinduism, the *Mahabharata*, written in the fourth century BCE, sacred places were described as follows: "Just as certain links in the body are purer than others, so are certain places on earth more sacred—some on account of their situation, others because of their sparkling waters, and others because of the association or habitation of saintly people."[19]

In India there are seven sacred rivers, the Ganges being the most important, and four *dhamas*, or dwelling places of the gods, located at the four corners of the subcontinent.[20] There are also the Buddhist sites (discussed in chapter 2), that are associated with the Buddha's birth, enlightenment, ministry, and death, and are marked with temples. In ancient Egypt there were sacred sites identified as places where parts of Osiris's dismembered body were placed. There is Mount Sinai, where God appeared in smoke and thunder to Moses with the words, "I am the Lord your God," the first of the Ten Commandments (Exod. 20.2). In Jerusalem the Mount of Olives is where Christ instructed his eleven disciples a final time and ascended to heaven. "Then the Lord Jesus . . . was taken up into heaven, and sat down at the right hand of God" (Mark 16.19).

Center of the World, Axis Mundi, Primordial Mound

The sacred place often symbolized the center of the world, the omphalos or navel of the world, the place where the primordial creation took place. Frequently these sites are associated with sacred mountains, like the Greek sacred site at Delphi, as we shall see later. In Christianity,

Golgotha was seen as a place of creation, where not only the crucifixion took place but where Adam was created and buried. Judaism held that Jerusalem was the center of the world, and the Midrash Tanhuma states, "Just as the navel is found at the centre of a human being, so the land of Israel is found at the centre of the world. Jerusalem is at the centre of the land of Israel, and the temple is at the centre of Jerusalem, the Holy of Holies is at the centre of the temple, the Ark is at the centre of the Holy of Holies, and the Foundation Stone is in front of the Ark, which spot is the foundation of the world."[21] Mecca, as previously mentioned, was also seen as a place of original creation, and the world radiated from its center marked by the Kaaba.

There were many rituals associated with the construction of a temple or a house, many of which symbolized a primordial act. Groundbreaking rituals often included animal and, in some instances, human sacrifices. Analogous rituals are still performed today in the "crypto-religious" ceremonies associated with groundbreaking and topping-off ceremonies mentioned earlier.

Sacred mountains, where humans and the divine meet, often represent a place of original creation in many of the world's faiths. There are also replicas of sacred mountains, such as the Sumerian Ziggurat at Ur-Nammu, which not only served as a sacred mountain, but physically and symbolically created a path to the sun. Cultures that worshiped sun gods, such as the Egyptians and the pre-Columbian cultures of Mexico and Central America, built sacred mountains in the form of the pyramid and ziggurat. For example, the Pyramid of the Sun at Teotihuacán, Mexico, was axially oriented to the setting of the sun during the summer solstice and was only one part of a vast temple and city complex. Borobudur is also cited as a sacred mountain, symbolizing a place of transcendence at the center of the world.[22] Another example is the Neolithic Silbury Hill in Wiltshire, England, which is the largest human-made mound in Europe dating from this time (fig. 12). This earthen mountain rises 130 feet above the surrounding countryside and is said to have been either a gigantic burial mound or an astronomical observatory that charted the path of the sun.[23]

Fig. 12. Sacred mountains were often humanly made, as was the one shown here at Silbury Hill, Wiltshire, England (Neolithic Age).

For the Egyptians the construction of sacred mountains could be said to have begun with the Pyramid of King Zoser in Saqquara and culminated with the pyramids at Giza. In the latter example, the pyramid of Chephren, with its gold apex burning bright in the day, pointed the way to the omnipotent sun god Re. The rays of the sun symbolized a sacred path to the gods, as in the words of the pharaoh described in the *Pyramid Texts:* "I have trodden these thy rays as a ramp under my feet whereon I mount up to my mother Uraeus on the brow of Re."[24]

As previously noted, the sacred place was also seen as an *axis mundi*—an intersection of the three zones of heaven, earth, and the underworld—a point in space, a center where communication with God or the gods was possible. Sometimes this connection between worlds was symbolized by a sacred column, and the world consequently radiated from its cosmic axis. Eleanor Munro has described this as a "hinge structure . . . an actual object or monument, an expanded geographical structure, or an intangible essence or symbol that joins sky and earth."[25] For example, the foundation of the Temple of Jerusalem, the center of the Jewish people, was reputed to descend to the underworld. In New Guinea, the "men's house" is typically located at the center of the village and symbolizes the universe—its roof, the dome of the sky; the walls, the four cardinal directions. The early Buddhist stupas similarly represented the cosmos, established a center, and consecrated a sacred reliquary. Their shape is said to have derived from the form of earth heaped around a germinated seed. At the Great Stupa at Sanchi the spherical dome symbolizes the "cosmogonic egg," establishing a vertical connection between heaven and earth, and its four gates mark the horizontal cardinal points. Often the sacred enclosure had an opening to the sky, a symbolic connection to heaven, an element powerfully present in the oculus of the Pantheon in Rome (fig. 13).

Image of the Cosmos, Celestial City

The sacred place was also commonly created as an image of the cosmos, an *imago mundi*, or an earthly representation of a celestial city. It was often seen as the work of the gods, a tangible symbolic rendering of the divine. "Man constructs according to an archetype," Eliade points out; "his city and his temple have celestial models."[26] In some cases, the plan of the temple was revealed by God. Such is the case of the temple plan revealed in a dream to King Gudea of Lugash. Today on a statue of the king, one can see the plan inscribed on a tablet that rests on his lap. Similarly, the Temple of Jerusalem was revealed to Ezekiel in a vision. "The hand of the Lord was upon me, and brought me in the visions of God into the land of Israel, and set me down upon a very high mountain, on which was a structure like a city opposite me" (Ezek. 40.1–3). In the Old Testament, God also specifically describes the materials and dimensions of the Ark and the Tabernacle to Moses. "And let them make me a sanctuary," he commands, "that I may dwell in their midst. According to all that I show you concerning the pattern of the tabernacle, and all of its furniture, so you shall make it" (Exod. 25.8–9). In the Western Gothic cathedral, the interior of the church was often cited as a representation of the Celestial City as

Fig. 13. The dome and oculus of the Pantheon in Rome (ca. 120–127), marks the sacred center, the *axis mundi,* of this home of the Roman gods.

it appeared in the Revelation of Saint John. In the Byzantine church, the door to the altar set in the east is called the Door of Paradise and is symbolically opened during Easter week.[27] Indian cities and temples, designed according to the laws of Vastuvidya, a branch of knowledge devoted to architecture, were believed to reflect a deified order.[28]

The sacred place also expressed a "nostalgia for paradise"[29] and symbolized a primordial place of spiritual redemption and peace. The cosmic model of the sacred place often represented a pure place at the beginning of time. This might take the form of the primitive hut, such as is used in the Jewish Feast of the Tabernacles (Sukkoth). "You shall dwell in booths for seven days; all that are native in Israel," commands the Lord, enacting a return to primordial time. Concepts related to the notion of the primordial hut have regularly surfaced in the history and theories of architecture; theoreticians from Vitruvius to Frank Lloyd Wright have included references to the "first architecture" in their discourses on architecture. For example, Marc-Antoine Laugier in his 1753 *Essai sur l'architecture* wrote:

> Man wants a dwelling (and so) some branches broken off in the forest are material to his purpose. He chooses four of the strongest, and raises them perpendicularly to the ground, to form a square. On these he supports four others laid across them; above these he lays some which incline to both sides, and come to a point in the middle. This kind of roof is covered with leaves thick enough to keep out both the sun and rain: and now man is lodged.[30]

Places of primordial creation have also been attributed to cave sites. Earliest known examples are found at Lascaux in southwestern France and other prehistoric cave sites in this part of Europe. Just as there were humanly made mounds to re-create sacred mountains, there are also many examples of constructed caves. The Indian subcontinent holds many striking examples, such as the Buddhist rock-cut caves at Ajanta and Karli which were built between 642 and 150 BCE, or similarly hollowed-out sites created by the Jain faith.

Sacred Geometry

Often the cosmic model for the sacred place was expressed by its divine proportions or precious materials. Solomon's Temple, as described in 1 Kings, was built of stone, timber, and gold to specific dimensions; it became the exemplar of the sacred place until years later when Emperor Justinian was said to proclaim upon the completion of the Hagia Sophia, "O Solomon, I have surpassed thee!"

The use of geometry and proportion could be said to have been for two principal reasons. The first was to create a self-contained and unified whole, a pure sacred form distinguished from the "formless" profane surroundings. The second reason was to re-create or reflect God's omnipotence and perfection. In the latter case, the theme of discovering the sacred place, as distinguished from creating it, is reiterated. The sacred temple became a hierophany, a visible manifestation of the deity. Various geometrical and numerological systems fall under the loose category of sacred geometry. There are musical proportions, the golden section, the Fibonacci series, as well as forms such as platonic solids, the squaring of the circle, and *vesica piscis*. Numerous analyses of ancient monuments have been performed in the hope of revealing these sacred relationships; they range from the well grounded to the merely speculative. The study and practice of geometry and proportion was held to be a spiritual practice itself, as noted by Plato in *The Republic:*

> You amuse me, you who seem worried that I impose impractical studies upon you. It does not only reside with mediocre minds, but all men have difficulty in persuading themselves that it is through these studies, as if with instruments, that one purifies the eye of the soul, and that one causes a new fire to burn in this organ which was obscured and as though extinguished by the shadows of the other sciences, an organ whose conservation is more important than ten thousand eyes, since it is by it alone that we contemplate the truth.[31]

I have previously mentioned the Old Kingdom Egyptian pyramids at Giza and their pure geometry which distinguished them from their surroundings. Over its span of three thousand years, Egyptian civilization was distinguished, among other things, by its expertise in geometry and proportion. This likely arose from the need to survey the arable land on the banks of the Nile each year following the river's annual flooding. Certainly the Egyptian monuments throughout the breadth of their culture are distinguished by their precise siting, orientation, geometry, and proportion. The great Pyramid of Cheops, for example, is precisely oriented to the cardinal points. The entry shaft on its north face is said to point directly to the polestar of its time, Alpha Draconis. It has also been suggested that if one superimposes the section and plan of the Pyramid of Cheops, the proportion known as *squaring of the circle*[32] is evident; others state that the pyramid corresponds to golden sectional proportions.

Greek temples from the classical era display a strong reliance on geometry and proportion to establish them as plastic, self-contained entities. For example, the Temple of Poseidon at Sounion, perched on a promontory overlooking the Aegean Sea, is clearly an "object in space," its form delineated by proportional interrelationships. The proportions of the Parthenon on the Acropolis of Athens correspond to the golden section, its formal clarity accomplished by the utilization of *entasis* throughout (fig. 14). Similarly, the Mughal-era Taj Mahal in Agra is the result of an interrelated proportioning system. It rests on a raised platform, self-contained in space, and radially aligned to its entry avenue and surrounding buildings.

The Renaissance period in the West utilized proportioning systems to create the sacred as an interrelated whole similar to the above examples. At the Old Sacristy of S. Lorenzo in Florence, Brunelleschi mounted a hemispherical dome on a cubic base to form both the principal space and its adjoining chapel. Furthermore, the room surfaces are subdivided by moldings that proportionally interrelate the plan and the elevations. After beginning construction on the sacristy, Brunelleschi was commissioned by his patrons to rebuild the original Romanesque Basilica of S. Lorenzo (fig. 15). Here the cubic spatial module of the nave is repeated and subdivided to create a powerful,

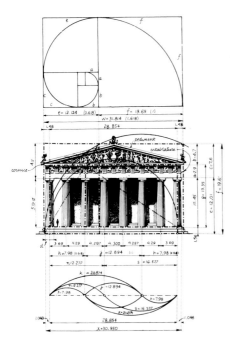

Fig. 14. The Parthenon on the Acropolis of Athens, the proportions of which correspond to the golden section.

Fig. 15. The nave of the Basilica of S. Lorenzo, Florence, Filippo Brunelleschi (1421–60).

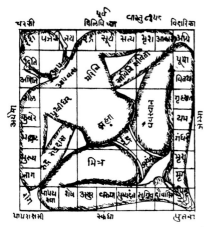

Fig. 16. The human body superimposed on a mandala, from the *Vastu-purusha*, an Indian architecture manual.

interrelated whole. One quarter of the square of the crossing forms the side aisles; two of these, one bay of the nave. Three squares equal to the crossing square form the transept and choir. The proportional module is reinforced throughout by the *pietra serena*, the surface decoration of dark stone. Here the mystical, vertical geometry of the medieval cathedral was supplanted by the mathematical precision of the Renaissance to create an intensely spiritual space.

Leonardo da Vinci's drawing after Marcus Vitruvius Pollio, which related the human figure to the geometries of the square and the circle, has become the symbol of the human-centered order of the Renaissance. Proportions derived from the human body, however, appear in cultures from many periods and places. The plan of Luxor Temple is said to correspond to a standing human figure, and the pilgrimage church of the Western Christian church with its outstretched transepts similarly mimics the human body. In the East there is the mandala plan, the roots of which are the Indian *Viatuvida*. In the Indian cosmology, the circle, corresponding to the earth, represented the perfection of the universe, but the square incarnated the supreme principal of Brahma. In the Indian manual of architecture, the *Vastu-purusha*, the human body is shown superimposed on a subdivided square mandala (fig. 16).[33]

Saint Bernard of Clairvaux stridently encapsulated the Cistercian reform with the dictate, "There must be no decoration, only proportion." The Cistercian order, founded in the twelfth century as a reform movement to the Cluniacs, were a silent order, spending their days occupied with labor, prayer, and music. The interiors of their churches were proportioned such that they functioned as colossal "sounding boards," reverberating the cadence of the sung mass. Cistercian monastic architecture is characterized by the absence of decoration, including stained glass. Regarding decoration and iconography, Saint Bernard is quoted as saying, "We forbid there be any statues or pictures in our churches or in any other rooms of a monastery of ours, because, when attention is paid to such things, the advantages of sound meditation and training in religious gravity are often neglected."[34] Geometry is the other outstanding feature. Responding to Saint Augustine's assertion that music and geometry were effective meditative devices, and that architecture responded to the same principles as music, the proportioning of the buildings, in particular the church, was done according to strict geometrical proportions, some of which were inherited from Greco-Roman antiquity. The musical ratios of the octave, or 1:2; the fifth, or 2:3; and the fourth, or 3:4, were the ones most commonly employed.

One of the first Cistercian monasteries was Fontenay, which was founded in 1118. By the end of the Middle Ages there were 742 Cistercian monasteries in all. Located in the Burgundy region of France, Fontenay is one of the most extant of the surviving monasteries. As was typical, it was located in a remote area next to a good source of water. The approach to the monastery was through a wooded valley. The church is the most striking feature of the monastery and expresses many of the Cistercian laws regarding their architecture. It is a low building without any towers, the antithesis of Cluniac architecture. When one enters the west door and proceeds down the nave, the power of its ordering is profoundly apparent. The interior is proportioned according to the square and the cube, and the ratio of 1:2. Similar to the much later S. Lorenzo, the module for the architecture is established by the crossing. This is repeated to form the choir and is halved to create the cadence of the piers of the nave. A quarter of the square is used to form the bays of the side aisles, which are capped by a string-course on the aisle piers to form a series of repeating cubes (fig. 17). The result was, quoting Saint Bernard, "Geometry at the service of prayer."

Saint Bernard and his contemporary, Abbot Suger, are cited as setting the stage for the Gothic that followed.[35] During the Gothic era the wealth of mathematical knowledge, rediscovered by the medieval world as a result, in part, of the Crusades and nourished by the School of Chartres, found its full application in architecture. The proportioning of the cathedral at Chartres, among many of the monuments of this spectacular age, has been attributed to the application of sacred geometry, from its plan, section, and elevation, to the complex geometry of its rose windows.

Fig. 17. Geometry in the service of prayer. A view down a side aisle, looking west, of the church of Fontenay Abbey (Cistercian), France (1139–47).

Setting for Ritual

Lastly, the sacred place is today, as in the past, a setting for ritual observances, a symbolic narrative facilitated by the architectural setting of the path and place. "A ritual is an enactment of a myth," Joseph Campbell points out. "By participating in a ritual, you are participating in a myth."[36] Through ritual, one is able to approach and perhaps commune with the divine. Often it provides the means for a transcendent experience. Ritual, to be effective, needs to be performed within a sacred setting, whether it is a simply demarcated space or an immense temple. Without this sacred setting, the ritual has no context and thus loses its meaning. Spiro Kostof describes this function: "Public architecture at best aspires to be just this: a setting for the ritual that makes of each user, for a brief moment, a larger person than he or she is in daily life, filling each one with the pride of belonging."[37]

Rituals, performed in groups or between an initiate and a teacher, were often kept secret in the form of mysteries. Dire warnings pertaining to the penalty for revealing the mysteries to the uninitiated often were connected with their ceremonial transmission. From an Egyptian mystery cult we read, "Thou shalt not divulge it. He who divulges it dies a sudden death. . . ." Similarly, the rituals had to be carried out precisely, or they could be very dangerous. The temple was a very powerful place, and the sacred ground had to be approached with specific actions.

Because there is often a strict requirement regarding the exact enactment of the ritual, the acts became canonized. Thus we find rituals that were passed on, virtually unchanged, from generation to generation. Rituals were never spontaneous, but were symbolic of timelessness and continuity. Over time, the enactment of the myth through ritual typically came to require a prescribed set of actions, dress, body movements, and speech.

Rituals also symbolize a return to primordial time or *in illo tempore*, the Golden Age, a time when the gods were present and the religious myths were initially enacted. Similar to sacred space, sacred time is perceived as an interval in the surrounding profane time. This sacred time generally takes the form of religious festivals, structured by the seasonal rhythm of the year. During festivals the myths are ritually enacted, often facilitated by the architectural setting. Sites such as Avebury seem to have grown directly from the ritual, as we will observe later. Often the mythological narrative is expressed by the path and the place. Rituals also often reenact a mythological event. For example, at the Convent of Saint George in Cairo, one can arrange to be wrapped in chains, symbolically repeating the persecution of the saint. Pilgrimage, as we have observed earlier, is a consummate example of ritualized religious behavior that is practiced by all of the world's major faiths. It is a symbolic and physical journey from the profane to the sacred with the express purpose of communing with the god.

Water often possesses strong symbolic content in religion, and the practice of ablution is a ritual that is shared by all of the world religions. In the Shinto faith, ritual purification is performed by washing one's hands and rinsing out the mouth at the water trough located at the entrance to the shrine. Zen Buddhist temples and teahouses also have places for ritual ablution. Christianity has a similar practice centering around the font of holy water in the narthex of the church. Islam is distinguished, in part, by its ritual acts of ablution before one enters the mosque. A particularly beautiful setting for this act is found at the Mosque of Sultan Hassan in Cairo, at its fountains set within an internal courtyard (fig. 18). Nearby is the Ibn Tulun Mosque, which has a stark fountain in the middle of its vast courtyard providing a place for the faithful to wash before prayers. Sacred springs often have provided settings for ritual ablutions, as we will observe later at the Greek site at Delphi. Ablution is common at Hindu temples as well. For example, there is the Great Bath at the ancient city of Mohenjo-Daro in Pakistan, and the Great Temple of Modhera in India.

The crossing of the threshold at the sacred place also typically requires an attendant ritual. In addition to ablution, other acts of purification and supplication are often required at the border between the profane and the sacred, such as prostrations, taking off one's shoes, and other related acts and rituals.

Fig. 18. The fountain of the Mosque of Sultan Hassan, Cairo (1356–63).

Often rituals were enacted by the community according to a yearly schedule of festivals and celebrations. These had the principal function of rededicating and resanctifying the temple. All the major religions have an annual calendar of observances and their associated rituals. These observances have traditionally included some type of processional within the sacred enclosure. In addition to these group enactments, daily rituals and ministrations are carried out by the priesthood.

Ritual drama often was ritually performed at sacred sites during specific times during the year. The Greek theater is said to have developed from early Dionysian rites. These apparently would center around an omphalos stone, such as is found at Delphi, with the participants ritually dancing around it, depicting Dionysus and thus suggesting the attainment of immortality. Similarly, Egyptian Osirian mystery plays were performed at Abydos, with actors depicting the many deities.[38] Christianity, especially during the Middle Ages, was distinguished by the rituals and drama enacted within the cathedral. Some of these were irreverent and playful, others reflected the incorporation of pagan practices into the Christian faith. During the Feast of the

Fig. 19. Telesterion, Sanctuary of Demeter, Eleusis, Greece (fifth century BCE).

Holy Innocents, for example, choir boys would switch places with the clergy and conduct the service. During the Feast of the Circumcision, an ass would be led down the nave and the service would include loud hee-haws issued by the clergy.[39]

Ritual, enacted within the sacred place, often was means of initiation as well. Here the initiates would be led through a series of rituals to effect what was often radical personal transformation. A Greek ritual site located at Eleusis was identified with the earth goddess in the form of Demeter, goddess of agriculture. This was the setting for the enactment of the Eleusinian Mysteries, a ritual that began with a procession along a sacred way that led from the Dipylon Gate in Athens to Eleusis. Here the serpentine path passed through a threshold to twin propylaia and concluded in the interior of the Telesterion. This columned hall, unlike the later temples to the Olympian gods, was to be entered and used by the participants. There, standing in crowded rows on steps that surrounded the central space, the initiates would watch and participate in the secret sacred rites (fig. 19).[40]

The Paleolithic cave sanctuaries found in France and Spain are believed to have provided settings for male initiation rites. At Lascaux, for example, it is thought that adolescent boys were led down the dark, winding, and descending passages to the inner womblike chambers. Here, Joseph Campbell states, "the boys became no longer their mother's sons but their father's sons."[41] This powerful place is perhaps one of the earliest examples of the spiritual path and place. One enters by means of a narrow, steeply sloping passage that leads to the Hall of the Bulls. Here paintings of four giant bulls created by thick black outline are shown: three are viewed sideways, the fourth faces the viewer. The most powerful space lies deep within the earth and is reached by a precipitous passageway called The Apse. At its bottom is the Shaft of the Dead Man, where a huge wounded bison is shown and at his feet, a small, mortally wounded man. These paintings of bulls and other animals of the hunt perhaps assisted in initiating the boys into the knowledge of hunting, a skill necessary for the clan's survival. The boys would emerge from this dark, damp womb of initiation into knowledge, no longer boys, but men.

The sacred place, through a multitude of forms and meanings, typically represented a sacred center, differentiated from the surrounding profane world. This sacred place, consecrated or inhabited by the gods, or located at the axis point of the world, could only be entered by the initiated through paths and gateways—the spiritual path and place.

CHAPTER 5

Many Paths, Many Places

We have observed the pan-cultural phenomenon of pilgrimage to the sacred place, as well as a variety of origins and symbolisms of sacred sites and their means of entry. In chapter 2, we identified several types of path and place plans found at sacred sites. Principally, these fall into two categories: the linear path and the segmented path; both comprise a number of organizations. Types of linear paths include axial paths, bifurcated paths, radiating paths, grid path systems, and circumambulating paths. Segmented paths take many forms, from "connected series," to labyrinths. Of course, all of the examples cannot be fully explained only by this means, nor do all of them fit neatly into specific categories. The following is an examination of a range of examples based on these typologies, however, as a point of departure for discussion.

The Axial Path

Japanese Shinto shrines are often axially organized, and Shimogamo Shrine in Kyoto and the Naiku Shrine at Ise Jingu are two variations of this path type. *Shinto*, or "way of the gods," is a word derived from the Chinese *shentao*, which means "mystic rules of nature."[1] It can best be described as a "native" religion, and it displays characteristics of similar faiths around the world. Unlike the other major religion of Japan—Buddhism, which arrived from China and Korea—Shinto is

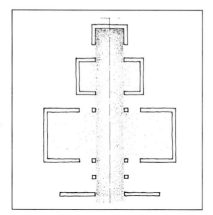

Fig. 20. The axial path.

indigenous to Japanese culture. The primary components that comprise Shinto are an animistic and pantheistic attitude about nature; and a belief in the promise of divine response to prayer. Regeneration, fertility, and ritual purity characterize its beliefs and practices. As in other native faiths, Shinto was a manifestation of needs arising from the anxieties and exigencies of an agrarian culture.

The beauty and diversity of Japan, and its often capricious, dramatic weather, predominantly formed Shinto. The desire to supplicate animistic deities and to bind together the community grew out of the communal, agrarian culture of rice farming. Natural objects such as mountains, stones, and trees symbolized a clan's local *kami*, or spirit. Early shrines were a simple clearing in the forest, marked, separated, and purified by a priest to prepare for the reception of the *kami*. Strips of paper, or linen, were tied to a sacred rope which was strung from four bamboo poles set in the ground. This marked a sacred space for the temporary presence of a deity, which early Shinto rituals called to the earth. Later the shrines came to house the personified gods themselves.[2]

The types of shrines one finds today can be divided into three groups: shrines for a local *kami*; shrines for specific requests (such as marriage, children, and success in business); and shrines of national and political importance. The first type is usually associated with a local natural landmark. Stones, or groupings of stones, as at Futami noted earlier, are typical of Shinto sites."[3] The second type exemplifies the Shinto belief in the response of the gods to specific requests. The Fushimi Inari Shrine in Kyoto, for example, is dedicated to success in business. Ise Jingu is the consummate example of the third type of shrine, and is associated with the deification of the emperor and royal family.

Typical Shinto shrines are characterized by axial symmetry and are commonly oriented north-south. The formal organization and orientation of Shinto shrines is similar to early Buddhist temples that influenced their development. The sequence of the axial path creates a series of thresholds and spaces that are increasingly sacred. The sacred place at the end of the path is the home of the gods, reserved solely for the deities and the priests.

The path typically begins with the characteristic *torii* gate, and beyond this threshold is often marked by opposing lanterns or protective talismans in the form of *koma-inu*, or "lion dogs." Usually before one enters the first courtyard, there is a water trough, or *chozu-sha*, a place of ritual ablution, where one uses a wooden dipper to wash the hands and rinse out the mouth. After this preparation, one is ready to enter the first precinct, or courtyard. The courtyards, enclosed by high walls and entered by prominent gates, generally contain the *kagura-den*, the sacred dance hall; the *haiden*, or worship hall; the *kannushi*, a building for the religious official and shrine manager; and a number of *massha*, or small offertory shrines. The inner courtyard is reserved for the ritually purified priests and encloses treasury and worship buildings.

At Shimogamo Shrine in Kyoto, the axial path is marked initially by a large *torii* (fig. 21). The gravel path leads to a place of ablution outside the first gateway. This two-story gateway firmly establishes a spatial threshold to the first courtyard. There follow two outer courtyards; the first contains the dance and worship halls (fig. 22); the second outer-courtyard, attained by a smaller gateway, contains a number of offertory shrines. Next is a wide, raised passageway with a central gateway that leads to the inner courtyard; within are a number of treasury and worship buildings (fig. 23).

Ise Jingu, located on the Shima-nanto peninsula, one of the longest inhabited areas of Japan, represents the soul of Shinto. There are two adjacent sites at Ise Jingu: Geku, the "Outer Shrine," and Naiku, the "Inner Shrine." The more important Naiku Shrine is dedicated to Amaterasu, the sun goddess and guardian deity of the Japanese nation.[4] The initial path sequence at Naiku is basically a segmented path, which follows the Isuzu River and the topography of the hilly, thickly forested site. It is only at the sacred enclosure itself that the path and architecture are organized axially. The path begins at the Uji Bridge over the river and leads past *torii* to a place of ablution on the opposite river bank. Beyond, it winds through the site, marked by a number of *torii*,

Fig. 21. The entrance *torii* at Shimo-gamo Shrine, Kyoto.

Fig. 22. The outer courtyard and dance platform, viewed through the main gateway, Shimogamo Shrine, Kyoto.

Fig. 23. The inner courtyard, viewed through its enclosing passageway. Shimogamo Shrine, Kyoto.

Fig. 24. On the right, the Naiku Shrine at Ise Jingu, Japan, is shown. On the left is the second site, used every twenty years for the ritual rebuilding of the sacred buildings.

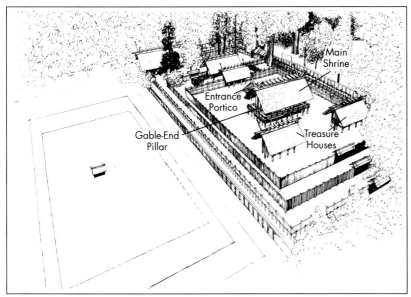

and flanked periodically by buildings dedicated to particular functions and rituals. The goal of the path is the sacred precinct, enclosed by four concentric rows of wooden fences, inside of which is the Main Hall flanked by the East and West Treasuries (fig. 24). Originally, the buildings held the sacred mirror, sword, and jewel, symbolizing the sun, moon and thunder. These artifacts are associated with the myth of Amaterasu, who, angered by her younger brother Susa-No-O, plunged the world into darkness by hiding in a cave. She is lured out by the laughter of the assembled gods who are watching a provocative dance and by her reflection in the sacred mirror, and thus light is restored. The small, traditional, indigenous-style buildings have no space for congregation; only those specially anointed and purified can intercede with the goddess. Worship in the form of prayer and obeisance takes place outside its walls. There are actually two sacred sites at the Naiku; the second is a building site used for the rebuilding of the sacred buildings every twenty years.

Shinto sites involve a linear progression from the secular world to the sacred, each space purer and holier than the preceding one, culminating in the inner courtyard. Typically, there are sequential domains of enclosure with attendant threshold gateways, a typology evocatively expressed by the concentric rectangular spaces at Naiku. Often, Shinto shrines are located in natural surroundings where the path becomes a journey into the landscape. The Shinto belief that the holy is present in natural objects and phenomena found symbolic expression not only in Shinto shrines, but also in Buddhist architecture as well. This pantheistic respect found powerful resonances in Zen Buddhism. Shinto architecture also expresses the transitory nature of life, its growth and decay. The periodic rebuilding of the sites at Ise Jingu, though principally derived from purification rites, powerfully symbolizes the impermanence of human works and, by implication, the constancy of the forces of the natural world. Lastly, the archetypal act of marking sacred ground, first by very simple means, later by enclosing walls, marks the place where the divine and the human can interact in meaningful and portentous ways.

Egyptian architecture, particularly Late Kingdom sites, provides many examples of axial paths. The axial nature of Egyptian sacred sites, such as the Mortuary Temple of Queen Hatshepsut (ca. 1500 BCE), is related to their proto-three-dimensional space conceptions. Egyptian sculpture, comprised of a composition of right-angle planes with a dominant front face, typifies the extent of three-dimensional space conception in Egyptian art and architecture.[5] Parallel planes, as in pylons in typical pylon temples, in one aspect were two-dimensional and legible surfaces, their hieroglyphics intended to be read as one passed along the path.

Queen Hatshepsut was the only female ruler of dynastic Egypt. She ruled during a notably peaceful twenty years during the Late Kingdom, and her reign was distinguished by an emphasis on the arts and domestic affairs. She intended her temple as an earthly rendition of the paradisiacal home of the gods, including Amun, to whom the temple is dedicated, replete with terraced gardens of myrrh trees. The story of the expedition mounted by Hatshepsut's architect Senmut to the land of Punt in search of the myrrh trees is depicted on the walls of the Punt Colonnade on the upper terrace.[6] The complex was located next to the Middle Kingdom Mortuary Temple of Mentuhotep, built five hundred years before, and apparently used its neighbor as a quarry for materials. Mentuhotep's temple also featured an axial causeway, enclosed on both sides by high walls flanked by statues of the king, and open to the sky. This path led to a forecourt, where a ramp ascended to a terrace on which a pyramid, hypostyle hall, and burial chamber were located.

The path at Hatshepsut's Temple began at the Nile and headed due west (fig. 25). A sphinx-flanked causeway led to an outer courtyard that was enclosed by walls and a colonnade to the west. A still extant, axially aligned ramp leads to the upper terrace, which is similarly bounded on its western side by a colonnade and by chapels to Hathor and Anubis. The final terrace, reached also by a ramp, contained a colonnaded court, on either side of which is a mortuary chapel and the Hall of Amun. The inner sanctum of the temple aligns with the path

Fig. 25. The plan and axonometric drawing of the Mortuary Temple of Queen Hatshepsut, Deir el-Bahri, Egypt (ca. 1500 BCE).

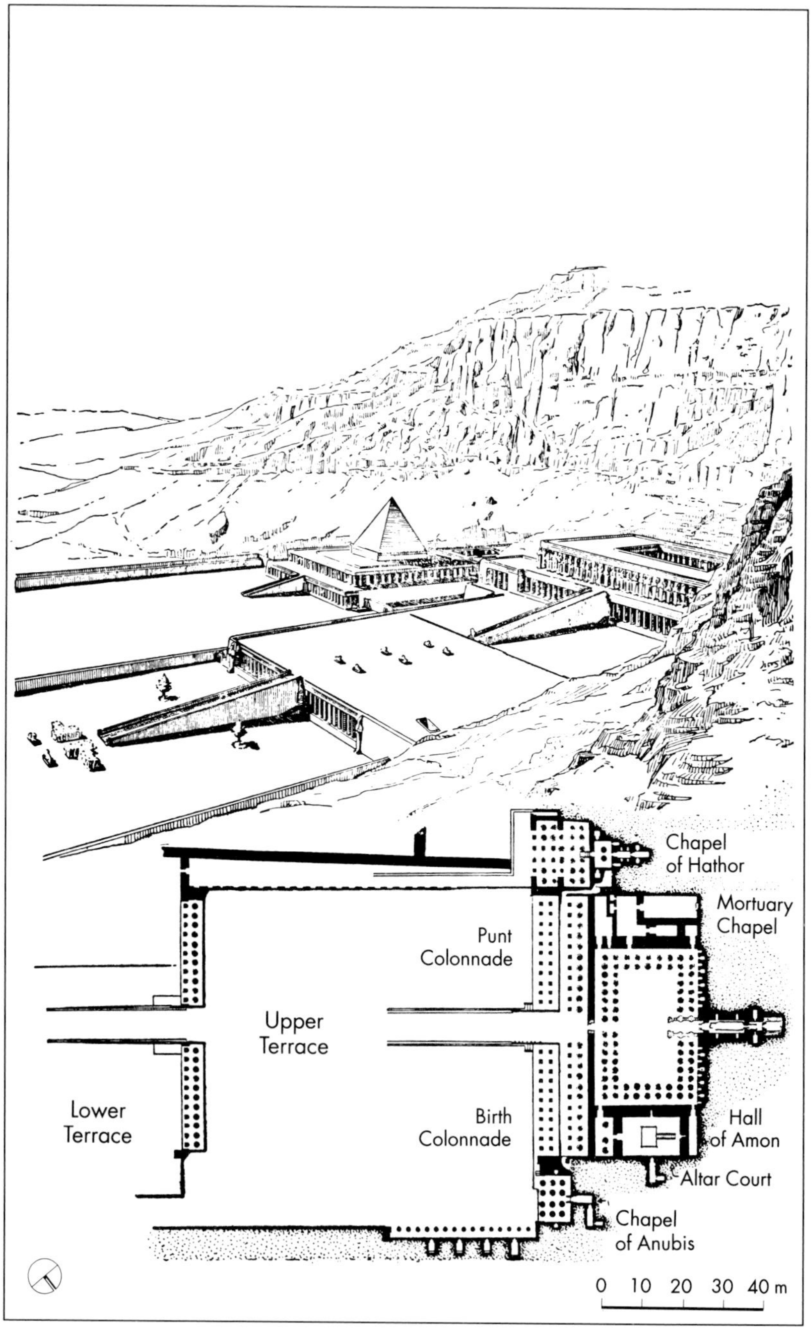

and is carved into the surrounding cliffs. Indeed, as is apparent today, the entire complex seems to be a continuation of the imposing backdrop of the cliffs (fig. 26).

The path was articulated by edges, guardian figures, thresholds, and the cadence of light and shadow—elements also at Karnak, discussed later. The deep, double colonnades of the terraces provided a dramatic edge and delineated one area from the rest. The place took the form of increasingly enclosed and sacred places, culminating in the dense, dark, and small inner sanctum.

The axial path at Deir el-Bahri was aligned with the east-west path of Karnak, located across the Nile on its east bank. This alignment symbolized the annual visit of the god during the Festival of the Valley, who would be symbolically ferried across the Nile on a sacred barge to the west bank to greet the dead. A yearly cycle of festivals were an integral part of Egyptian religion, the settings for which were provided by sites such as Hatshepsut's Temple. Processionals would begin with the symbolic trip across the Nile and continue up the causeway to the inner sanctum. The spaces became increasingly sacred, with the inner sanctum reserved only for the priesthood.

Fig. 26. The ramps, terraces, plantings, and colonnades of the Mortuary Temple of Queen Hatshepsut were designed to depict a paradisiacal garden. The inner sanctum of the temple is carved into the base of the rock cliff. To the left are the remains of the Middle Kingdom Mortuary Temple of Mentuhotep.

The dramatic effect of sequentially aligned, increasingly small and dark spaces is most effectively observed today at the temple of Hathor at Dendara, a Ptolemaic-era temple. It is remarkably preserved, with most of its walls and roof still extant. As one walks along the axial path at Dendara the floor gradually rises, ascending a series of terraces, while the roof simultaneously lowers (fig. 27). The inner sanctum is a self-contained enclosure, oppressively small and dark in comparison to the immense, bright outer courtyard (fig. 28).

Dendara, dedicated to the goddess Hathor, was the setting for the beginning of the annual Festival of the Reunion when Hathor, who was associated with the moon, was symbolically reunited with Horus, a god associated with the sun. The procession would begin in the inner sanctum of the temple, attended only by the priesthood. It would proceed along the axial path, passing finally through the outer colonnade of the temple, the column capitals of which were adorned with the likenesses of Hathor. There, through the opened gates of the walled enclosure, the common people would get their first glimpse of the retinue. The lengthy procession of priests bore at its rear the small, golden sacred barge of Hathor. The procession traveled to the Nile, where the barge was loaded onto a ship for the long sail upriver. Followed by pilgrims on foot and in boats, the procession first stopped at Karnak, thirty-seven miles upstream, where ceremonies were performed. After another stop at Komir, the festival concluded at the Temple of Edfu, where the harvest festival was concluded with music, dancing, and feasting.[7]

Fig. 27. A longitudinal section of the Temple of Hathor, Dendara, Egypt. (Ptolemaic era).

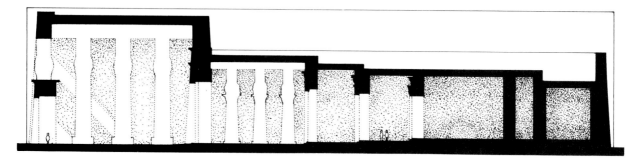

a   b

Fig. 28. (a) The inner sanctum (on the left) of the Temple of Hathor, Dendara, where during the Festival of the Reunion the procession would begin. (b) The axial path leading from the inner sanctum. (c) The entrance to the temple, viewed from the main courtyard. It is here that the common people would have first viewed the retinue of the priesthood.

c

Fig. 29. The entrance to the Treasury of Atreus, Mycenae (ca. 1400 BCE).

Examples of Mycenaean funerary architecture also display an axial alignment of the entry path, though on a much smaller scale. The entrance to the *tholoi* of the Treasury of Atreus at Mycenae (1400 BCE) is a straight, linear path formed by cylopean walls on either side (fig. 29). Inside the dromos, or beehive-shaped tomb, in a rectangular antechamber, were the remains of the king (fig. 30). On the day of the king's interment, the funerary procession would have traveled down the axial path, its walls rising incrementally higher as the path cut into the hillside, an intensifying experience of enclosure and sacrality. An imposing gateway, set within a battered wall and still partially extant

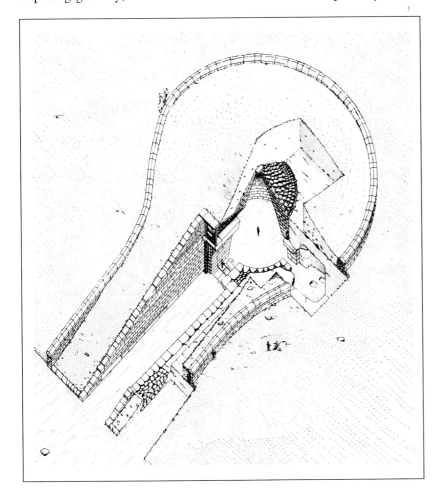

Fig. 30. The Treasury of Atreus, Mycenae, showing the beehive-shaped *tholoi* and the rectangular antechamber, where the remains of the king were entombed.

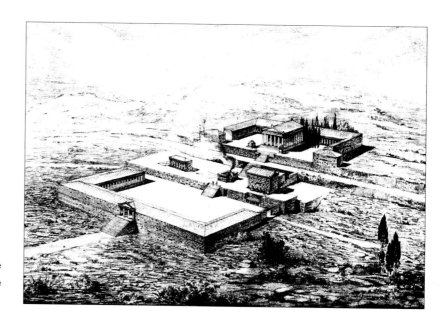

Fig. 31. The axial path leading to the upper terrace and temple at the Temple of Asklepios at Kos (300–150 BCE).

today, marked the entrance to the inner sanctum. The doorway was flanked by a pair of green downward-tapered limestone columns, above which were set two smaller columns and a decorated panel. Inside was the dominant space of the *tholoi*. In the antechamber space, the king would have been lowered into a pit beneath the floor level and surrounded by his earthly treasures. After the ceremonies were completed, this chamber would have been sealed up.[8] It has been suggested that the entire path and *tholoi* were subsequently covered with earth, but it is possible that they were retained for repeating ceremonies and rituals.

The Hellenistic Greek temple of Asklepios at Kos (300–150 BCE), added to later by the Romans, displays a striking similarity to the terraced temples of Queen Hatshepsut and Mentuhotep (fig. 31). There were three axially oriented terraces; the final terrace held the temple, which was surrounded by a colonnaded stoa on three sides. The site was dedicated to Asklepios, the god of healing, and to the physician Hippocrates (who was born on the island of Kos). The first terrace was a large courtyard surrounded on three of its sides by rooms for the sick and by a southern retaining wall that contained fountains. The second terrace contained an altar and several temples. The entire complex served the pilgrims who arrived there in search of a cure for their ailments. The path is not exactly axial as the placement of the stairs shifts from terrace to terrace. It is a series of volumes, marked by the thresholds of the stairs and temples placed within the courts. The strict axiality of the final section of the path that led to the temple itself, however, provides a stark contrast to the segmented path of the earlier Temple of Apollo at Delphi. The final axial alignment is looking north from the temple itself. There, aligned with the final set of stairs, is a conical mountain across the seas. According to Vincent Scully, "the process of healing or seeking to be healed is now found to lie far beyond the self, as the temple and the landscape reveal together and show it to lie in the earth's keeping."[9]

Roman temples, such as is typified by the Temple of Fortuna Virilis in Rome (200 BCE), and the Maison Carrée in Nîmes (19 BCE), exhibit a similar frontal axiality. In both cases the entire temple is raised on a podium and is reached by a wide set of stairs; a deep colonnaded porch forms an entry volume to the cella beyond. Even the Pantheon in Rome (118–128 CE), with its dominant central space, was entered along an axial path, first through a courtyard and then a colonnaded temple front located on its south side. The path is aligned with the circle/sphere that creates its central space.

The axial plan of the Roman basilica accommodated and was transformed by the rituals and liturgy of early Christianity. The apse, formerly reserved for the Roman priests and sacrifices, now became the place for celebrating the Eucharist. The central nave of Santa Sabina in Rome (422–32 CE) was formed by flanking aisles, and its path culminated in a simple hemispherical apse. Similarly, S. Giovanni in Laterano in Rome, which dates from just after Constantine's declaration of 313 CE, was based on the basilican plan. Here, an axial path occupied a central rectangular colonnaded space, leading to an apse at the far end of the building. Similarly, San Zeno in Verona is characterized by a basilican plan, except in this example the sanctuary is raised above

Fig. 32. View from the nave looking toward the sanctuary, which is raised above the crypt. The Basilica of San Zeno, Verona.

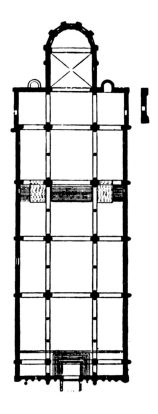

Fig. 33. Plan, San Zeno, Verona.

the crypt and is reached by stairs, a spatial device that we will see at Vézelay (figs. 32, 33). The plan of an idealized monastery known as Saint Gall (820 CE) shows a church of basilican plan and an axial path that leads to a now more articulated apse. Later buildings, such as the cathedral at Speyer (1029–61 CE), Santiago de Compostela (1075–1125 CE), and the Abbey Church of Saint-Pierre, also known as Cluny III (1088–1121 CE), display the same axial path, its entrances, thresholds, and spatial sequencing growing increasingly more sophisticated.

The lengthy axial path typified the Western Roman Catholic cathedral. In the Eastern church, linear axiality was subordinate to the centralized domed space. It was the Gothic that lengthened and accentuated the axial path of the Western Christian church. This is especially evident in English medieval cathedrals such as Canterbury, Norwich, Saint Albans, and Peterborough (fig. 34). The cathedral was the center of civic life in medieval Europe and host to a yearly schedule of pageants and festivals. The processional path of the cathedral facilitated and accommodated a variety of functions, from daily services to marriage and burial rites.

In Western architecture the axial path continued throughout subsequent historical iterations. Renaissance churches such as S. Spirito in Florence (begun 1436 CE) and Sant 'Andrea in Mantua (begun 1472) display similar, if not so accentuated, linear paths. Indeed, all the major faiths contain examples of axial paths in some of their monuments. Certain mosques, such as the Külliye of Süleyman I, display a strong axiality of path and place. There are numerous Hindu temples, such as the Golden Temple of Vishwanath Khajuraho, India (eleventh century), that display a similar organization. Temple cities, such as the Forbidden City in China, as well as early Buddhist temples in Japan, also display an axial layout.

The Woodland Cemetery located outside of Stockholm was designed by the architect Gunnar Asplund and landscape architect Sigurd Lewerentz. It provides an example of a modern axial path in a parklike setting. This funerary complex, which initially resulted from a 1915 competition, initially suggests aspects of classical radial planning.

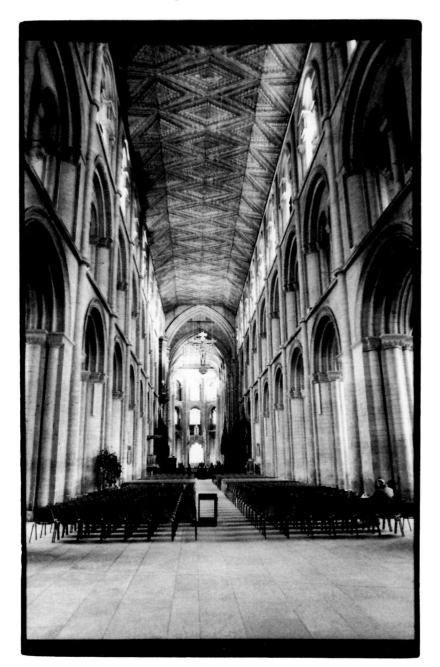

Fig. 34. The nave of Peterborough Cathedral, England.

Fig. 35. Site plan, Woodland Cemetery, Stockholm (1935–1940), courtesy of Canadian Centre for Architecture, Montréal.

However, the main entrance path is axial in plan, though markedly different in organization from many of the previous examples. The most striking aspect of the main entry path, called the Way of the Cross, is that it does not have an articulated termination space. Instead, it traverses a space with buildings on one side and landscape on the other, passing them by on its journey (fig. 35).

The complex is surrounded by high stone walls that permit limited views into it at controlled points. The path begins on the north side at a semicircular exedra and a gateway set within the wall, delineating the passage from secular to sacred. The Way of the Cross ascends a gradual incline, initially passing on the left a wall fronted by an earth berm, and on the distant right, the raised earthworks of the Meditation Knoll (fig. 36). The path itself is created simply, by stones set in the grassy landscape. Further along the path, another threshold is formed by the cross that is just to the right of the path, with a crematorium complex on the left. This group of buildings contains the crematoriums and two small chapels. The journey concludes with the larger Chapel of the Holy Cross. Its open portico, first glimpsed from the distance, is entered on the left of the terminus of the Way of the Cross. The square opening of the roof of the chapel's entry portico marks the threshold to the space within.

Throughout the complex of Woodland Cemetery, there is an interplay of the natural and the humanmade. Perhaps this is illustrated by the earlier Woodland Chapel, which is located to the south and east of the principal buildings. The pure geometry of its interlocked squares, its whiteness contrasted with the dark surrounding forest, and the circular inner sanctum with its hemispherical dome, establish it as a place apart. The surrounding plantings of the chapel underline its separateness and produce a dramatic entry threshold, while simultaneously blurring the edge between it and its surroundings. This dialectic is also apparent at the Way of the Cross, where there is a complex interplay between the landscape, path, and architecture. The surface of the path itself exists in a zone that is neither landscape nor architecture. The path and its destinations are comprised of a series of thresh-

olds followed by open volumes of landscape and architecture. As one climbs from the gateway at the street to the crest of the hill, framed views along the journey are consistently directed skyward, toward the ethereal unknown.[10]

Another modern example of the axial path is the Roman Catholic church of Pastoor van Ars-kerk in the Hague. This building was architect Aldo van Eyck's second major commission and was completed in 1969, ten years after the Orphanage in Amsterdam. I have chosen this early work of van Eyck's because of the way he has consciously reinterpreted the interior path of the Western Christian church. He had in fact explored similar ideas in an earlier project entitled the Wheels of Heaven, a Protestant church that was never built. Writing about the

Fig. 36. The Way of the Cross at the Woodland Cemetery, Stockholm, viewed from the entrance. On the left is the crematorium complex, on the right the Meditation Knoll. The goal of the axial path is the open portico of the Chapel of the Holy Cross.

planning of both projects, van Eyck states, "Far from wishing to secularize, i.e. neutralize or banalize, what for others is sacred, I have in both cases tried, as an outsider, to mitigate the old worn-out hierarchy's irreversibility; persuading it to become reversible—or relative."[11]

This church, as in the previous examples, demonstrates ways in which the Western Christian plan type can be transformed. At Pastoor van Ars-kerk, there is a strong directional "sacred way"[12] running east to west, but instead of leading to the destination of the sanctuary, it passes by a number of semicircular chapels while ascending five levels (fig. 37). Van Eyck describes it as a "tall space—neither narthex nor nave, but something of both," and it also serves to divide the public side of the church, or "congregation space," from the private side, which contains a general use or extension space, offices, and a priest's apartment.

The path begins at a set of double doors on the western facade of the church, marked on one side by the cylindrical massing of an expressed chapel (fig. 38). The entrance is not anticipated by any other massing or path articulation on the outside. Van Eyck states that the site and an early planning decision of a rectangular plan sacrificed "the idea of extended or gradual entry a complex periphery allows. This time entry is so sudden that the nature of the church doors becomes that idea's last resort." The dual use of the entry, as both a place to arrive and a place to leave, is symbolized by unequally sized doors—a small one for entry, a large one for exit. "One slips in from the side one after another and leaves with others after mass through the large ones. . . . Entry starts, as it were, once one is inside! An unavoidable limitation, but a limitation still."[13]

Once inside the door, one enters a low, dark foyer space and is presented with a choice of either turning left toward the private area, or turning right and heading toward a light-filled space marked by one of the chapels. Shortly after turning right, one attains this space, which is 36 feet (11/m) high and spans the entire east-west axis of the church (fig. 39). This space, formed by a cadence of concrete block piers and semicircular chapels, is lit from above by four round skylights and has

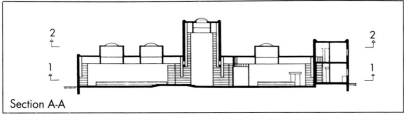

Section A-A

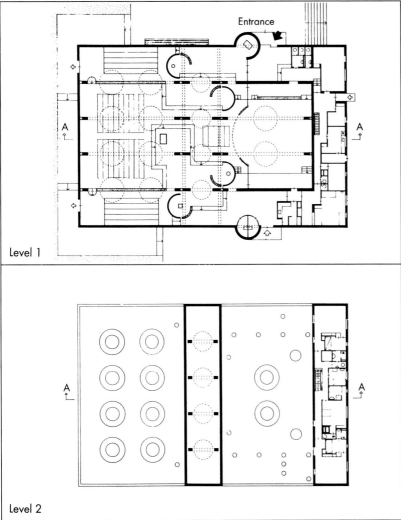

Level 1

Level 2

Fig. 37. Site plan (below), longitudinal section and floor plans (left), Pastoor van Ars-kerk, The Hague, The Netherlands, Aldo van Eyck (1969).

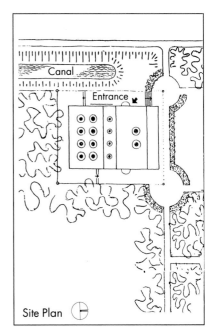

Canal

Entrance

Site Plan

Fig. 38. The approach and entrance to Pastoor van Ars-kerk. The entry doors are to the left of the projecting chapel.

the effect of compelling one to walk up its steps and traverse its entire length.[14] Shortly, however, the ambiguity of the space becomes apparent as one realizes that the path is passing by the destinations instead of leading toward them. The eastern end of the path is handled no differently than the western end, except that the flanking chapel becomes a confessional. According to van Eyck, "The tall space . . . became a kind of interior street with all sacred places strung along it. People filter out of and into it from end to end between the semicircular chapels, piers, and outer walls."

The congregational space displays its own form of ambiguity (fig. 40). It is predominantly formed by the low, hovering circular skylights. Each of these cylinders is bisected by a structural beam suggesting a directionality toward the altar. However, the pattern of openings also inscribes a static space, not unlike that found in the repeating domes of Islamic architecture (known to have been an influence in van Eyck's early work). Regarding the relationship of this space and the "street," van Eyck explains, "I wished to combine the quality of the low crypt-like space with that of the tall gothic-like one. Low when

Fig. 39. The sacred way at Pastoor van Ars-kerk, looking east.

Fig. 40. The repeating pattern of sky-lights in the congregation space at Pastoor van Ars-kerk. The sacred way is visible beyond the altar.

seated during mass; tall when walking (after entry and before leaving)."

Thus there is a clear articulation between places for movement and places for repose. This in part explains the directional neutrality of the "sacred way." It also creates the dynamic interplay between the path and the sanctuary and altar of the church. The ambiguity of path and place in Pastoor van Ars-kerk is deliberate. "It is my belief," van Eyck states, "that architecture should respond to emotional extremes more readily by containing them. It can thus help to mitigate whatever inner stress is caused by forced compliance with only one half (and neglect of the other) of twin phenomena maliciously split into conflicting-false-alternatives. It is for this reason that ambiguity and paradox have from the start played their part in what I make."[15]

We have looked at a broad range of axial paths, from the ancient to the modern. All have evidenced similarities in plan and organization, though there are many variations between the different faiths and historical periods. In ancient examples there is a surety and confidence communicated by an axial path, perhaps expressing the belief that if certain rituals are performed faithfully, then wishes will certainly be granted. Shinto, for example, is a faith that believes in the divine response to prayerful requests and rituals, and in this sense the path reinforces and symbolizes the liturgical intent. In the modern examples, the axial path often is transformed, and ambiguity and plurality of meaning are the result.

The Split Path

The split path is variant of the linear path—a type in which the path either diverges into two or a number of paths, or approach paths converge onto a single avenue. Early examples appear in the ziggurats of Mesopotamia during the Sumerian period. In particular there is the Ziggurat of Ur-Nammu at Ur (2000 BCE), where three ascending paths meet at the first terrace to form one stepped path (fig. 42).

Ziggurats appear early in Mesopotamian culture, examples dating from the Protoliterate period (3500–3000 BCE). They symbolized a path to the heavens, their apexes a meeting place between heaven and earth. In this way they symbolized the hope of reconciling the split between heaven and earth told in their myths. Typically the ziggurat complex was surrounded by a defensive wall within which were treasures and storehouses for food. It was symbolically the last defense of the city, for if the home of the god was destroyed, the city would perish as well. There was often a ground-level temple that contained an image

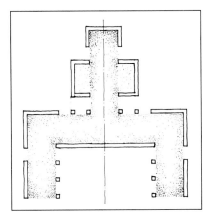

Fig. 41. The split path.

Fig. 42. The split path ascending the Sumerian ziggurat to its sacred apex.

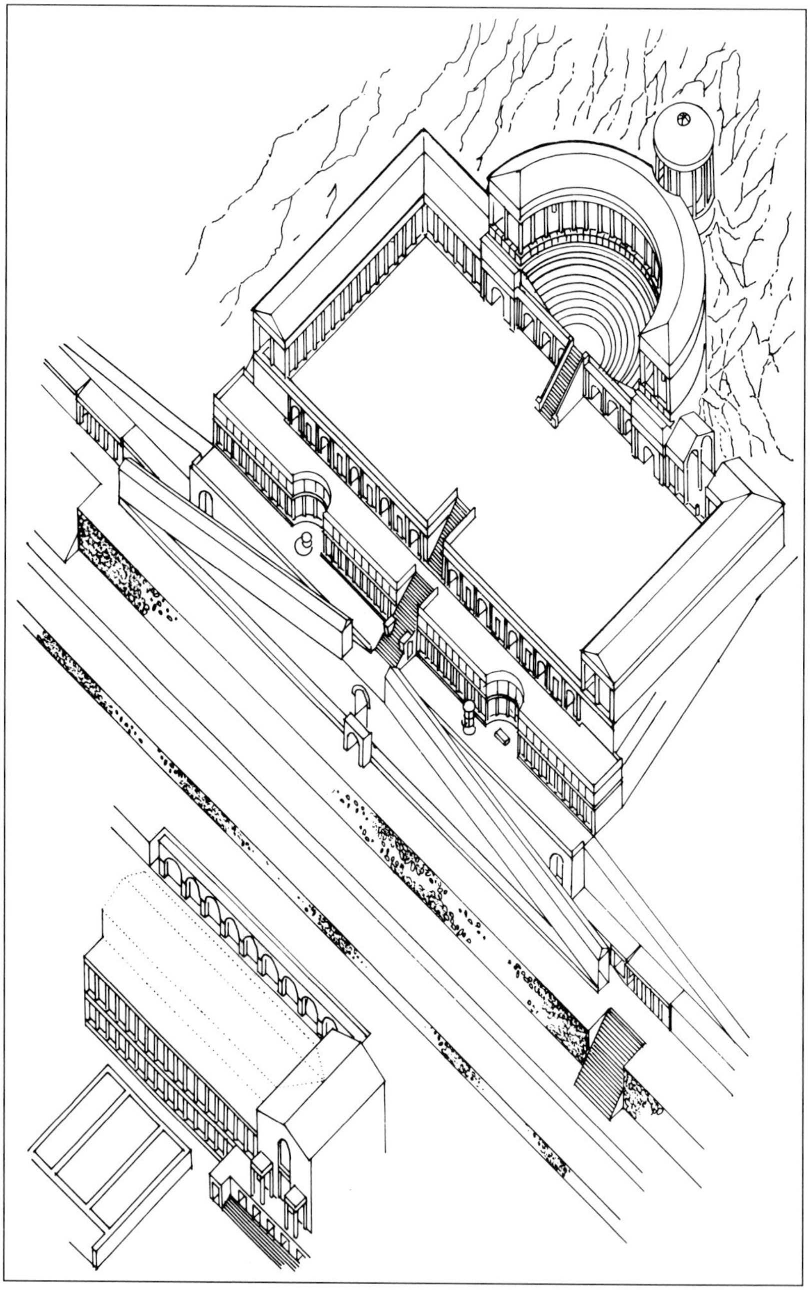

Fig. 43. At the Sanctuary of Fortuna Primigenia, Praeneste (Palestrina) (ca. 80 BCE), the two halves of the split path are enclosed causeways.

of the deity, though its countenance was hidden from the uninitiated. However, at the summit of the ziggurat, the goal of the ascending path, the deity would be revealed in its totality, presumably to those sufficiently prepared to gaze upon him.

Ascending the Ziggurat at Ur-nammu at the point where the three paths converged, there was an enclosure, a threshold volume. The path ascended axially from this point, attaining the second and then the third terrace, before finally reaching the temple at the top of the ziggurat. Here the god was said to descend; in some myths, to sleep with a virgin and thus ensure the fertility of the land for another year.[16]

We can observe a Roman example of the split path at the Sanctuary of Fortuna Primigenia at Palestrina (formerly called Praeneste, ca. 80 BCE), which is located near Rome on a steeply sloping site. Here, an axial path led to a temple dedicated to the Roman goddess of fate; it was a place of divination (fig. 43). The path began at a pair of stairs, symmetrically disposed about the central axis. These attained a terrace, where in a threshold space fronted by colonnaded enclosures, the paths turned at right angles toward the central axis. Next, a pair of enclosed ramps ascended, running perpendicular to the axis of the site. Both arrived at a central space, where dramatic views of the valley below were first afforded. Now the singular axial path continued its ascent and passed by two colonnaded terraces to attain a large open terrace. This space was enclosed on three sides by a colonnaded enclosure and was the setting for ritual dances. Another set of axial steps led to a series of semicircular steps that were related to the space below. These later steps were enclosed by a colonnade, its semicircular plan almost tangentially meeting the cylindrical temple beyond. The path, as in many of the linear examples, provided a tightly controlled spatial sequence. This was especially accentuated in the two enclosed ramps, a dark, tunnel-like experience that gave way to the openness of the terrace landing beyond.[17]

The pilgrimage church of Saint James at Santiago de Compostela displays a similar converging path, where a pair of paths ascend to a platform that fronts the western facade. Pilgrims entered the city by

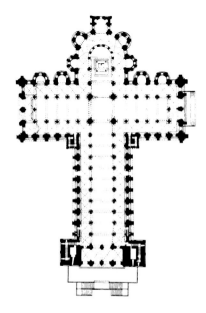

Fig. 44. The split path at the Cathedral of Saint James, Santiago de Compostela (1075–1125), leads from the piazza to the exterior platform of the west front.

one of seven gates and proceeded to these exterior stairs. At the raised exterior platform the axial path begins by passing through the western doors and beneath the carved tympanum into the narthex (fig. 44). In the nave, one of the best preserved Romanesque spaces, the axial path proceeds, marked by the rhythm of the flanking aisles. The transept at Santiago de Compostela is especially elongated, a typical feature of pilgrimage churches. The axial path culminates with arrival at the sanctuary and the statue of Saint James. Here, today as in the past, the pilgrims customarily embrace the statue from behind and perhaps place their pilgrim's hat on its head.

The Piazza of Saint Peter's in Rome, by Bernini (1657), provides another Christian example of a split path. Here, twin paths created by oval colonnades create an entry forecourt. "With arms wide open to embrace, the entry of the human race" (fig. 45). It could be argued that these colonnades were created more to bound the piazza than to form two approach pathways. Certainly the piazza dominates, both physically and in its use. (It is here that on Easter the Pope gives his blessing from the central balcony of the western front, the *urbi et Orbi*, to the assembled pilgrims.) However, the paths also serve as a means of approach, as is evident when one visits Saint Peter's today.

The approach to the Vatican actually begins as one crosses the Pont Sant'Angelo. Traveling across this bridge one passes stone angels on either side, each holding objects of Christ's passion. Lastly, statues of Saint Peter and Saint Paul mark the entrance to the Vatican precinct. Here, in a space fronted by the Castel Sant' Angelo, the path turns left and leads to the broad approach avenue of Saint Peter's, the Via d. Conciliazione completed in 1940. (In Bernini's time, two narrow avenues led to the church.) At its end one enters the Piazza S. Pietro. Four rows of columns form each colonnade, and the middle pair create a central path. All are aligned with radiants from the center of the square so that if one stands in the middle, only the closest row of columns is actually visible. An obelisk marks the center of the square and the approach axis. This prominent marker—as well as the orientation of the elliptical space, which is counter to the direction of the path—visually and physically slows one's approach. A trapezoidal space fronts the western facade of the church. Its angled side walls create a false perspective that makes the space seem shorter and taller than it actually is. A set of stairs leads to five doors, but the one on the far right is locked except during jubilee years. It is during a jubilee year that the papal procession ritually opens this door and enters the church. Through the doors, one enters the nave; its rectangular volume aligned with the direction of the path serves to lead one forward. At the crossing, underneath Michelangelo's great dome, is Bernini's baldachino and the high altar—the destination of the journey.

The altar marks the sacred place where Saint Peter fulfilled the commands of Jesus to found a church, and where his relics are interred. The path, through a spatial narrative and a series of thresholds and approaches, including the split path of the Piazza S. Pietro, leads to this sacred place.

A modern example of the split path is Unity Temple, located in Oak Park, Illinois, and completed in 1906. Along with the Larkin Building, Unity Temple is one of the most important buildings of Frank Lloyd Wright's early career. Built for the Unitarian faith, the building is characterized by a double entry route and a sequence of spatial experiences that culminate in a centralized space. Unity Temple is located on a rectangular site the size of which would not easily permit a lengthy entry sequence (fig. 46). However, the massing of the architecture expands the otherwise small site; the binuclear plan and the articulation of the architecture create a building that is less of an object and more a series of coordinated architectural events.

It is the expressiveness and detailing of the massing that accentuates the sense of passage present in the entry sequence. The two entry paths, symmetrically disposed about the longitudinal axis, may have had separate functions, or perhaps were a device to accentuate the transparency of the linking foyer volume. The principal entry, however, is along the western facade, and it is this sequence that I will describe.

The path begins at the northwest corner of the chapel, where the massing of its cubic form is fully apprehended (fig. 47). Running parallel to the chapel's western face, the path passes the mass of a stair

Fig. 45. Piazza S. Pietro, Rome, looking toward the Via d. Conciliazione and the Pont Sant'Angelo.

Fig. 46. Frank Lloyd Wright's Unity Temple, Oak Park, Illinois (1906).

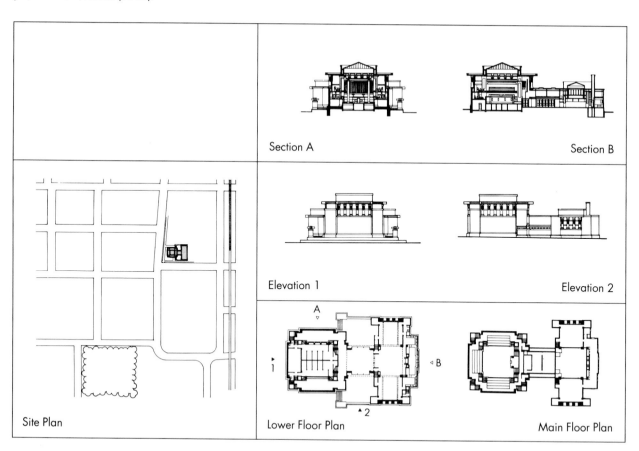

Section A

Section B

Elevation 1

Elevation 2

Site Plan

Lower Floor Plan

Main Floor Plan

Fig. 47. The western half of the split-entry path, viewed from the northwest corner of Unity Temple. The chapel is on the left.

Fig. 48. The deep overhang and entry doors of the east entrance to Unity Temple.

tower, then the chapel enclosure wall (at the top of which appears the cadence of a series of deep openings), and then another stair tower. At this point an exterior stair appears, set between the stair tower and a wall, the top of which is approximately 12 feet above grade. This is a clearly articulated volume, further inscribed by a sculptural form at the thickened end of the wall (absent in early photos of the building), and it functions as a transitional zone. Six steps lead to an outdoor space framed by the enclosure wall, the two wings of the building, and the entry foyer. The openness of this "outdoor foyer" is focused on the deceptively tight entry to the foyer proper. A deep overhang at the entry, which frames a set of three small pairs of doors, creates a constricted intermediary volume (fig. 48). Once inside the foyer, the space opens up again, creating a place to pause along the path. Turning right at this point, one gains access to the large community space. If one turns left, there is again a constricted intermediary volume that appears between the foyer and the chapel. Inside this space one ascends another six steps to the main floor of the chapel.

At Unity Temple, as is common in modern sacred architecture, the plan of the sanctuary is transformed from typical Christian models.

Fig. 49. The sanctuary of Unity Temple, looking toward the lectern.

One enters by walking past the altar/lectern, seeing first the seated congregation instead of the minister and altar. The chapel itself is spatially nondirectional, the result of its cubic form and the symmetrical layers of space and levels that form it (fig. 49).

The path at Unity Temple lacks a clearly defined point of entry, unless one considers the exterior stairs to mark that point. The path, as we have seen, is a series of spatial experiences, characterized by compression followed by expansion, a component of the spiritual path present in many examples. Similar to the archetypal spiritual path, the route offers a sequence of events and choices along the path that serve to accentuate the distance and time of travel. When one arrives in the chapel, one is actually close to the beginning of the path. The experience is one of having traversed a distance of much greater length than is actually the case. The surface and edges of the path throughout are clearly inscribed. It is also interesting to note that by perceiving the mass of the chapel at the beginning of the path, the goal is anticipated but must be attained by first passing through a number of increasingly "private spaces." Wright was clearly aware of the spatial emphasis of Unity Temple when he wrote about it. "The reality of the building is not in the four walls and roof but in the space enclosed by them to be lived in. . . . (at) Unity Temple to bring the room through was consciously a main objective."[18]

The split path is in essence a transformation and elaboration of the axial path. Thus it shares many of the characteristics noted previously. Its added complexity, however, can serve to further accentuate points of decision along the entry sequence. Therefore, perhaps its typology could be related to the mystical axiom: "many paths, one God."

The Radial Path

Radial paths radiate from or converge on a central space; they act as spokes of approach that radiate from the hub of the sacred place. The causeways, earthworks, and stone circles at Avebury in Wiltshire, England, provide an example of an early path and place and this type of path organization.

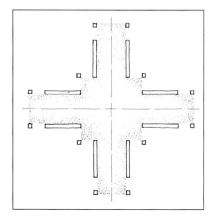

Fig. 50. The radial path.

There are over nine hundred stone-circle sites still in existence in the British Isles. Of these, the causeway, earthworks, and stone circles located in Avebury in southwestern England, which date from 2800 to 2200 BCE, comprise the largest megalithic site in the British Isles. There are various explanations for Avebury's purpose and use, including that it was the mythological burial place of the knights of King Arthur's court who died in the Battle of Mount Badon. Concerning henges in general, Caroline Malone cites "causewayed enclosures" as the precursors of the later henges. According to Malone, they may have been used as early corrals for livestock, defensive settlements, or markets and meeting places.[19] Aubrey Burl also outlines various theories to explain the phenomenon of stone circles, which range from places of sacrifice and burial sites to astronomical calendars, convergences of ley lines and power spots, and geometric compositions. However, there are no definitive facts for any of the possible uses for the sites.

The stone circles were added to, changed, or desecrated over the centuries, and because the Neolithic people that built them left no record of their beliefs, it is extremely difficult to determine what these sites meant at the time of their use. Burl argues that the stone circles were essentially places for communal ritual. These rituals, centered around cycles of death and fertility, included ancestor worship and celestial observances facilitated by the alignment of certain sites to the sun and/or moon. Charred, often partial remains of corpses as well as fertility carvings have been discovered at many sites. Most likely, seasonal rituals connected with cycles of planting and harvest were enacted at these sites, as well as rites related to fecundity and procreation.[20]

With a few exceptions, stone-circle sites did not have approach avenues. However, Stonehenge had an avenue that began at the northeast periphery of the circle and led out to the river Avon. Avebury had two known approach routes, one of which in part still survives today. The huge circular earthworks at Avebury are approximately 1,400 feet (427 m) in diameter (fig. 51). They are comprised of an outer bank, parts of which were as high as 18 feet (5.5 m), and an inner ditch, which

Fig. 51. Radial paths converged on the neolithic earthworks and stone circles enclosure at Avebury, Wiltshire, England. West Kennet Avenue is seen at the bottom of the site.

is 69 feet (21 m) wide and 30 feet (9 m) deep. Inside the earthworks is the Great Circle, originally formed from ninety-eight standing stones, of which only twenty-seven remain. The space formed by the great circle contained two smaller henges—the south and north circles. There are four openings in the earthworks at its north, south, east, and west periphery, two of which served as the terminus for causeways. A western avenue, barely discernible today, ran out for at least a mile. The second avenue, called West Kennet Avenue, ran south for approximately 1.5 miles (2.5 km) to the Sanctuary on Overton Hill.[21]

The bank, ditch, and Great Circle of standing stones provided the principal means of enclosure of the sacred ground at Avebury. At the entrances, the height of the bank increased and the path was lowered, forming a threshold to this ground. West Kennet Avenue was formed by opposing pairs of pillar and lozenge-shaped standing stones that ranged in height from 5 to 13 feet (1.5–4 m). Originally there were approximately one hundred pairs of stones placed 49 feet (15 m) apart. These stones would have been chosen for their particular shape but could have been shaped as well by grinding and chipping. Otherwise, there is little in the way of existing elements that gives clues to the articulation of the approach path.

It cannot be known for certain what purposes the earthworks, stone circles, and approach avenues at Avebury served. It is likely that rituals and processionals connected with cycles of planting, harvest, and the constant rhythm of life and death were part of its use. It is safe to assume that, like other agrarian people, the generations of builders of Avebury felt a strong connection to and dependence on the land, and sought ways to appease and explain powers beyond their control and comprehension. Shared rituals served as a means of appeasing the forces of nature to which these people were subject; their very lives depended on a good harvest.

Evidence of human bones within the inner circles suggest that Avebury was a site of ancestor worship and fertility rites. The opposing pillar and lozenge shapes of the standing stones of Kennet Avenue could have represented male and female forms and suggest that this avenue was used for processionals related to fertility rites. West Kennet

Avenue might also have been used as a processional for the bearing of the dead to places within an inner circle where the corpses were left to decay on platforms in the open.[22] In this light, Avebury serves as an early example of architecture, in a very primitive form, facilitating and accommodating shared symbolic acts.

The Roman quadrata is perhaps the consummate radial plan; its four avenues converging on a central space. The enclosed area was called the *templum* and was bisected first by the north-south *cardo*, then by the east-west *decamanus*. Gates at the enclosure wall marked entrance at the four cardinal points. The sacred center of the Roman city was the intersection of the *cardo* and *decamanus*, and was called the *mundus*, or "the world." According to Eliade, a square quartered in such a way represents an *imago mundi* and symbolizes the four quarters of the world. Additionally, just as the Roman basilican form was transformed in the early Christian church, the four-quarters organization found expression as well. We have observed how the axial nave dominates the path organization in the Latin Cross plan. In the Greek Cross, or quadrature-plan church, the path orientation is more multi-

Fig. 52. Radial paths, the courtyard and fountain at Ibn Tulun Mosque, Cairo.

115

directional. Four equal arms radiate from the center, as is illustrated by Bramante's original plan for Saint Peter's in Rome.

The paths that converge on the central ablution enclosure at the Ibn Tulun Mosque in Cairo are also radial in organization. The mosque, built by the ninth-century ruler that bears his name, is one of the largest mosques in the world; its inner courtyard was sized so that it could house most of his army and horses if need be. The thirteenth-century fountain enclosure is set in the center of this court and is approached by radiating paths that subdivide the courtyard (fig. 52). Today the mosque is entered on its northeast side through a massive enclosure wall. Three sides of the enclosure are bounded by a colonnade; on the fourth is the mosque. Those coming to worship first remove their shoes and then proceed to the ablution fountain at the center. There, after ritually washing, they proceed back on one of the paths to the mosque, which is located on the southeast side of the courtyard. A similar arrangement is found at the Moorish Court of the Lions at the Alhambra in Granada, Spain. Here, quadrant paths converge on the fountain, centrally located in the colonnaded, rectangular space.

One of the outstanding characteristics of radial paths is that they establish a strong sense of center and destination. At Versailles, for example, the radial paths all converge on the bedroom of King Louis XIV, symbolizing his omnipotence and implying his location at the center of the world. Often, as in the quadrature church plan, the center point is left open, establishing the central holy place. Departing from or arriving at a central point, radial paths establish a strong sense of both departure and arrival, and of place.

Fig. 53. The grid path.

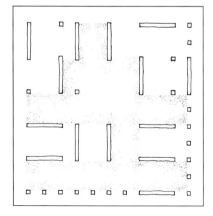

The Grid Path

A grid arrangement of paths, conversely, suggests either an absence of center or a number of centers. The grid of columns and lack of a strongly defined path in mosques such as the moorish *Mezquita*, or Great Mosque in Cordoba (1328 CE) perhaps reflect the Islamic concept of god as everywhere and nowhere (fig. 54).[23] In other words, if

Fig. 54. A grid of columns define the interior space of the Great Mosque of Cordoba (1328).

God is omnipresent and elusive, then a path to come in contact with the deity is seen as pointless and possibly blasphemous. At Cordoba, the contrast of this belief system with Christianity and its well-defined path and goal is strikingly apparent when one leaves the mosque and enters the Baroque church inserted later at its center. The mosque includes a magnificent garden that one first enters with fountains originally used for ritual ablution.

Often, the grid, like the Roman quadrata, is aligned with the cardinal points and thus has cosmic connections. This is seen in pre-Columbian cities such as Teotihuacán and in Chinese cities such as the Forbidden City. Though it has been utilized throughout the history of architecture, it was the grid that in many ways came to symbolize modern architecture. Its suggestion of limitless space and absence of place perhaps may be seen to parallel the modern condition. This is a subject to which we will return in the conclusion.

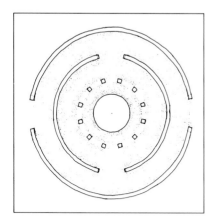

Fig. 55. The circumambulating path.

The Circumambulating Path

Circumambulating paths either surround a central space or form the space itself. I will examine a number of paths of this type as found in different faiths around the world.

An early example is the original Church of the Holy Sepulchre in Jerusalem, where a two-level ambulatory surrounded the tomb of Jesus. Roman mausolea perhaps were precursors of the centrally planned sacred building with surrounding ambulatory, as is found at Santa Costanza in Rome (ca. 350 CE). This was built as the mausoleum of Constantine's daughter Constantina, and its form accommodated the Roman custom of circumambulation around the place of burial.[24] (Later, it became the martyrium of Saint Costanza, a saint that likely never existed.) The building has a basilican section adapted to a centralized plan, the central dome rising above the surrounding aisle. The effect is a bright, light-filled interior, a vision of heaven contrasted with the dark, earthbound ambulatory[25] (fig. 56).

Many Byzantine churches featured an ambulatory that surrounded a central space covered by a dome that rose lightly from pendentives.

H. Sergios and Bakchos in Constantinople (begun ca. 525 CE), the Church of Zwartnots in Armenia (641–66 CE), and San Vitale at Ravenna (547 CE) display the same central planning associated with Christian martyriums and Byzantine churches. At San Vitale, similar to the Dome of the Rock, an octagonal outer form surrounds an inner colonnade.

The Dome of the Rock (691 CE), with a circumambulating path, marks a sacred center—the place of Muhammad's ascension to heaven. Its approach is actually axial and begins with the El-Kas Pool, a place of ritual ablution (fig. 57). The path then ascends a set of steps to the platform on which the mosque stands. Entering into the octagonal space, however, the path becomes circular. We have observed earlier the importance of circumambulation at the Kaaba at Mecca, and similarly here the path inside the domed space circles but never attains the sacred center (fig. 58).

Just as the centralized plan with surrounding ambulatory was adopted for early Christian martyria, the later baptistry also used this form. This can be seen in numerous examples such as the baptistry of the Cathedral at Pisa (1063–1118 CE). In medieval churches the ambulatory defines the sanctuary at the end of the basilican space. The term itself—from the Latin *ambulare* "to walk"—suggests its processional use. French cathedrals featured the *chevet*, a chancel dominated by the ambulatory as found at Saint Denis, built by Abbot Suger beginning in 1134. Christian monasteries also featured a circumambulating path which in these examples defined the cloister. The Cistercian Fontenay Abbey has a cloistered space that was a distinguishing element of the ideal abbey as set out by this order (fig. 59).

One needs to travel to the East, however, to find perhaps the most evocative and symbolic examples of the circumambulating path. Sites such as the ancient Khmer temple of Angkor Wat located in present-day Cambodia were built to symbolize holy mountains, with concentric rings of avenues scaling their heights, ascending toward divinity and enlightenment. The Buddhist temple of Borobudur on Java is a well-documented and restored example, and speaks vividly about a circumambulating spiritual and symbolic journey.

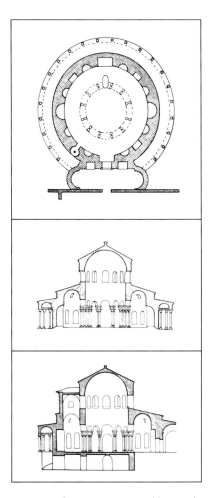

Fig. 56. Plan, transverse, and longitudinal section of the circumambulating path of Santa Costanza, Rome (Ca., 345 CE).

Fig. 57. The approach to the Dome of the Rock in Jerusalem (691 CE) begins with ritual ablution at the El-Kas Pool. From here an axial path leads to the mosque and the circumambulating path within.

Fig. 58. Inside the Dome of the Rock, Jerusalem, the central and holy Rock of Abraham is surrounded by a circumambulating path.

Fig. 59. Christian monastic cloisters are defined by a surrounding arcaded path. Cloister, Fontenay Abbey, France.

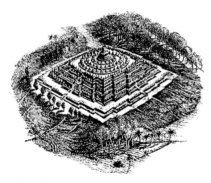

Fig. 60. Borobudur, Java (eighth and ninth centuries).

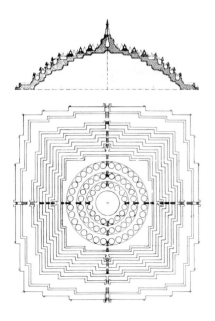

Fig. 61. The plan and section of Borobudur show the concentric circumambulating paths that ring this mandala-shaped sacred mountain.

Angkor Wat, located outside the Khmer capital of Angkor Thom, was built during the twelfth century and is the crowning achievement of this culture, known for its building prowess. In the fifteenth century, the Khmer were conquered by the Thais, and their monuments fell into ruin, covered by the encroaching jungle until centuries later. Ankor Wat's plan and circumambulating path are based on the mandala, a diagram traditionally used in meditative practices.[26] (Similarly, the Kum Bum Chapel at the Gyangtse Monastery in Tibet, is based on a mandala plan.) Oriented to the cardinal points, the base of the temple is set on an island formed by a moat that is 650 feet wide and 2½ miles long. Five square terraces form the main temple, rising at the center to a height of 215 feet and crowned by five towers. Its image is said to symbolize the mythical Mount Meru. The approach to Angkor Wat was by a raised causeway that was originally 36 feet wide and 1,500 feet long and led to a bridge over the moat. This led to the first terrace, where one would enter a sculpture-lined gallery with friezes depicting Hindu deities. Here a ritual circumambulation of the temple would begin, a common feature of the venerative practices at Hindu temples. The entire sequence covered a distance of 12 miles and symbolized spiritual trials and lessons.

Borobudur offers a striking example of the circumambulating path, its sequence symbolizing a journey toward enlightenment. Built in the eighth and ninth centuries by the Buddhist Sailendra dynasty, it rises from the Kedu Plain on the island of Java just south of a range of volcanic mountains. The temple at its apex attains an altitude of 100 feet, and its remote location suggests a pilgrimage to a sacred mountain (fig. 60). Similar to Angkor Wat, the temple is a series of increasingly smaller terraces that form in one aspect a massive stupa. At Borobudur there are six square terraces; the top four contain galleried passageways, on top of which are four round terraces, the last one holding the central stupa. The complex is aligned to the cardinal points and has stairs at the center of each face that ascend to the successive levels. The entire complex was meant to be circumambulated in a clockwise direction, ascending from the lower levels to the central stupa at its summit (fig. 61).

The temple was approached from the east by means of an axial path through surrounding gardens. A set of stairs flanked by mythical guardian deities led to the first and second terraces. (The bottom terrace is 370 feet (113 m) square. A frieze called the "hidden foot" originally adorned the face of an abandoned lower terrace and depicted scenes from a Buddhist scripture on heaven and hell.) Next, the first of the four galleries was reached by means of stairs up and through a passageway adorned with other guardian figures. At this point the pilgrim would turn left and begin the ritual circumambulation of the temple (fig. 62).

The galleries are approximately 6.5 feet (2 m) wide and are adorned on either side with friezes, a legible and temporal narrative whose stories unfold as one walks along. The myriad of serene faces and complex scenes on the first level contain mythical stories and folktales, and the story of the Buddha's many lives. Each side of this gallery has two sets of panels and so must be traversed four times to receive its entire message. One then passed through another portal guarded by carved figures to the next terrace. The next three terraces depict an increasingly complex and esoteric story about the quest for wisdom by

Fig. 62. On the left of the first gallery at Borobudur are two of the four bands of friezes.

the pilgrim Sudhana, taken from the *Gandavyuha* Buddhist text, a message of growing spiritual enlightenment. Each gallery on these levels contains two sets of panels, and so before one reaches the first round terrace, six more circumambulations must be completed. Following are three round terraces (which are not perfectly circular), which contain a total of 72 Buddha figures, all shown sitting in meditation and placed within bell-shaped stone stupas. The stupas have diamond and square-shaped openings that allow the Buddhas to be glimpsed inside. These three terraces would have been circumambulated as well until the pilgrim reached the uppermost and central stupa. Inside this stupa, hidden from view, was the figure of the *Adibuddha*, the primordial Buddha in Buddhist cosmology from which everything originates.[27]

The overall plan and symbolic path sequence at Borobudur are derived from a mandala.[28] On the outside balustrade of the terraces are placed Buddha figures, originally 432 in all; the number of figures perhaps symbolizing the length of one *kalpa*, or world age, which is 4,320,000 years.[29] The Buddhas display different *mudra* positions,[30] and on the first three levels there are four types, relative to the direction they are facing. The fourth terrace has Buddhas in the *vitarka mudra* hand position, symbolizing the act of teaching. The circular terrace Buddhas, 72 in all, sit in the *dharmacakra mudra* which signifies the "turning of the wheel of doctrine." All of these correspond to deities depicted in mandala designs. Similar to the mandala and its use in spiritual practices, Borobudur contains guardian figures to exclude evil forces, provides a setting for the appearance of deities, and creates the setting for an initiatory experience of passing through the various realms of spiritual enlightenment. It is not a place to venerate the Buddha but to actively participate in the journey of becoming enlightened oneself, to become a bodhisattva.

The total number of circumambulations though the galleries is ten, or a distance of three miles. Each section of gallery has a number of right-angle shifts so that only limited segments are able to be seen at each given point. This zone of darkness and constriction gives way to the light and openness of the upper terraces. It is a journey from the "world of illusion" to the "sea of immortality." For the monks and pilgrims that ascend this temple today as in the past, its complex messages symbolize in part a journey up a sacred mountain, ascending from the lower realms to its sacred summit. Borobudur is a signposted path, with places to pause or turn back, guardian deities, and Buddha figures suggestive of mountainside ascetics or the gods on mythical mountains. Its message is complex and its use has changed over the years, but in essence its experience is didactic, a lesson of life and spiritual development.[31] According to Eliade, "Ascending it is equivalent to an ecstatic journey to the center of the world; reaching the highest terrace, the pilgrim experiences a breakthrough from plane to plane; he enters a 'pure region' transcending the profane world."[32]

The circular path perhaps grew out of archetypal devotional and religious acts. Romans encircled their tombs, Christians their crypts and chancels, Moslems their holy rocks, and Hindus and Buddhists their holy mountains. In this aspect it symbolizes a respectful and gradual approach to the divine. One walks around the sacred center, close but not too close, and in some cases the center is never reached. At the Dome of the Rock, for example, one can never walk on the Rock of Abraham, but can descend to a grotto below it called the Cave of the Spirits. The circumambulating path also suggests unity because of how the path and place simultaneously create each other. The sacred place and the path to it form an integral whole.

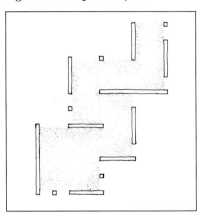

Fig. 63. The segmented path.

The Segmented Path

Segmented paths comprise our last category of path and place organizations. They can be defined as a multidirectional connected series of paths that lead to the sacred place. Examples range from one or two twists and turns, to a labyrinthine journey.

Classical Greek sites offer a number of examples of this type, one of which is the sacred way at the Temple of Apollo at Delphi, which we will look at in depth later. The Acropolis in Athens also displays a sophisticated version of the segmented path, each segment offering specific views and orientations as it approaches and passes through the Propylaia and continues upward to the Parthenon and its neighboring monuments (fig. 64).

The use of the Acropolis of Athens dates from Mycenaean times when it was a fortified city, as was the citadel at Mycenae. In the political setting of classical Greece, however, this mountaintop site, which rose up from the plain below, was deemed inappropriate for the houses of any one individual or group, and instead became the home of the gods; in particular, the virgin goddess Athena, warrior and guardian of the city. Athena could not protect Athens from its sacking by the Persians in 480 BCE, however, and the present remains date from the rebuilding of the site after this sobering event. The temple precinct contained temples dedicated to the multiple personalities and roles of the goddess.

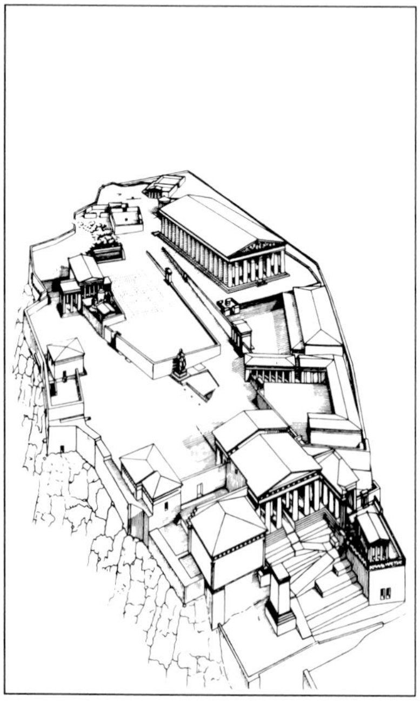

Once a year during midsummer, the birth of Athena was celebrated during the Festival of Panathenaia. This event included athletic games and a procession that led from the main gate of the walled city. It was just outside the Dipylon Gate, located next to the cemetery, that the procession would gather at dawn.[33] Leading the procession was an emblematic item—a large "tunic," called a *peplos*, that had been knitted during the previous year by a select group of maidens. It depicted scenes of the battles of the gods and was raised on a cart in a manner that suggested a ship. Following in the parade were men on horseback, chariots, elders carrying olive branches (the sacred tree of Athena), musicians, and young men carrying jugs of oil and wine and leading sacrificial sheep and cows. The procession itself was depicted on the inside frieze of the Parthenon. The road from the Dipylon was called the Dromos, and from the distance, the temples and monuments on the Acropolis would have been fully visible, their bright whiteness and glowing colors radiant in the early morning light. However, as the procession wound its way past the agora and came closer to the mountain, the sight of these monuments would disappear, to be regained only upon attaining the summit.

At the base of the Acropolis the *peplos* was removed and carried by hand as the participants continued on foot. As they ascended, the Tem-

Fig. 64. A segmented path led up the steep incline to the Acropolis in Athens (reconstruction, ca. 400 CE).

ple of Athena Nike appeared on the right; dedicated to the goddess
Athena as warrior-protectress, it was perched on massive walls. Viewed
at an angle that revealed its three-dimensionality, it formed the first
entry threshold. The path headed straight from here to the symmetrically disposed propylaia. Inside this structure the bright openness outside gave way to constricted gloom, the volume of the space growing
smaller as the steps continued to rise toward its ceiling. The north
wing of the propylaia was an area to pause and take refreshment; the
south wing led to the Temple of Athena Nike. Through the Doric
facade of its east front, the temples of the summit were glimpsed, their
brightness contrasting with the gloom of the propylaia.

Passing though this threshold space, the procession marched into
this bright open space. The propylaia faced the space fronted by the
two major temples; the Parthenon on the right and the Erechtheion
on the left, both dedicated to Athena as protectress of the city. In the
middle of the space, just to the right ahead, was the statue of Athena
Promachos ("the champion"), beyond which was the altar of Athena
where the beasts would be ritually sacrificed. Most likely the procession would have visited the Parthenon first, its sculptural west front
depicting battles of the gods; its great east doors opened to reveal the
forty-foot gilded statue of the goddess standing in the gloom within.
Eventually the procession would reach the Erechtheion where the
tunic would be draped on a wooden cult statue of the goddess. Looking
outward, the participants would have beheld the great city below them
and the surrounding countryside, and the segments of the path that led
them to this home of the goddess.

Japanese Zen Buddhist temples also make use of the segmented
path, often with powerful symbolic affects. I will discuss this in depth
in chapter 6 through the example of Koto-in, a subtemple of Daitoku-
ji Zen Buddhist Monastery in Kyoto. Daisen-in is also a subtemple
of Daitoku-ji and displays a sophisticated entry sequence, involving a
connected series of paths that include passage through the monastery
itself (fig. 99).

Daisen-in is located at the northeast corner of the monastery and
was founded in 1509 by Kogaku Soko. Today it consists of a collection

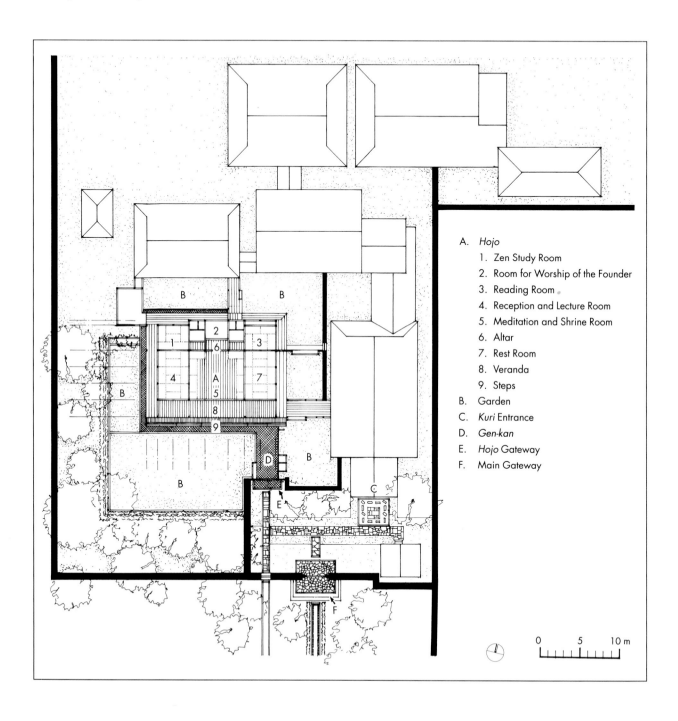

A. *Hojo*
1. Zen Study Room
2. Room for Worship of the Founder
3. Reading Room
4. Reception and Lecture Room
5. Meditation and Shrine Room
6. Altar
7. Rest Room
8. Veranda
9. Steps
B. Garden
C. *Kuri* Entrance
D. *Gen-kan*
E. *Hojo* Gateway
F. Main Gateway

of buildings that house an active community of monks. It is known for its main temple building, the *hojo* or abbot's quarters, and its surrounding *kare-sansui*, "dry gardens."[34] The path that leads to the *hojo* includes a sequence of paths, gateways, and spaces of a richness and complexity that suggests a symbolic journey.

The *hojo* in the subtemple functions as the living quarters and reception area for the abbot and serves as a place where monks in training can meet with their teacher. It is also a place where the abbot gives talks to the community of monks and where *sutras* are chanted.[35] The *hojo* is typically oriented south, has a rectangular plan covered by a single overhanging roof, and is divided into two rows of three rooms each (fig. 65). The internal space divisions are accomplished by means of either fixed clay walls or sliding screens and have functions that vary from *hojo* to *hojo*. However, the plan typically accommodated the dual functions of secular and sacred functions.

The entry path to Daisen-in leaves a secondary path (which also serves an adjacent subtemple) at a right angle. Traveling north, it passes a planted garden on the left and ascends three steps to reach the main gateway. This gateway marks the entrance to the domain of the subtemple, which is surrounded by solid clay walls (fig. 66). After passing through the gateway into an outer courtyard, one is presented with two right-angle choices. To the right the path leads to the *kuri*, or kitchen building; to the left is the main gateway to the *hojo*, distinguished by its *karahaphur* roof, a style favored by the military aristocracy (fig. 67). Once inside this entrance, one enters an entry foyer called the *gen-kan* and continues north to attain the *hojo* at its southeast corner (fig. 68). Here the garden, first glimpsed through a small "firelight window"[36] in the entry foyer, is fully viewed (fig. 69).

The path is marked by a series of edges and a variety of paving patterns. Each section of the path utilizes a unique combination of granite slabs and paving stones. For example, the path as it enters the entry foyer is paved with smooth tiles (which are also used at the edge between the *hojo* and the main southern garden). The spatial sequence begins with the first volume, formed by the surrounding trees and

Fig. 65. The plan of Daisen-in Temple (founded 1509), Daitoku-ji Zen Buddhist Monastery, Kyoto, showing the entry path and *hojo*.

Fig. 66. The path leading to the main entrance gateway at Daisen-in Temple.

Fig. 67. Inside the main gateway of Daisen-in Temple, one path leads to the *hojo* gateway. Visible beyond the southern garden wall and the entrance is the *hojo*.

Fig. 68. The *gen-kan*, looking toward the *hojo*, Daisen-in Temple. *Gen-kan* means "an entrance that extends deeply into the heart of the house," and it serves as a transitional volume of the sequence of entry.

Fig. 69. Southern veranda and garden looking back toward the *gen-kan*, Daisen-in Temple.

plantings outside the first gateway. The second volume is inscribed by the gateway itself, through its depth, overhanging roof, and raised platform. The third volume is the outer courtyard within which are a number of small gardens and a bell tower. The fourth volume is the entry foyer, which penetrates into the temple building itself.

At Daisen-in the volumes sequentially decrease in size, creating the experience of compression and anticipation. The sequence of gateways establish thresholds to increasingly sacred spaces. Along the path incomplete glimpses of the temple and its gardens are afforded, underlining the experience of passage and anticipating the attainment of the spiritual place. The entry foyer acts as a symbolic bridge to the *hojo*, the effect of which is accentuated by its asymmetrical approach. Inside the *hojo* the modulation of floor and ceiling levels in part delineates a series of internal volumes.

The *hojo* is the final segment of the path and yet is also a separate entity. Through its siting and articulation the *hojo* at Daisen-in is further established as a place apart. This is accomplished through a variety of means: First, the plan and form of the *hojo* underline its appearance as an object building set within the stone and planted landscape of the gardens. Second, the building, surrounded by *kare-sansui*, symbolically "floats" in a sea of gardens. The form and articulation of the *hojo* create a series of volumes that delineate a series of concentric and increasingly sacred spaces. A wide veranda surrounds the building, forming one of a number of volumetric edges. On its southern edge, steps descend to the garden; tile and granite paving form an additional edge (fig. 70). The entire surrounding volume is further inscribed by the prominent overhang of the roof.

As is apparent at Daisen-in and will be observed at Koto-in, the subtemple gardens complement and expand on the symbolic themes of the path and the *hojo*; together they form a complete composition. The *hojo* is experienced as a series of compressed volumes, and there is a distinct edge formed between the edge of the *hojo* and the surrounding gardens. Inside, the experience of the *hojo* is dark, introverted, and compressed, an orientation that gives way dramatically to the perceived

Fig. 70. The layers of tile and stone paving at the southern garden of Daisen-in Temple serve to further delineate the edge of the *hojo*.

Fig. 71. The view from the meditation and shrine room toward the southern garden of Daisen-in Temple.

expansiveness of the temple gardens (fig. 71). At Daisen-in the quiet presence and completeness of the main building is juxtaposed with the animated and active garden.

The gardens are used as meditative objects, viewed from the *hojo*. From inside the shrine room, for example one may gaze outward toward the garden. Inside, it is dark and compressed; outside, the garden and its ambiguous scale suggest a limitless vista. The raked stones and surrounding two layers of hedge and low clay wall in the garden enclose a space of indeterminate size, and a view is offered beyond, above the wall to trees in the distance. The asymmetrical arrangement of the garden elements themselves, in particular the two enigmatic gravel cones, compliment the symmetrical ordering of the architecture.

The relationship of the garden and architecture establishes particular psychological responses. The horizon created by the garden space, reinforced by the orientation of the main building and its effect of framing specific views, creates a world that is completely enclosed and yet appears limitless. A garden technique called *shakkei*, or "borrowed landscape," includes specific distant views and is an integral part of the garden's design. It is a powerful interplay of compression followed by release, also present in the path sequence to the *hojo*. The effect is a release of tension, a letting go, an effective trigger for spiritual experiences.

In the garden, the unity of opposites is a recurring theme reminiscent of Taoist philosophy. The vistas offered by the garden tend to ground the sense of place within the main building and the greater world beyond. A sense of oneness with the earth and the cosmos is engendered by the manipulation of scale and vista. An opposition or interplay between the building and the garden is also present, however. Whereas the subtemple architecture is ordered, symmetrical, and modular, the garden is deliberately asymmetrical. Thus a relationship of interplay, ambiguity, and tension is formed—opposites that demand attention but also speak about ultimate unity. The relationship of the architecture and the garden also suggests the cosmic interplay of opposites, the yin and the yang of Taoist philosophy—the masculine strength of the ordering of the main building raised above the ground on foundation poles, contrasted with the feminine, mysterious garden growing out of the earth.

The gardens have been called built *koans* because of the need for the viewer to interact with and "complete" the arrangement of the garden[37] (fig. 72). The fact that the garden is not to be occupied but only viewed adds to this experience. The interplay of the garden and the architecture demands mental participation. The monk sitting on the veranda, gazing at the garden, is not passive but actively engaged in the environment, exemplifying the Zen principle of mindfulness. A quality of mindfulness is also present in the dynamic relationship engendered by the environment of the *hojo*, its segmented entry path and gardens. The demands and choices of the path, the transition from outside to inside, the interrelationship of the architecture and the garden, all insist on awareness and engagement from the participant. The simple ordinary materials, arranged and ordered it appears by a force deeper than that of everyday life, speak about the possibility of the sacred for those that desire and ask.

A modern example of the segmented path is Le Corbusier's chapel of Notre Dame du Haut. Completed in 1955 toward the end of the

Fig. 72. The northeastern garden of Daisen-in Temple. The enigmatic relationships of the rock groupings of Zen gardens have been called "built koans" because of their use in meditation.

architect's long career, it is a seminal work of his "third career." It was built on the ancient site of a pilgrimage church that had been destroyed during World War II. Le Corbusier was very conscious of the site as place of pilgrimage and considered the east exterior chapel that he created as the goal of contemporary pilgrimage. He wrote about the building:

> Pilgrimage
> The witness is there facing the lawn covered
> with men and women
> beside the altar
> where the consecration of the host is about to be celebrated again.[38]

Sited at the top of a prominent hill, Ronchamp is very visible from a distance. Unlike Unity Temple, for example, it offers the opportunity for a lengthy entry sequence. The first view of the church tells one that the dominant white mass of the architecture puts it in the overall category of "object in space." This is even more apparent when one gets close to the building and the backdrop of the surrounding hills recedes from sight. Moreover, it is a plastic mass with a distinct front and back, the "front" two sides facing toward the direction of entry.

The path begins at a point down the hill where the chapel is just visible, the exposed concrete "hat" of the roof hovering above the white gunnite walls. The entry to the path is undefined—there is neither an articulated threshold, nor an enclosed sacred enclosure, though one might make the case that the hill itself serves this purpose (fig. 73). As one progresses from this point, the path continues to be undefined, marked only by paving and by low shrubbery. About halfway up the slope, the path passes the curious monk's building on the right. Its rectilinear language and low squat form might have been designed as a humble counterpoint to the chapel itself, but it appears simply as a visual detraction from the otherwise undisturbed view of the chapel, and the mass of this building is not utilized in any spatial way as a means of inscribing an event along the path. Its relationship to the path is at best ambiguous.

Fig. 73. Notre Dame du Haut Chapel, Ronchamp, France, Le Corbusier (1950–55).

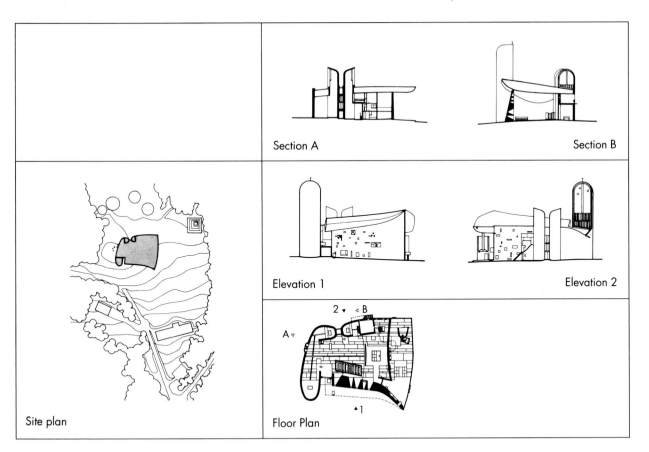

Section A

Section B

Site plan

Elevation 1

Elevation 2

Floor Plan

Fig. 74. The southeast corner of the Notre Dame du Haut Chapel, intended as the principal view of the building.

After passing this building, the southeast corner of the chapel becomes fully visible, clearly designed to be the dominant edge of the mass (fig. 74). Shortly thereafter the path turns to the right and approaches the main entry doors. At this point a clearly inscribed entry is present, the brightly colored doors located within a recess formed by the vertical light well on the left and the thick south wall on the right.

Once inside, the path's direction is perpendicular to the east-west axis of the chapel and does not have a clear termination point to facilitate reorientation. In fact, the experience of the interior throughout is one of directional ambiguity. The western chapels seem to draw the pilgrim as much as the eastern altar, and the overall experience lacks a focus or termination point. Rather than a dominant directionality, there are a number of destinations, including the numerous recesses in the southern wall, suggesting where individuals might find their place. Here again the Western Christian axial plan type has been transformed, in this case more radically than at Pastoor van Ars-kerk and Unity Temple. The chapel space—inscribed by the curved and canted walls, the parabolic hovering roof, and the sloping floor—has an unbalanced and diffuse character. The only focus of an otherwise undefined altar is a visual one, a statue of the Virgin Mary, set in a transparent box in the eastern wall. However, the overall experience of the interior of the chapel is one of enclosure and provides a sense of arrival. It is a dynamic space with many visual and spatial directions present. The strongest component is the thick southern wall; its light-filled openings provide a luminous quality that imbues the entire interior with a feeling of spirituality.

Le Corbusier was clearly influenced by the possibilities the site suggested in relationship to pilgrimage. However, throughout the entry sequence, spatial sequences are noticeably absent; the focus seems to rest entirely on the mass of the church itself. No attempt is made to separate the outside from the inside, except when the path reaches the main entry doors. Consequently, the potential for an evocative and symbolic entry path remains more or less unexplored.

There are places created outside the church, the eastern altar in particular, but these have little connection to the entry path sequence or the space inside. The main door is well articulated, but here there is a curious symbol painted on the doors. Instead of "universal symbols" of Christianity or pilgrimage, there is instead an original work of art by the architect, including a drawing of his own hands. However, once inside, amid the conflicting directions and symbolism, there is a feeling of enclosure and a distinct sense of place, accentuated by the geometry and materials of the sanctuary. Concerning the path, William Curtis has pointed out that "Le Corbusier managed to capture the spirit of the place. The gradual ascent up the hill has a ritualistic character, which the architect turned to good effect by organising the building as a sequence of *événements plastiques* (sculptural events) incorporating the setting and the surrounding horizons."[39]

Two chapels designed by E. Fay Jones are approached by subtle segmented path sequences. At the Thorncrown Chapel in Eureka Springs, Arkansas (1980), and the Mildred B. Cooper Memorial Chapel in Bella Vista, Arkansas (1988), an essentially axial approach is manipulated to create a segmented path that offers only partial views

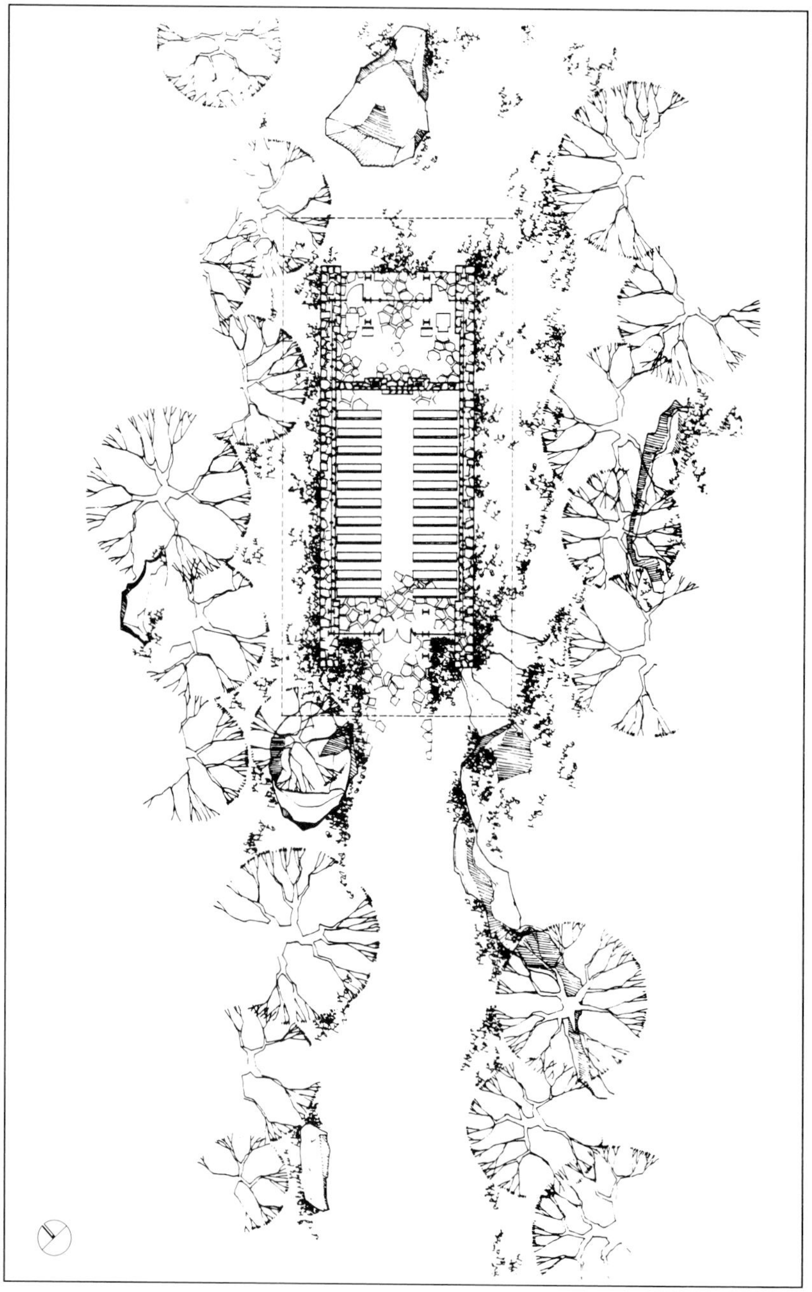

Fig. 75. The plan of Thorncrown Chapel, Eureka Springs, Arkansas, by Fay Jones and Associates Architects (1980), showing part of the approach path.

of the chapel along its route. At Thorncrown, the approach is essentially in two segments. The first section leaves a parking area and travels toward the structure at an oblique angle to its axially aligned space. The threshold to the path is marked by a small concrete and wood office that is set into the hillside on the right. Along the first section of the stone path, strategically retained trees on the wooded hilly site prevent direct views of the chapel.[40] Suddenly, however, the path shifts and heads on axis toward the front entrance (figs. 75 and 76).

The chapel itself displays many archetypal characteristics of sacred space in terms of threshold, enclosure, spatial articulation, and orientation. The building's structure is comprised of only 2×4, 2×6, and 2×12 wood members.[41] Its form is delineated by a dominant gable roof with a pronounced overhang. The entry threshold is created by twelve 2×12 composite columns placed in three rows of four columns each. The overhang of the gable end of the roof and the expressed structural cross bracing further inscribe the threshold space. The glass-and-wood enclosure and the wooden doors are located at the middle bay of columns. This placement effectively transforms the entire three rows of columns into a deep threshold sequence that exists both inside and outside the chapel.

Past the compression of these comparatively heavy columns and the low doors, one enters a surprisingly diaphanous and dynamic space (fig. 77). It exhibits a simultaneous sense of enclosure and openness. The enclosure is created by the low stone walls that surround the space and the opaque, overhanging roof. Between these elements of the earth and sky is a composite, cross-braced structure of 2×4 wood studs. Twelve thin composite wood columns line each side of the single space and are connected by a series of horizontal bands and enclosed by glass. Between these two walls, two sets of cross braces span the central space. The effect is a compression of space and an expansion both upward, outward, and along the axis of the nave. The crossing of the principal cross-bracing members is articulated by diamond-shaped metal brackets. Their repetition visually directs one toward the sanctuary and beyond.

Fig. 76. A dominant gable roof and deep threshold space in part define Thorncrown Chapel as viewed from the entrance pathway.

141

Fig. 77. The complex cross-braced structure of Thorncrown Chapel creates a dynamic, diaphanous space. Looking east, the sanctuary and the landscape beyond are visible.

Fig. 78. The sanctuary of Thorncrown Chapel.

The sanctuary is raised three steps above the nave floor and is further enclosed by a low cross-axial wall. At the far end of the sanctuary, the three rows of 2×12 composite columns reappear, establishing both its enclosure and another threshold. Wood members and glass provide enclosure at the middle row of columns, similar to the entry threshold. Beyond this point a powerful and evocative space is formed as the floor, columns, and roof extend beyond the sanctuary borders. This space, apparently inaccessible, creates and symbolizes a sacred inner sanctum and in this way is joined with the long lineage of meaningful sacred sites. Still further beyond, a single cross is set in the landscape, partially framed by a stone escarpment (fig. 78).

The "double threshold" of entry and its symbolism of passage to the ineffable sacred ground beyond is more clearly defined at the Mildred Cooper Chapel. Here, both ends of the building are more fully enclosed. At the end of the path, a deeper and more succinctly delineated space is created beyond the confines of the sanctuary, which is further defined by a cross-axial stone wall.[42]

Thorncrown Chapel is visited by thousands every year who make a pilgrimage to its remote location in the Ozark Mountains. They travel the winding mountainous roads, walk the entry path, and enter its shimmering, light-filled space. The chapel was named by the architect who thought that the cluster of structure in the nave suggested the "crown of thorns" that Jesus was forced to wear on his path to Calvary. According to the chapel's brochure, the entry path is a symbolic "walk with our Lord" and the chapel's setting is on "holy ground—all ground is holy if Jesus is present." As the sun sets, and the birds and surrounding landscape become quiet, the chapel is lit by twenty-four wall sconces that line both sides of the nave. Their cruciform reflections endlessly repeat in the flanking glass walls, suggesting infinity and eternity. The presence of this place and its steady stream of visitors confirms the enduring and meaningful power of sacred architecture in any age.

A path of labyrinthine organization might be said to be epitomized by the Minoan Royal Palace at Knossos on Crete (fig. 79). (The word *labyrinth* itself has roots in the Cretan language.) This site perhaps

Fig. 79. Knossos, the Royal Palace (ca. 1600 BCE), axonometric drawing with plans of major rooms shown at selected levels.

1. Lower Level
2. Central Court
3. Piano Nobile
4. Workshop Area
5. Royal Domestic Quarter
6. Theatral Area
7. Official Entry
8. Throne Room (below Piano Nobile)
9. Corridor of the Procession
10. Stepped Causeway
11. Pillar Hall
12. Hall of the Double Axes
13. Queen's Megaron

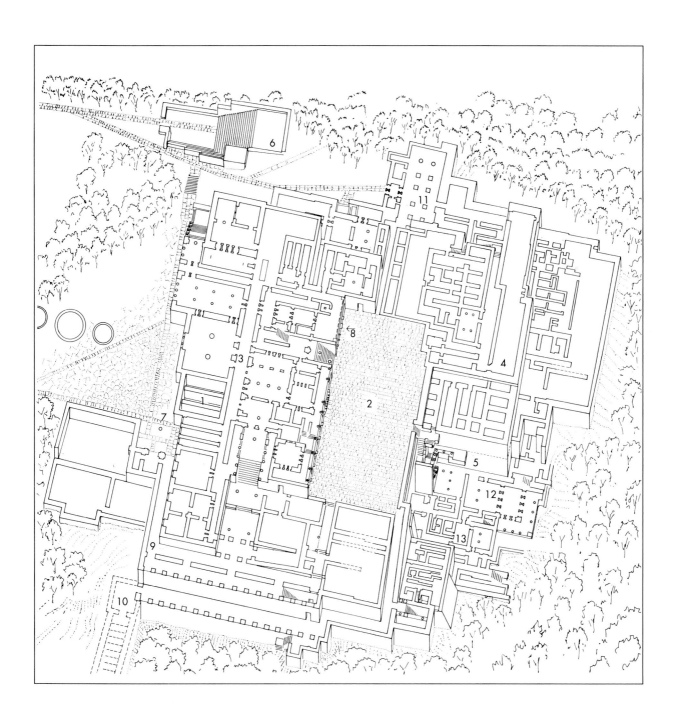

was the setting for the myth of Theseus and the Minotaur's labyrinth. Theseus was the son of the Athenian king Aegeus, whose city at this time was bound to King Minos to deliver seven young men and seven young maidens every nine years to be sacrificed to the Minotaur. This creature, half man and half bull, was the progeny of King Minos's wife Pasiphaë and a beautiful enchanted bull. In his shame the king had the architect Daedalus construct a labyrinth; in its depths resided this strange and deadly creature. According to Ovid, the architect

> famous for his skill, constructed the maze, confusing the usual marks of direction, and leading the eye of the beholder astray by devious paths winding in different directions. Just as the playful waters of the Maeander in Phrygia flow this way and that, without any consistency, as the river, turning to meet itself, sees its own advancing waves, flowing now towards it source and now towards the open sea, always changing its direction, so Daedalus constructed countless wandering paths and was himself scarcely able to find the way back to the entrance, so confusing was the maze.[43]

When the time of tribute came around again, Theseus volunteered to be one of the victims, telling no one that he intended to kill the Minotaur. When the victims were paraded before the Minoans on the way to their doom, the King's daughter Ariadne saw Theseus, fell immediately in love with him, and vowed to save his life. She went to Daedalus to learn the way out of the labyrinth and then secretly met with the hero, making him vow marriage to her if he escaped. Following Ariadne's directions, when Theseus entered the labyrinth, he tied the end of a ball of string to the door and unrolled it as he worked his way deeper and deeper into the labyrinth. Presently, he found the Minotaur and killed it, followed the string back out, and escaped with Ariadne and his countrymen.

According to Kostof, the palace at Knossos might appear more ordered than it does to us today if the upper levels were reconstructed.

Moreover, there is an overall organization centered about the central courtyard, the goal of the entry sequence. The approach to the palace was by way of a "stepped causeway" that negotiated a ravine below. The entrances to the palace were located on its north and west sides. The north entrance was fronted by a paved path, the width of which required those approaching to walk single file. The enforced processional might have been watched by spectators in the palace, as suggested by the myth of Theseus.[44] At a threshold called the theatral area, the path split. One segment headed east, entered the Pillared Hall, and then continued south down a narrow corridor toward the Central Court. The other path segment led south to the west entrance, which was fronted by a large paved courtyard and defined by a single column porch. The following path sequence was more labyrinthine and ceremonial. A narrow corridor painted with frescoes depicting processionals led east into the darkness of the palace. Turning north and passing through a threshold space, the path then ascended a monumental stair to a hall. Through the hall to the east the path ascended a narrow set of stairs to the Central Court. The path twisted and turned, passing by ritual spaces, ascending and descending to the various state and residential spaces. Its destination, the Central Court, provided the setting for the daring Minoan Bull Dance in which young men and women would vault themselves over a charging bull by grasping its horns. Its ritual enactment is said to have been in celebration of the goddess. Subsequent paths and destinations to the east, according to Scully, similarly depicted the journey from light to dark, from the outside to the "womb" of the great goddess.[45]

The segmented path and labyrinth underline the rigors and trials of the spiritual path to the sacred place. Perhaps more than other path types, through its numerous thresholds and path segments, an expansion of time and sense of passage is created. It is a journey to the unknown that mirrors the stages of the spiritual quest. It symbolizes the hero's journey through its segments of increasing sacredness, its boundaries to protect the uninitiated, and the trials and decisions along the path that lead to the sacred place.

• • •

As we have observed throughout the previous examples, the path and place in sacred architecture typically includes the following components: There is a clearly articulated entry, a sequence of increasingly sacred spaces long the path, a clear marking of path surface and edges, a consistent ordering of constructive elements and materials, anticipation of attainment of the sacred place, and a symbolic story expressed by the path and place. We will continue to focus on these elements in the following examples, as well as to address more comprehensively the relationship between belief and form. This will entail understanding the fundamentals of the particular culture's belief system and its historical context, and documenting the characteristics of the sacred site and the architectural elements of which it is comprised. We will then examine possible correspondences between the sacred place and the religion, philosophy, or mythology that it served. Each architectural example will be examined according to its *characteristics*, or the overall composition of the spiritual path and place, including plan type and orientation; its *articulation*, or the constructive and space-forming elements of which it is comprised, including geometry-proportion, physical and spatial properties, and construction and materials; and lastly its *meaning*, or the significance, symbolism, and experience of the path and place in their religious context.

The first two categories, in essence, intend to establish the "what it is" and "how it is" of each example. It will document the overall composition, its constituent parts, and its religious and historical setting. The third category is more complex but basically attempts to explain "why it is" through examining interrelationships between belief and form. I argue that the architecture of the sacred place is fundamentally "built myth," both symbolizing the belief system and accommodating the enactment of shared rituals.

CHAPTER 6

A Journey to Selected Sites

The Temple of Amun-Re

The Temple of Karnak, dedicated to the god Amun-Re, the principal deity of the Late Kingdom, was located in the ancient capital of Thebes on the east bank of the Nile in Upper Egypt. It was called the "collector of holy places" because so many cults found their place here[2]; at the height of Theban power and wealth, it was the most important temple in all of Egypt. During this time the temple had hundreds of priests attending to its daily functions and rituals. The cult statue of Amun-Re itself was ritually purified each day by the priests, who began by ceremonially cleansing themselves in the Sacred Lake, located within the temple complex. They then entered the temple and, bearing censers of charcoal and incense, proceeded to the inner sanctum where the cult statue and sacred barges of the royal family were located. Ceremonies were then performed in front of the statue and its flanking offertory chapels, including offerings of food, and the statue was ritually undressed, purified, and then readorned.[3]

The Egyptian calendar had many religious festivals throughout the year. They all shared rituals associated with the symbolic reaffirmation of the pharaoh as god and the regeneration of the land. One was the *Sed* Festival, the pharaoh's jubilee festival which was performed thirty years after his coronation; it renewed his authority and divinity, as well

I am he who made heaven and earth, formed the mountains and created what is above.
I am he who made the water and created the celestial waves. . . .
I am he who made the bull for the cow. . . .
I am he who made the sky and the mysteries of the two horizons, I placed there the souls of the gods.
I am he who opens his eyes, thus the light comes forth.
I am he who closes his eyes, thus comes forth obscurity;
On the order of whom the Nile's flood flows abroad, whose name is not known to the gods.
I am he who made the hours, thus the days were born.
I am he who opened the New Year's festival, who created the river.
I am he who made the living fire.
    I am Khepri in the morning, Re at his noontide, Atum in the evening.

    —Amun-Re,
    Egyptian creation myth[1]

as the mythical union of Lower and Upper Egypt. The Great Festival Hall of Tuthmosis III at the eastern end of Karnak was built for this purpose. The agrarian Egyptian society had many festivals that included ritualistic processions, dancing, music, and feasting. For example, the Great Festival of Min celebrated the harvest and included the ritual enactment of the union of the pharaoh and the queen. Often the festivals included a journey on the Nile, followed by a procession along the linear axis of the temple. As we observed earlier, the Festival of the Valley entailed a journey across the Nile from the Temple of Amun-Re at Karnak to Queen Hatshepsut's temple which was expressed and facilitated by the alignment of their two axes.

The Temple of Amun-Re at Karnak was one of many Egyptian examples of processional architecture. When one visits the temple today, it is clear that it is one of the more extensive, elaborate, and powerful examples, as well as perhaps one of the more notable renditions of the path and place in sacred architecture. In its time it evocatively expressed Egyptian religious beliefs and provided the setting for a yearly round of religious observances and festivals. Much of the imagery of the Late Kingdom temple complexes were concerned with the act of journey. Carvings on the walls depicted the sacred barge of the god on his yearly journeys, and the path sequence in part symbolized the journey from life to the afterlife. Death itself in Egyptian religion was also a journey with way stations along the route. *The Egyptian Book of the Dead*, which first came into use in the Late Kingdom, provided instructions for the path to the underworld and thus was often placed in the sarcophagus. The goal of the journey was the meeting with Osiris, the god of the underworld. The *Book of the Dead* provided instructions for the initiation rites that followed, which included the weighing of the heart of the deceased and the answering of questions regarding conduct in life. There were also initiatory questions and the dead were required to recite the secret names of the door to the afterlife.[4]

The temple precinct at Karnak was enclosed by a precinct wall. Inside the temple complex were numerous subtemples, all dominated by a long, axial east-west path that passed through a series of spaces and events and culminated in the inner sanctum of the god Amun-Re

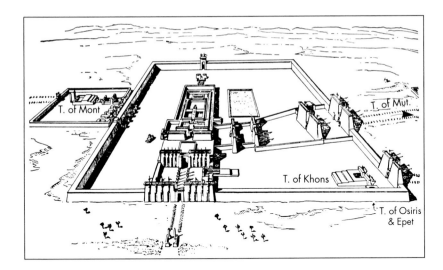

Fig. 80. A precinct wall surrounded the Temple of Amun-Re.

(fig. 80). The temple complex at Karnak was also linked with the earlier, smaller temple at Luxor. This temple was dedicated to the Theban Triad of Amun, his wife Mut, and their son Khons and was connected to Karnak by an avenue of ram-headed sphinxes. Between the two temples were also palaces and administrative buildings. The site of the temple at Karnak had been a sacred place since the Old Kingdom, but remains of earlier structures have been lost.[5] The principal temples at Karnak were begun in the Eighteenth Dynasty (1562–1308 BCE). On the west bank of the Nile across from Thebes there are numerous temples and tombs, a vast necropolis including the Mortuary Temple of Queen Hatshepsut. It symbolized the land of the dead located in the mountains where the sun set.

Mortuary temples such as Queen Hatshepsut's provided a place for the pharaohs to worship their patron gods and, after their death, served the function of a mortuary chapel. The Late Kingdom temples served a different purpose, being places for the communal worship of one or more gods, and often added to by successive pharaohs. The elements that comprise the Temple of Amun-Re at Karnak at are typical of Late Kingdom temples, which are also called pylon temples. These characteristics are exemplified by the earlier Temple of Khons, who was the moon god and son of Amun-Re and Mut. It was located

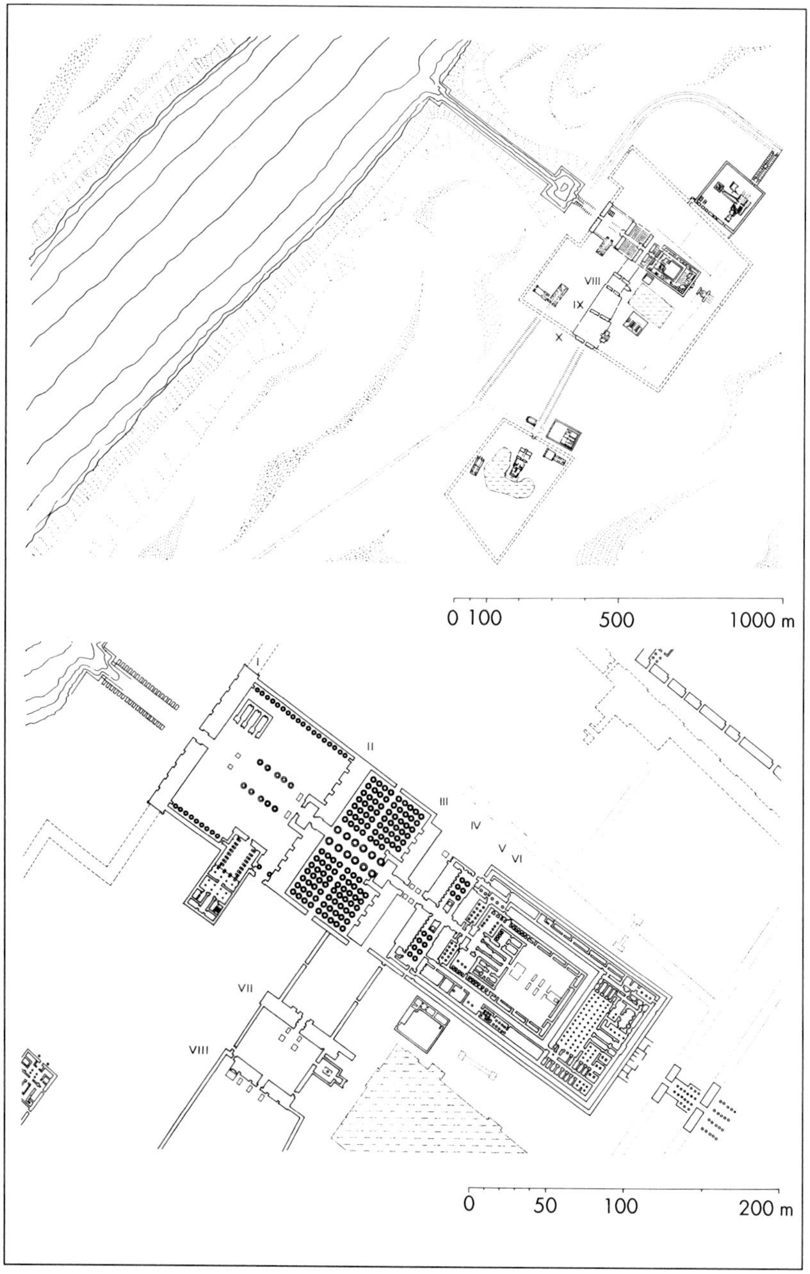

Fig. 81. Site plan and floor plan. (Numbers indicate pylons.)

within the Karnak temple precinct and built around 1100 BCE[6] (fig.81). In pylon temples an axial, symmetrical path dominated the organization which began with an approach avenue flanked by recumbent sphinxes. The overall complex included pylons, colonnaded open courtyards, hypostyle halls, and a series of spaces that became darker and more compressed as one progressed along the path. The inner sanctum at the end of the path held the cult statue and the sacred barge used to transport it to other temples.

The Temple of Amun-Re at Karnak was constructed in phases and began with the sanctuary, which was constructed during the reign of Tuthmosis III (1525–1512 BCE) (fig. 82). The original sanctuary was fronted by a pylon (known as Pylon VI) and contained many of the characteristics common to Late Kingdom temples. Later additions were built around this sacred center. The sequences of spaces built toward the west served to increase and accentuate the pylon temple characteristics. The result was a long axial processional way that began at the Nile and concluded with the sanctuary of the god Amun-Re. Throughout the complex the path dominates, the architecture is mas-

Fig. 82. The trabeated entry gate and pylon.

Fig. 83. The approach avenue (right), flanked by ram-headed sphinxes, led to Pylon I. Originally, an immense trabeated opening delineated the entrance.

Fig. 84. The courtyard between Pylons I and II (below, right), looking toward the hypostyle hall.

Fig. 85. Pylon II with hypostyle hall beyond (below).

Fig. 86. The incised surfaces of the hypostyle hall were originally brightly colored. The space was lit from above by means of clerestory openings.

sive and monolithic, and the spaces are generally tight and constricted.

As is still partially apparent today, the journey began at a landing dock at the terminus of a canal that led from the Nile where two rows of opposing ram-headed sphinxes led to Pylon I (fig. 83). This typical pylon was composed of two massive battered walls, 150 feet (45 m) high and 50 feet (15 m) thick at their base. Between them was set a massive trabeated entry, capped with a lintel bearing the image of the sun (see Temple of Khons). Beyond this was a large rectangular open courtyard, formed by Pylons I and II on its west and east sides, respectively, and colonnades on the remaining edges (fig. 84).

Pylon II established the entrance to the hypostyle hall of Seti I and his son Ramses II (fig. 85). This is the largest of all Egyptian hypostyle halls and one of the more significant and notable spaces in Egyptian architecture. Its grandeur is still apparent today, measuring 340 feet (104 m) in its north-south dimension, 170 feet (52 m) east-west. Its size and scale was anticipated by the earlier hypostyle hall of the Mortuary Temple of Mentuhotep at Deir el-Bahri which featured eighty octagonal columns arranged in ten rows.[7] At Karnak the hypostyle hall contains 134 columns in all, the tallest forming the central aisle are 69 feet (21 m) high and 12 feet (3.5 m) in diameter at their base. Originally, the entire hall was roofed with monolithic stone slabs, and the roof of the three central aisles was raised to allow for clerestory light to enter the space (fig. 86). Beyond the hypostyle hall, one then passed through a series of increasingly constricted spaces marked by pylons, obelisks, and colonnades to the Sanctuary of Amun-Re which contained his sacred barge (figs. 87 and 88).

The path at Karnak was a tightly controlled series of spatial events. This longitudinal axial path, traveling from west to east, comprised a number of linked, additive spaces. The articulation of the path relied on symmetry and frontality to communicate a sense of passage, order, and continuity. Egyptian architecture has been accused of being nonspatial, but this is not entirely true. Certainly the early pyramid sites, such as at Giza, were predominantly plastic in nature and were perceived as objects in space. Even at Giza, though, the spatial nature of Late Kingdom temples was anticipated by the Mortuary Temple of

Fig. 87. The path as it leaves the hypostyle hall.

Fig. 88. The inner sanctum of the temple.

Chephren and its approach path from the Valley Temple on the banks of the Nile. It was in the Late Kingdom that the axial path came to dominate the organization of the temple complexes, however, continuing into the Ptolemaic era as found at sites such as the Temple of Hathor at Dendara and the Temple of Kom Ombo. The path in pylon temples was essentially a series of linked spaces, not to occupy or even to pause in for long, but simply to pass through along the linear route.

The path at Karnak was articulated by a number of space-forming and constructive elements. These included a series of massive, battered pylons, colonnaded inner courtyards, hypostyle halls, and three-dimensional markers in the form of guardian colossi, flanking recumbent sphinxes, and obelisks. Pylon I, which initiated the path sequence, was quite possibly one of the most powerful thresholds found in the history of architecture. It established an intermediary space inscribed by its 50-foot depth and the entry portal. Subsequent pylons reinforced the experience of the path as a series of thresholds and spaces that sequentially marched toward the hidden sanctuary. Pylon VI, the earliest and smallest of the pylons, created the final threshold at the Sanctuary of Amun-Re.

Pylons I and II had recesses near their tops in which banners on poles were mounted. They were also capped by a cavetto cornice, which cast shadow, accentuating the solidity and massiveness of their form. The pylons read frontally as thickened planes and were also legible, containing messages on their surfaces. The incised surfaces were brightly colored, as were most of the surfaces in the temple complex.

The courtyard between Pylons I and II was bounded on its north and south sides by massive colonnades, many of which still remain. It was a large space, larger by half in plan than the hypostyle hall; succeeding pharaohs and building programs gradually infilled this space with a number of temples and objects. The experience of this space set up a fundamental element of the articulation of the path, a cadence of light and dark. From the shadow of Pylon I, one entered a large, dazzlingly bright space bounded on its sides by the colossal architecture and by the consistently blue Egyptian sky above. Religious rites were performed in this courtyard at the Temple of Seti II, which contained the shrines of the Theban Triad; their sacred barges were placed here during processions. Late Kingdom temples typically contained shrines of this type, which were associated with the divine marriage and its symbolic promise of regeneration and fecundity. At the southern side of the Great Court is the Temple of Ramses III. At its eastern side was Pylon II and the entry to the hypostyle hall, flanked by guardian colossi.

Many of the elements that comprised the articulation of the path were present in the great hypostyle hall. The first was the rhythm of light and dark; the hypostyle hall was predominantly a dark space, lit only from above by clerestories at the outside edge of the three taller central avenues. These clerestories, one of the many remarkable features of this space, rose up from the smaller outer columns to the height of the tall columns of the central avenue and were constructed from bars of solid stone. Entering this space from the bright outer courtyard would have initially plunged one into darkness. Slowly, as the eyes adjusted, the colossal hall would reveal itself, shafts of light stabbing into the gloom, the colorful incised surfaces depicting scenes of the pharaoh with various deities.[8] Though the space was a multidirectional network of paths, its central avenue headed resolutely forward.⁹

The monumental scale of the temple, introduced by the pylons, was reinforced by the hypostyle hall. The scale throughout was colossal and otherworldly, as evidenced by the massive columns, the principal constructive element, which in turn rested on stone bases half the height of a human. The columns themselves are wider than the spaces between them (fig. 89). Two types of papyrus-form columns were used in the hypostyle hall. The first, which formed the central avenue, was the open-lotus flower type with its distinctive bell-shaped capital. Because the roof support was hidden by the capital, they appeared to be growing unencumbered toward the light. The second type, the closed-bud columns, comprised the rest of the darkened hall. The ceiling was constructed of monolithic slabs of stone, the underside of which were painted blue with the stars of the night sky represented.

As is characteristic of Egyptian architecture of this time, this was not a place for static contemplation, but one to be ritually passed through. As one proceeded along the linear path, the compression of space and cadence of light and dark continued. Passing through Pylons III, IV, and V, one went through a subsequent open courtyard and a small hypostyle hall before approaching the Sanctuary of Amun-Re. Here, as at the Temple of Khons (see also Dendara), the floor level rose incrementally as the ceiling was lowered, creating a series of increasingly darker and more constricted spaces. The sanctuary itself would have been a completely enclosed "stone box," dark and compressed. In essence, this was a "room within a room," a completely separated inner sanctum—the holy of holies in Late Kingdom temple architecture. At the eastern wall of this space a false door was incised, a further symbolic reinforcement of the continuance of the path. Also, as the highest point in the temple, it represented the primordial mound, The First Place of the Egyptian cosmology, and thus was both a threshold and a goal.

It was at the Temple of Amun-Re at Karnak that the annual Feast of Opet was held. The architecture symbolized mythological meanings and facilitated the enactment of ritual communal celebrations. The

Fig. 89. There is more stone than space in the hypostyle hall, which further defines the axial path.

festival commemorated the mystical marriage of Amun-Re and his wife, Mut, a symbolic rite to assure the repeating fertility of the land. During the celebrations, the sacred barges of Amun-Re and his divine family journeyed to Amun-Re's Southern Harem at the Temple of Luxor. The elaborate festival was enacted by the pharaoh and the priesthood of Karnak, but the inhabitants of Thebes and pilgrims from all over Egypt also participated. The procession began at the sanctuary, the inner sanctum of the god, where the pharaoh and priests in full regalia would perform preparatory rites. The barges were then carried on their shoulders in a colorful and reverential procession that marched past the pylons, courtyards, hall, and obelisks of the path sequence before entering the hypostyle hall. Here they would be met by more participants to continue along its axial path and into the bright light of the Great Courtyard. After further rites at the shrines of the Theban Triad, the now fully swelled retinue would pass through Pylon I and down the avenue of the sphinxes to the canal from the Nile. There the barges would be loaded onto a ship for a short sail to Luxor. The townspeople lined the banks of the Nile to cheer the water-borne processional and may have even pulled the ships along with ropes. There were six stops along the route for celebrations at shrines. Its destination was Luxor Temple where the reverse order of the processional occurred, the retinue getting progressively smaller as the spaces grew more sacred. Finally, only the priests and the pharaoh entered the dark and compressed inner sanctum of the temple to perform final rites at the golden cult figure of Amun-Re, resplendent in the gloom, lit from above by a single shaft of light.[10]

The enactment of the mythical divine marriage suggests order and continuity, and Christian Norberg-Schulz has suggested that representing "order and consistency" was the ultimate goal of Egyptian architecture.[11] Egyptian culture and architecture is remarkable for its consistency over a period of thousands of years, though there were certainly distinctive eras as well as times of social upheaval when little building was done. Egyptian religion did not have one definitive text but was composed of a rich and at times conflicting mythology that has proven difficult to understand in its totality. Like most archaic religions, it featured creation myths and a pantheon of gods associated with various aspects of life and mythical events, often centered at specific geographical areas. Many of the myths were concerned with the cyclical nature of the cosmos and the seasons and served to provide assurance of its annual regeneration.[12] It was the Nile that defined the Egyptian cosmology, the life-giving river surrounded by the vast and undifferentiated desert, except for the mountains in Upper Egypt. The regularity of the yearly flood, the consistent clear skies with the sun charting its regular course, the flat and barren desert, all communicated the phenomena of continuity. It was the sun, however, that came to dominate the Egyptian religion, and the Egyptians are credited with inventing the solar calendar. The god Amun was one of eight gods worshiped at Hermopolis, but by the Twelfth Dynasty he became associated with the sun god Re and became the principal deity named Amun-Re. By the Eighteenth Dynasty his "solarization"[13] and omnipotence was complete and a "solar theology" with its attendant powerful priesthood firmly established. Eliade has stated that "solar cults" emphasize continuity, and "Solar hierophanies give expression to the religious values of autonomy and power, of sovereignty, of intelligence."[14]

Thebes and the Temple of Amun-Re at Karnak became the center of this solar theocracy. The temple was oriented so that the rising sun would emerge between the two halves of Pylon I, just over the heraldic sun disk at its entry threshold. The path of the sun symbolized the journey from life to death as it rose in the east and set in the land of the dead in the west. The sun god was said to journey to the underworld and its perils each night, and to emerge victorious the following morning. The omnipotence of Amun-Re was not challenged until the reign of Akh-en-Aton (1379–1362 BCE), who established a purer form of sun worship in the deity Aton and moved the capital to Akhetaten (Tell el-Amarna), north of Thebes. His successor Tut-ankh-Amon, however, restored the god to power and reestablished Thebes as the religious and political capital of Egypt. The Eighteenth Dynasty was the apex of Egyptian civilization, a time of cultural flowering and political expansion, but with the death of the young Tut-ankh-Amon, it ended never to flourish again.

The vast regularity of the Egyptian landscape and sky, played against the mystery of the Nile's yearly flooding, created a communal mythological and ritualistic response that served to explain the environmental phenomena. It was a typical response of an agrarian society's intimate and at times precarious relationship to the land and its life-sustaining harvests. Communal rituals articulated the human need to participate in the rhythms of the cosmos. Through participation in the ritual, humans became symbolically joined with the cosmos and thus the anxiety of their dependence was lessened. Acts of devotion and supplication were performed in the belief that they would guarantee the continuity of the beneficent environment. The priests, playing the roles of the gods, enacted the myths of cosmic order, death, and regeneration. The temple at Karnak, through its yearly cycles of festivals, observances, and daily ministrations, symbolized and accommodated the myths of the Egyptian cosmogonic cycle. Four major themes appear in the architecture of this temple and the rituals that it held: order and continuity, symbols of life and death, symbols of fertility and fecundity, and increasing levels of the sacred along the path.

The Egyptian cult of the dead and its necropoles were one manifestation of a belief system that conceived of the cosmos as ordered and timeless. The architecture communicated these values through a number of means. The first was through its construction and materials, a "durable megalithic mass,"[15] that expressed victory over the corruption of the body and the eternal order of the cosmos. Secondly, these values were also supported through the formal ordering of the constructive and space-forming elements. According to E. Baldwin Smith, "The endless repetition of halls and corridors, as well as the New Kingdom's desire for magnitude, were the instinctive result of the primitive desire for certainty."[16] Lastly, there was the certainty of the linear path, with its unwavering route to the sacred place. The linear and orthogonal organization of Egyptian architecture is related to the physical presence of the Nile, a linear axis that bisects the country, along which were the gridded fields and cities of its longitudinal oasis. The temple replicated the Egyptian cosmos with mountains, in the form of the pylon, that rise on both sides of the longitudinal "river" of the axial path.[17] Eliade argues that the temples were "microcosmic images of the country." All of these elements gave what Christian Norberg-Schulz has described as "existential security" amid the enormity of an, at times, turbulent and unsure world.

The path sequence and its articulation also symbolized the transitory nature of life. The linear, linked spaces of the path expressed the belief that life progressed unremittingly toward an everlasting postmortem paradise. Thus, as I have noted, the spaces were not to be paused in or contemplated for any length of time, but passed through. The false door that appeared at the eastern wall of the Sanctuary of Amun-Re very powerfully symbolized continuity. The *ka*, or life spirit, of the pharaoh gods were said to travel forth daily from their colossal abodes—thus the need for all of one's worldly possessions in the crypt, as well as the sacred barge typically found at mortuary sites. The architecture symbolized this "eternal wandering," the brief passage through the dream of life to awakening in the world beyond. Death itself came to be seen as the true reality.[18] Conversely, or one could say concurrently, the path symbolized this paradise itself. Thus, as each generation built its part, the cosmogonic symbolism of the path was elaborated on.

In archaic societies attitudes about death are typically paired with myths and symbols concerning fertility, fecundity, and regeneration. Myths of death and resurrection were found in Egyptian religion (as in other archaic faiths and still in contemporary religions). The myth of Osiris, Isis, Seth, and Horus is perhaps one of the earliest examples of a resurrection theme.[19] The Osirian myths and their timeless themes of death and resurrection were associated with the annual flooding of the Nile and the regeneration of the land. Both Osiris and Isis are fertility symbols, and the goddess was an early "madonna figure," often depicted suckling the child Horus.[20]

Many of the elements that comprised the path and architecture at Karnak spoke about themes of regeneration and fecundity. First, the temple precinct, surrounded by an impenetrable wall, was an internalized sacred world separated from the secular external world.[21] The temple itself was a series of concentric enclosures, the last being the inner sanctum itself. The interior spaces of the temple symbolized a divine oasis, replete with plant forms, water, and the night sky. The plant-form columns speak about growth and regeneration, and their placement in the massive, round stone bases, an echo of residential architecture, served as fertility symbols.[22] The columns appeared to grow up toward the overarching sky depicted on the ceiling of the hypostyle hall.[23] Their papyrus forms suggested the sacred grove in which Horus was born and spoke about fecundity and resurrection. The path as the stage on which regular repeating rituals were enacted also spoke about repetition and renewal.

At the Festival of Opet the common people would have first glimpsed the procession in the hypostyle hall and the Great Courtyard. The retinue would emerge from the darkness and constriction of the inner sacred spaces where only the priests were permitted. The priesthood in archaic societies was a powerful element in the development and transformation of mythology and religion, and thus the architecture. Indeed, the symbolic language in this example, as well as others, cannot be explained as simply the result of a shared belief system. There is a fundamental base to all religions and their edifices, but in time they also take on a life of their own.[24] Similar to the structuralist theory of "*langue* and *parole*," there is a dialectic interrelationship between the fundamental beliefs of a religion and its multifaceted expressions. There is also another way to consider the role of the priesthood: They were powerful actors as well as creators of the developing myths and rituals, at times for self-serving reasons. The empowerment of the priesthood could be said to be a necessary part of the myth, a handing over of the task to the designated "hero."

Lastly, the path at Karnak communicated and facilitated a symbolic journey. Along the route, the levels of sacrality increased as one progressed further into the temple and a mythological narrative unfolded legibly, spatially, and temporally. This is a phenomenon shared in various ways by the following examples of the sacred path and place.

Delphusa, here I entertaine suppose
To build a farr-famed Temple and
*   ordein*
An Oracle t'informe the mindes of
*   Men,*
Who shall for ever offer my love
Whole hecatombs—even all the Men
*   that move*
In rich Peloponnesus and all those
Of Europe, and the Iles the seas
*   enclose,*
Whom future search of Acts and
*   Beings brings—*
To whom I'le prophecie the truths of
*   things*
In that rich Temple where my oracle
*   sings.*

—Hymn to Apollo[25]

The Sacred Way and Temple of Apollo

The sacred way and temple complex located at Delphi on the Greek mainland was dedicated to the god Apollo, though other gods were worshiped here as well. The site is in a dramatic, mountainous setting, situated on the northern shore of the Bay of Corinth, on a steep slope that is part of the foothills of Mount Parnassós. When one first sees the site and its striking, severe natural beauty and commanding views, it is easy to see why it was long known as a sacred site. Delphi was regarded as the "navel" of the ancient Greek world, and this center was marked by a sacred *omphalos* stone. Its use dates from Mycenaean times when it was first identified as an oracular site. Like most sacred sites, it was built upon numerous times, each stage elaborating on religious themes, such as a journey from the profane to the sacred. The first-known structure, a wooden temple, was erected in the eighth century BCE. The present remains date from around 350 BCE, though some parts, including the temenos enclosure wall, date from the sixth century BCE.

Like many Greek sacred sites, Delphi needs to be understood in relation to its site. Greek architecture and its siting, like many examples of ancient architecture, was a response to its environmental setting. The landscape of Greece is strikingly different from the Nile Valley. The Egyptian environment was dominated by the axial oasis[26] of the Nile and, in comparison, offered little topographical and seasonal variety. The architecture in part expressed this constant, unchanging, eternal order. Egyptian monumental architecture was also more internalized, as exemplified by the hypostyle hall and its hermetic depiction of the symbolic oasis. The Greek landscape, in contrast, was characterized by variety and specificity. Moreover, the seasons in Greece are pronounced and often dramatic. Unlike Egypt, the landscape did not suggest uniformity and constancy, either architecturally or politically.[27] The plurality of Greek institutions and religions was expressed by its architecture. The Greek response to the landscape was varied and typically site specific, which has made it difficult to describe in general terms. Whereas Karnak was an internalized world, predominantly responding to the larger site characteristics of the Egyptian landscape, Delphi is a specific response to a particular site. As in other Greek sacred sites, the landscape retains a powerful presence. The path and architecture served to mark the sacred place, as well as responding to and transforming the site and its surroundings.

Originally the site was the sanctuary of Gaia, the goddess of the earth and fertility. It was identified by its sacred spring, where the goddess and her child, the serpent python, were worshiped. According to Greek mythology, the god Apollo killed the python and took over the sanctuary as his own, and it became the religious center of a powerful god worshiped throughout Greece. Apollo was the god of light and reason, and his presence was said to provide a reconciliation between nature and humans. Delos was the birthplace of Apollo and thus the other site important to his worship, but he journeyed to Delphi and there established his dominance. To do this, he had to kill the giant snake who guarded the oracular site. "Now rot here," the god exclaimed after his deed, "upon the soil that feeds man."[28] And so the god's name became Pytho, which derives from the Greek word for rot, and afterward Apollo was called Pythian Apollo.[29]

Greek sacred sites were typically associated with a particular god and commonly symbolized either human dominance or subservience to its physical setting. The association of a deity or a group of gods to a site most likely was based on the site's characteristics, but also determined the relationship of the architecture to the site. As described by Scully,

> not only were certain landscapes indeed regarded by the Greeks as holy and as expressive of specific gods, or rather as embodiments of their presence, but also . . . the temples and the subsidiary buildings of their sanctuaries were so formed in themselves and so placed in relation to the landscape and to each other as to enhance, develop, complement, and sometimes even to contradict, the basic meaning that was felt in the land.[30]

Sites where nature dominated were dedicated to the earth goddesses Demeter and Hera; where the forces of nature and man were balanced, to Zeus; and places of human community were associated

Fig. 90. Site plan, the sacred way and Temple of Apollo, Delphi (ca. 400 BCE).

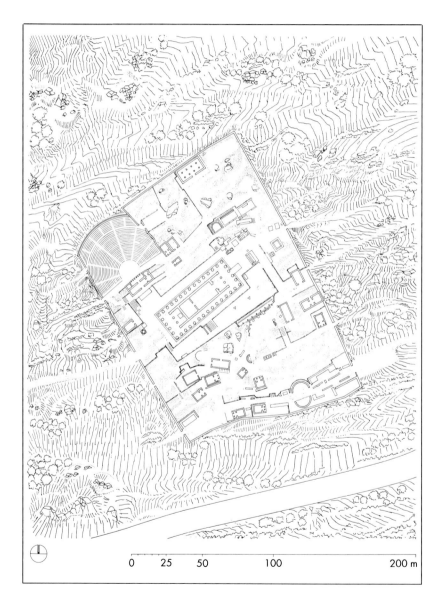

0 25 50 100 200 m

with Athena.[31] The association of Apollo at Delphi both complemented the ancient powerful chthonic forces and symbolized the dominance of the god. Scully argues that its path sequence expressed the struggle between the will of humans and the forces of nature. The architecture and the site need to be seen as a total composition that represented, at least in one aspect, the "conflict between the old way, that of the goddess of the earth, and the new way, that of men and their Olympian Gods."[32]

The presence of a monument-lined path, a dominant temple, a theater, and a stadium suggest that numerous events and rituals occurred at Delphi throughout the year, both of a state and religious nature. One of the yearly events was the Pythian Games, established to honor Apollo's slaying of the python and his self-imposed eight-year banishment to cleanse himself of this act. This act of expiation, in which Apollo toiled as a simple shepherd in the Vale of Tempe on the slopes of Mount Olympus, is significant—it speaks of a respect for, and reconciliation with, the earth forces. The panhellenic Pythian Games, which were held every four years beginning in 582 BCE, included both musical and athletic contests. The games lasted from six to eight days and included sacrifices, feasts, and music, as well as a processional along the sacred way to the Temple of Apollo.[33]

Delphi was also the seat of Apollo's greatest oracle and thus was a pilgrimage site for those desiring to consult her. It was here that Croesus, King of Lydia, asked the Delphic oracle if he should go to war against the Persians. The oracle replied that if he did, "he would destroy a great empire."[34] It was only after his defeat that it became clear the empire spoken of was his own. The myth of Oedipus is also intimately linked with the Apollonian Delphic oracle, who was said never to lie.[35]

The sacred way at Delphi was lined with monuments to the various wars between the city-states, as well as treasuries, and led to places dedicated to the gods. It was the interplay between these edifices dedicated to the ways of humans, the sacred spaces, and the dramatic site that characterizes the path and place. As we shall observe, this interplay is a prominent characteristic of the site.

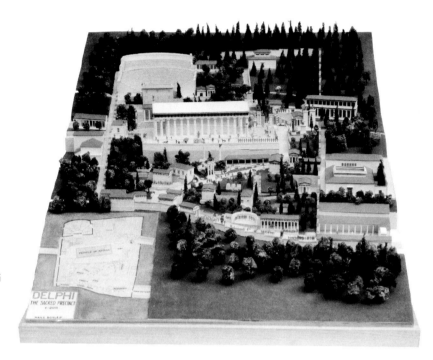

Fig. 91. Reconstruction model of Delphi in about 160 CE.

The principal site at Delphi is a temenos, or sacred site, originally enclosed on all sides by a precinct wall (figs. 90 and 91). Within this enclosure the segmented path of the sacred way traverses the site, zig-zagging up the steep south-facing slope. The principal entrance to the sacred precinct was at the southeast corner of the enclosure.[36] Close to this entrance was the ancient Castalia Spring, a place of ablution before entry. The main entrance did not provide the most direct route up the slope, but was located so that the path provided views of the temple above[37] (fig. 92). The first part of the sacred way ran west, gently traversing the slope. Along this segment were located numerous monuments and treasuries of the different city-states, which often commemorated intercity conflicts. Just before it reached the western wall, the path turned sharply to the right and headed northeast, more steeply up the slope. On the left at this junction was the prominent Treasury of the Athenians, previously partially glimpsed from below, now more fully revealed (figs. 93 and 94). This treasury is the only fully

Fig. 92. The sacred way looking toward the temenos entrance. To the right, the Temple of Apollo is visible on the hillside.

Fig. 93. The sacred way, approaching the Treasury of the Athenians.

Fig. 94. The Treasury of the Athenians.

restored structure on the site, and its prominence and siting provide a clue as to how the entire precinct might have appeared. Beyond this point, as one looks up the path, views of the mountains are offered.

Along this segment of the path, the Treasury of the Athenians slowly reveals itself as one passes by and glances back, until its Doric Order front becomes visible. As the path progresses upward, similar shifting views of the remains of the Temple of Apollo are afforded; at times they are partially visible, set against the mountains; at other times they disappear (fig. 95). Originally, as one drew close, its longitudinal elevation would appear to hover above its massive polygonal base wall. As the path reached the level of the temple, it turned sharply left, directly facing the temple's principal Doric facade. There, as one looked back, the facade of the Treasury of the Athenians would have been fully revealed, set against the distant mountains (fig. 96). The path, after turning, then passed numerous shrines before finally entering the temple by way of a shallow ramp. The path terminated inside the dark, mysterious cella and adyton of the temple, the seat of the oracle (fig. 97). Beyond the temple, via a steep set of stairs, the path climbed to the theater. Steeply up the slope from there was the stadium. The thoughtful and meaningful siting of the theater and stadium is still powerfully apparent today, and their attainment suggests a resolution of the humanmade and the natural as one looks over the sacred enclosure and the mountains and valleys to the south (fig. 98).

The sacred way at Delphi functioned as a series of volumes varying in their degree of enclosure and created by the edifices of the monuments lining it. The siting and organization of Greek sites has been explained in numerous ways and at times misunderstood. Often they have been examined merely stylistically and formally, and because interior space was often subservient to exterior form and articulation, the temples have been characterized as being merely sculptural. Because the external form was presumed to dominate, this has led to speculation that the landscape was unimportant. These theories have been challenged by Christian Norberg-Schulz, C. A. Doxiadis, and Vincent Scully. Norberg-Schulz argues that "it is essential to understand the

Fig. 95. The sacred way, with the Temple of Apollo on the left, framed by the mountains behind.

Fig. 96. Looking back from the Temple of Apollo, the principal facade of the Treasury of the Athenians is now fully revealed.

Fig. 97. The remains of the east facade of the Temple of Apollo. A ramp led to the entrance of the cella and adytum, the seat of the oracle.

Fig. 98. The theater is located above the Temple of Apollo and offers a dramatic view of the sacred precinct.

temple in relation to the total situation under which it was created. That is, it has to be related to its site and to the purpose it had to serve. . . . Siting then was anything but arbitrary."[38] Similarly, Scully states that the temples and other edifices at Greek sites were always intimately linked with their natural environment. Moreover, the buildings only composed part of the "architecture of the site."

The first segment of the path was densely enclosed by flanking monuments and treasuries. These buildings were placed so as to accentuate their uniqueness, and their edifices delineated a series of inscribed volumes on the path. Scully describes the placement of the treasuries as "like that of free persons in a crowd," each vying for attention. Their "irregular" placement he explains as follows: "The spaces between them are simply voids which are not yet filled and which, because they are irregular in shape among the regular shapes of the treasuries, cannot prevent the eye from seeing the treasuries as lively objects which are acting out their cities' will to witness the procession and to be seen themselves. Each of the little buildings is therefore an active individual participant in the life of the site."[39] Secondary threshold volumes were implied by the spaces between the monuments, establishing a cadence of thresholds and volumes as the path progressed up the hill. There were also nodal points along the first segment of the path—for example, the opposing semicircular niches, which originally were lined with sculptures of the epigones and mythical heroes (see site plan, fig. 90).

Greek spatial and site planning is apparent as one approaches the restored Treasury of the Athenians. Because it is set at an oblique angle to the approach, it is always viewed three-dimensionally. As one moves closer, its form shifts as different portions of its sides are revealed. This dynamic relationship of the architecture to the path and its complex spatial and temporal effects served to underline the uniqueness of each monument and the spaces that surrounded them. In fact, Greek temples did not utilize axial site organizations until the late Hellenistic era, as we have observed at the Sanctuary of Asklepios at Kos.

Tight, constricted passageways that give way to more open spaces is a common architectural theme in Greek sacred sites and their predecessors. At Delphi, the linear enclosure of the first section of the path gives way to the more open, spatial rendering of the second part which begins at the Treasury of the Athenians. Here the shifting views of the objects flanking the path, the Temple of Apollo above, and the mountains beyond, compel one onward. Doxiadis proposed sight lines to explain the "irregular" placement of temples at Greek sites, and a case can be made in support of some of his ideas. However, the relationships suggested by Doxiadis depend on a static viewing point and thus cease to exist when one moves through the sites.[40] The numerous monuments placed along the path suggest a series of discrete objects and, consequently, a series of adjacent spaces along the path. For example, the polygonal wall that creates the plinth for the Temple of Apollo, set at an angle to the path, effectively modulates the spatial experience of the route as one passes by. From a distance, where the path turns at the Treasury of the Athenians, the presence of the wall is dimly felt, shadowed by the remains of the temple above. As one approaches, however, its mass is accentuated and it increasingly encloses the path. As one walks past, its angle draws it closer and closer to the path, and the remains of the temple above recede from view. Originally, the Stoa of the Athenians was placed against part of this wall, which would have accentuated this spatial experience. Once beyond the wall, though, the spatial orientation and character of the path changes dramatically as it turns and faces the entrance to the Temple of Apollo. The east facade of the temple originally inscribed a space in front of it that was orthogonally oriented to the final section of the path. Suddenly, the wall revealed itself as a plinth, and the three-dimensional presence of the temple was fully revealed, framed by the mountains across the valley.

As far as can be discerned from the remains of the path itself, its surface marking did not respond to the objects that delineated its edges. In other words, the inscribed volumes created by the adjacent monuments and treasuries along the path were not reflected by the path surface itself. There are steps and platforms that do appear at certain points, but generally the path functions as a ramp, consistently flowing up the hillside, ending in the ramp that attains the sacred place of the cella. The path, it appears, was paved throughout with thick slabs of stone and was wide enough to accommodate a large processional on foot, as well as horse-drawn chariots.

The path at Delphi, as at other sacred sites, re-created the spiritual journey. It was a journey from strife, symbolized by the chaotic juxtaposition of buildings along the first section of the path, to the order and peace of the Temple of Apollo. It was a journey from the secular to the divine; from the path formed by the deeds of humans to the sacred inner sanctum of the cella and adytum. The journey was also from the lesser art forms to the highest, from the path flanked by sculpture and architecture to the theater above. Dionysus, the god associated with drama and the younger brother of Apollo, took the site as his own every year from November through January. During this time, when Apollo was said to journey to the Land of the Hyperboreans, the oracle was silent.[41]

Each spring, when Apollo returned to his site, his presence was greeted with renewed religious devotion. Those seeking a prophecy from the oracle were known as *theopropoi*, or pilgrims. Their pilgrimage would have begun far away and included the tortuous mountainous routes that approached the site from the east and the west after passing by other sacred sites. The route from Athens passed through Lebadeia, just beyond which was the gorge of the Trophonion, another oracular site that balanced the will of humans with the power of the earth.[42] Just south and east of the sacred way at Delphi was another sacred site, the Sanctuary of Athena Pronaia. Upon arrival at Delphi, there would first be a ritual cleansing at Castalia Spring; dues would be paid and at some point an animal sacrificed to the god. The pilgrims would then pass through the main gateway which was flanked by the colossal Bull of Korkyra and rows of statues. Treasuries, statues, and other colossi would be passed as the pilgrims traversed the path, climbing upward toward the mountains and the Temple of Apollo. Inside, the temple's adytum was located at the site of the ancient *bothros*, or offertory cave of the great goddess. Here, there was a stone *omphalos* that symbolized the navel of the world and established the site as sacred and central—an *axis mundi*. The oracle, also called the Pythia, is said to have sat on a tripod above a chasm of the earth, whose vapors contributed to her trancelike prophetic state. She was also said to chew laurel leaves and drink from Castalia Spring as ritual preparation. Here the pilgrims would approach to ask their questions, and the answers would be translated, often in verse, by attendant priests. The pilgrims would journey home wearing laurel leaves, which symbolized their sacred ordeal.[43]

Apollo's slaying of the python symbolized human dominance of the site.[44] Apollo as the "sun god" represented male attributes, and thus the battle was between the feminine earth goddess and the male sun god. The conflict was never resolved though, and the power of the site lies in this ambiguity and the messages it holds in regard to human strength and weakness. The eternal conflict is expressed through various relationships on the site, some of which have been previously discussed. The jostling of the treasuries speak about the hubris of humans, the might of the separate city-states, and the foolishness of their constant battling. Along the first section of the path, the various monuments communicated the folly and tragedy of the ways of humans. As described by Scully,

> If you were an Athenian you were forced to bear the monument put up by the Spartans after Aegospotami, and it was directly opposite your own monument to Marathon. If you were a Spartan you would have to endure the partial blocking of your monument by the one set up by the Arcadians to celebrate your defeat at Leuctra. And next to your monument would be another intended to throw yours into the shade, set up by the Argives to celebrate the refounding of Messenia, your former hard won possession. "Know thyself," which joined "Nothing to excess" as the god's motto at Delphi, clearly required a certain self-command here.[45]

The monuments and treasuries each inhabit their own space but collectively form the path that leads to an ideal higher existence. The path itself, by constantly offering views of the surrounding mountains, contrasts the works of humans with the might of nature. The site was known to be prone to earthquakes, as well as constantly changing and often violent weather. The Doric order of the Temple of Apollo—an order that possessed a cool rational ordering but also seemed to rise out of and be rooted in the earth—also speaks about the unresolved conflict between humans and nature.[46]

The temple itself offered no protection from this conflict; most rituals were performed outdoors in the space fronted by the temple. One such rite took place every eight years during the Septentrion Festival. This celebration ritually enacted the killing of the python and the pilgrimage to Tempe. It included a torch-lit procession up the sacred way to a place on the path near the Temple of Apollo. Here a wooden hut was erected, recreating the lair of the serpent. The python would then be symbolically killed, the hut burned, and the young male Apollo would travel north to Tempe along with his companions. Their pilgrimage was completed when they returned adorned with laurel leaves. The laurel tree, sacred to the god Apollo, symbolized purification, and garlands were also awarded to athletes at the Pythian Games.

The form, organization, and articulation of the temple expressed the qualities of the god. Its interior was not for humans but provided a sacred place for the deity, and the only view of its dark interior was through partially opened doors during ritual celebrations. As at other sacred sites, the architecture became a mediator between humans and their gods. According to Kostof, it "was the meeting ground between the human and the divine. At the same time that humans were lifted up by the proud soaring of the columns, deities came down to the level of human visibility."[47]

The site at Delphi, as at other Greek sacred temples, formed a unified whole. The interplay of humans and nature, humans and god, male and female, were in the end reciprocal. The path sequence and its destination articulated these complex and powerful relationships. Archetypal strivings and conflicts of human existence were thus made manifest, to the same end as the Greek pantheon of gods. Within its composition, the path and place accommodated and facilitated the telling of the story, the journey from one consciousness to another.

Koto-in Zen Temple, Daitoku-ji Monastery

Koto-in is a subtemple of Daitoku-ji, a Zen Buddhist monastery located in the northwest section of the ancient imperial city of Kyoto. Koto-in was founded in 1601, approximately one hundred years after

Daisen-in and the nearby temples and gardens of Ryoan-ji (1488), one of hundreds of Buddhist temples in Kyoto. Founded in 794, Kyoto was the spiritual and cultural center of Japan for over a thousand years and today is a museum of Japanese history, religion, and architecture. The monastery belongs to the Rinzai branch of Zen Buddhism. It was founded by Daito-kokushi in 1319 CE as a simple forest hermitage called the Hermitage of Great Virtue.[48] Here he attracted his first disciples and the monastery grew under imperial patronage. With subsequent support from military rulers, the monastery grew to become one of the most important in medieval Japan.

To reach Koto-in, one first walks through the monastery grounds, passing the main temple buildings and some of the twenty-three sub-temples for which it is famous, to reach its entrance. The monastery avenues are generally straight and open, but entering Koto-in, all this changes as the path twists and turns, its rough, dark paving stones leading into a dark, cool forest. The distance is short, a ten-minute walk, but by the time one reaches the main temple building it feels as if a much longer journey has been taken.

To fully understand Koto-in, however, we must first place it in the context of its monastic setting. Koto-in is only part of an overall monastery campus of buildings and grounds, referred to as the monastery or temple complex. In addition, monasteries have a grouping of main temples located prominently in the complex. At Daitoku-ji, these buildings include the *hatto*, the hall for novice monks; the *butsuden*, the Buddha Hall; the *san-mon*, the main gate; and the *chokushimon*, a smaller gateway. Typically, all are arranged axially, and at Daitoku-ji, the axial orientation is north-south (fig. 99).

The temple complexes are walled compounds, surrounded by high precinct walls with gated openings. There is a main entrance, and once inside, similar to Shinto shrines, there are a number of thresholds that must be passed to gain increasingly sacred ground. The walled compound grew out of two principal concerns. The first was the archetypal act of marking sacred ground, delineating a border between the profane outer world and the sacred place. The second had to do with practical considerations. Many Zen monasteries, such as Daitoku-ji,

Fig. 99. Site plan, Daitoku-ji Zen Buddhist Monastery, Kyoto (founded 1319), showing the main temples and principal avenues.

A. Main Gate
B. Secondary Entrance
C. Monastery Avenues

D. Main N-S Avenue
E. Main Temple Buildings
  1. *Chokushimon*
  2. *San-mon*
  3. *Butsuden*
  4. *Hatto*
  5. *Honbo*

F. Daisen-in Subtemple
G. Koto-in Subtemple

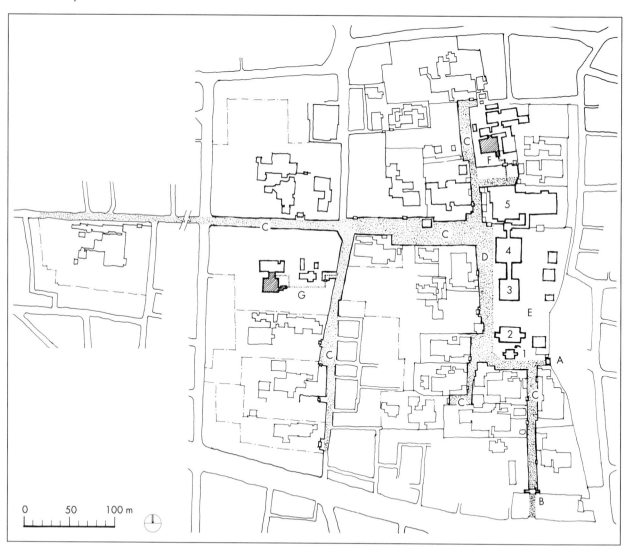

0   50   100 m

were built during Japan's medieval age (thirteenth to sixteenth centuries) which had periods of social upheaval and civil war; and similar to medieval monasteries in western Europe, they became refuges from a chaotic and dangerous world. Like their European counterparts, Zen monks preserved culture and knowledge that might otherwise have been lost. During the protracted periods of war, the monasteries attracted not only religious aspirants but feudal lords as well. In fact there are many examples of retired military leaders founding subtemples within temple complexes. Koto-in was established in such a way. Indeed, the choice of a monastic life may have been as strongly motivated by the quest for security as for spiritual reasons.

Daitoku-ji Monastery is an irregularly shaped, walled compound that, like the city of Kyoto itself, is oriented north-south. Its orientation, as well as its location at the base of the mountains, indicate that geomantic principles influenced its layout. Originally the monastery was set in the forest, remote from Kyoto; now it is surrounded by residential areas. The borders of the monastery are indistinct in places, the result of encroachments by Kyoto as well as loss of portions of the complex through fire and during periods of decay. Most of the monastery was destroyed by fire during the Onin War (1467–77) and was abandoned for a number of years afterward. During the Meiji Restoration, state support of Buddhism was eliminated and many monasteries, including Daitoku-ji, fell into decline and sold off properties and possessions to survive. There are a number of main avenues inside Daitoku-ji, which run either north-south or east-west. They occupy the central areas of the complex, divide the overall plan into smaller areas, and provide access to the subtemple entrances. A principal main avenue runs north-south and leads past the main temples of the monastery.

Today, there are two principal entrances to the complex; the main gate located at the eastern edge of the monastery and adjacent to the main temple buildings, and a secondary entrance located at the southeast corner. (There are also two lesser means of entry; one at the southwest, another at the west.) The main gate, or *somon*, establishes a threshold to the main path of the temple complex (fig. 100). As in other spiritual paths, the event of the main gateway is essential to de-

Fig. 100. The depth and height of the main gateway of the monastery establishes the threshold to the monastery's grounds.

Fig. 101. The secondary entrance to Daitoku-ji is reached by a long, shallow set of steps.

lineate the passage from outside to inside. The main gate, twice the height of the adjacent precinct walls, creates an entrance openning that is square in elevation. The depth of the entrance is established by flanking doors and the overhang of the wooden-and-tile roof, which forms an intermediary volume. From outside, partial views of the main temple buildings and the main pathway beyond are afforded. There is also the remains of a shallow moat at the main entry, crossed by a short, wide, stone "bridge."

The gate at the secondary entrance also establishes a clear threshold to the temple complex (fig. 101). Here, because a change of level needs to be overcome, the wall is raised on a battered granite base, and there is a long set of stairs with deep treads and shallow risers. Inside this gateway the path is an enclosed avenue that continues north, past a number of entrances to subtemples, to join with the main path at a point opposite the ceremonial entrance to the main temple buildings.

The main path, at this point, passes the *chokushimon*, the ceremonial entrance to the main temple buildings. This gate, formerly located at the Imperial Palace, traditionally is used only by the emperor and thus is normally closed. A ceremonial path is established by this entrance, which is on a north-south axis, and passes through the three main temple buildings: the *san-mon, butsuden,* and *hatto* halls, the latter two linked by a covered walkway. Flanking these buildings on their east side are the bell tower *(shoro)*, the storeroom for the sutras *(kyozo),* and a monk's bath house *(yokushitsu).*

Past the *chokushimon,* the path turns right to the main north-south avenue, which runs parallel to the north-south axis of the monastery temples (fig. 102). It passes by these temples on the right as well as a number of subtemple entrances on the left. The avenue at this point is wide and open to the main temple buildings, which establishes it as the most monumental place in the monastery. The next significant junction along the main temple complex path is just past the *hatto.* Here, in a space formed by the edifice of the *hatto* and the enclosure walls of the *honbo,*[49] and subtemples, is the entrance to a secondary path that leads to a number of subtemples, including Daisen-in. At this point the

Fig. 102. The main north-south avenue passes by the monastery temples. Visible on the right is the *butsuden* and *hatto* halls.

Fig. 103. Horizontal banding on a typical clay wall.

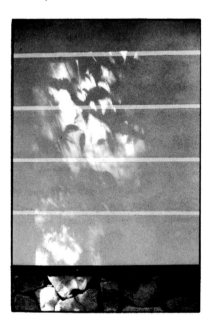

main avenue turns west, continuing past a number of subtemples. At the western end of this avenue, another path is reached that heads south, gaining access to the entrance of Koto-in.

The path is delineated by two principal means: enclosure and marking. It is enclosed by walls on one or both sides, usually between seven and ten feet high. These, as well as the precinct walls, are massive and solid. They are constructed of clay and stone, and are capped with wood and tile. At places, the walls have horizontal banding that accentuates their linear appearance (fig. 103). Beyond the walls, partial views of the subtemples are at times glimpsed.

The path is marked by a variety of edges and paving patterns. The first edge is articulated by the wall and a granite drain-way at its base. Often, in the gravel area next to the wall, conifer trees are planted (fig. 104). Symmetrically arranged, the avenues are created by stone paving laid in a rich variety of patterns. Long, narrow granite pavers form each edge, accentuating the linearity of the path. Inside, stone paving is set in regular and random patterns that change as one travels along the path (fig. 105).

Fig. 104. Monastery avenues are typically enclosed by high walls behind which are the subtemples.

Fig. 105. A range of paving patterns are used throughout Daitoku-ji.

The breadth of types of enclosure and marking provides unique identity to each path segment and establishes a series of spatial thresholds as one walks through the monastery. Linked spaces formed by segments of walls of varying heights (both contiguously and across the path), and their alignment, entry gates, and planting, create the experience of passing through different areas. The variety of paving patterns and other path-marking elements reinforces the sequence of discrete places. The walls, higher than eye level, accentuate the feeling of compression, enclosure, and introversion, relieved only by shifts in the path and entrances to the subtemples, and at the main north-south avenue. The repetition of all the path elements reinforces the experience of journey along the path and interplay with the rhythm of walking and moving through space.

The monastery walls mark the sacred ground within; they are in essence a consecration of the sacred place first established by Daito-kokushi. The path, which attains places of increasing sacrality, acts as a mediator, a guide to the sacred place that creates a sign-posted spiritual journey. Its sequence relates to the Buddhist Eightfold Path[50] and underlines the religious axiom that the path to God or Buddha is never simple or easy. As one proceeds deeper into the monastery, a sense of spiritual commitment grows. Finally, one arrives at the entrance to the subtemple where these themes are continued and elaborated on.

Koto-in and Zen-Influenced Arts

The entry path at Koto-in is a sophisticated series of spatial events, similar to the monastery avenues. Like Western state and religious buildings, the temple path and place were meant to express their importance to the dignitaries and religious aspirants who visited them. In this aspect, Koto-in is similar to many examples of sacred architecture, one being the re-creation of the experience of journey that is taken by pilgrims of all faiths. Moreover, the path and place at Koto-in is distinctly Japanese in that it symbolically expresses aspects of Zen Buddhist philosophy. The path, in this context, is a meaningful and evocative entry sequence that mimics a pilgrimage to the prototypic monk's mountainside hermitage depicted in Chinese landscape paintings favored by the Zen sect.[51] Similarly, the siting, austerity, and simplicity of detail of the temple architecture set amid the surrounding gardens symbolizes a meditation pavilion set in the landscape. Analogous to the *sukiya* style of the Zen teahouse and its "dewy path" entry sequence, the characteristics, articulation, materials, and construction of the entry path and temple inculcate Zen Buddhist beliefs in a powerfully symbolic way.

Zen is a word derived from the Chinese *Ch'an*, which means meditation, a fundamental activity of its practitioners. Zen philosophy eschewed formal doctrine and instead stressed a direct, intuitive, self-reliant, and austere path to enlightenment. Zen flourished in China between 700 and 900 CE (during the later half of the Tang dynasty) and came to Japan in the twelfth century during one of the fertile periods of religious and cultural exchange between the two nations.[52] The late twelfth century was the beginning of Japan's medieval age, when political power was transferred from the emperor of the Heian Court in Kyoto to a military government centered in Kamakura near Tokyo.[53] Zen found fertile ground to establish itself in Japan due in part to the political setting; Zen philosophy, including its emphasis on individuality, appealed to the *samurai* class of the feudal society with their *bushido*, or code of battle and chivalry. In time, a close relationship between Zen and the military class developed, and the Kamakura shogunate provided financial support for the first Zen monasteries, including Daitoku-ji. In return, Zen monks, many of whom were Chinese refugees, provided advice on religion, art, and trade. Zen monks became the arbiters of taste, providing the rulers with cultural information formerly reserved for the royal family. From this point on, Zen was to have a profound effect on many aspects of Japanese culture, including the arts and architecture.

The main temple buildings at Daitoku-ji are built in the "Zen style," their axial layout and complex bracketed roof systems derived from Chinese models. The architecture of a subtemple such as Koto-in, however, was built in the *shoin* style, a type of traditional residential architecture used by feudal lords during the Muromachi period (1392–1573) and adopted by the Zen sect which consequently influenced its later development.[54] Parallels can be drawn between Zen Buddhist philosophy and the architecture, entry path, and gardens of the subtemple.[55] Zen monastic life, among its many beliefs and practices, stressed austerity and simplicity and a rigorous schedule of work and meditation. Life was short and precarious, death never far away. Enlightenment therefore should be pursued constantly and was possible at any moment.[56] Perhaps at Koto-in this is evidenced by its ordinary, unfinished materials, the fragility of its construction, and the introspective and meditative quality of the spaces that comprise the path and its destination.

The simplicity, modesty, and minimalism of traditional Japanese architecture has been explained as a result of cultural characteristics of the Japanese.[57] However, both Edward Morse, in his book *Japanese Homes and Their Surroundings*, and Heinrich Engel point out that the primary catalyst for this particular attitude of dwelling came from the extreme poverty of the country during the period of its development. It was only later that Zen Buddhism transformed this situation into a spiritualized philosophy of building and habitation.

There is a fundamental difficulty in describing Zen because it has a profound mistrust of language and reason. However, though its philosophy may not be explicit, it is often implicit in its practices, writings, folktales, and mythology. Zen, and its philosophy of direct experience, freedom from attachment, acceptance, impermanence, openness, celebration of the ordinary, simplicity, process, nonduality, tension and release, naturalness, reverence for nature, and mindfulness, is symbolized to varying degrees by the temples and their entry paths.[58]

Zen-influenced arts such as landscape painting, literature, and the tea ceremony are similarly related to the form and experience of the subtemple. For example, Chinese landscape paintings from the Southern Sung dynasty, imported to Japan by Zen monks, often show scenes of austere mountainside dwellings, with a few hermits shown living in harmony with nature, far removed from society[59] (figs. 106 and 107). Subsequently, this style was practiced in Japan, and paintings of this type were often called *shosaiga*, or "paintings of the study." These mountainous landscapes often depicted a simple hut, a scholar's retreat, or Zen priest's hermitage, set precariously in the wilderness. Paintings of this type had historical precedents dating from the early period of Zen in China. During this formative time, the following was small—in essence, teachers with a few students each. The first Zen masters typically lived in simple dwellings set in remote and often mountainous locations. Students seeking the master would make a pilgrimage to them and, if accepted, would build their own dwellings nearby. In this way the first monasteries grew up,[60] including Daitoku-ji, as mentioned earlier. The architecture of the subtemple in part was a re-creation of the prototypical Zen hermitage, and the journey to it, a mimesis of the early pilgrimages to the Zen masters.

The ideal of the scholar retreat, which also has Taoist and Confucian roots, is depicted in certain Japanese folktales that extol the spiritual virtues of the remote hermitage. *An Account of My Hut* (1212), attributed to Kamo no Chomei, includes the following passage:

> The present hut is of no ordinary appearance. It is a bare ten feet square and less than seven feet high. . . . Since I hid my traces here in the heart of Mount Hino, I have added a lean-to on the south and a porch of bamboo. On the west I have built a shelf for holy water,

Fig. 106. The path to the remote hermitage was a popular subject of landscape paintings favored by the Zen sect. Okada Beisanjin (1744–1818), *Going to Meet the Noble Hermit.*

191

and inside the hut, along the west wall, I have installed an image of Amida. . . .[61] Above the sliding door that faces north I have built a little shelf on which I keep three or four black leather baskets that contain books of poetry and music and extracts from the sacred writings.[62]

Fig. 107. A scholar's retreat, shown in harmony with its natural surroundings. Bunsai (active mid-15th century), *Landscape* (detail), courtesy of the Museum of Fine Arts, Boston, Chinese and Japanese Special Fund.

The tea ceremony, among other arts associated with Zen, also influenced the symbolic aspects of the Zen Buddhist temple.[63] The earliest tearooms were inside the temple buildings; later they became freestanding rustic buildings, called *sukiya*, or "abode of fancy." The tea ceremony was popular with the *samurai* class during the medieval period. Sen no Rikyu (1521–1591), father of the Zen tea ceremony, was a close advisor to Hideyoshi, the last military ruler of the medieval age. It was during Sen no Rikyu's time that the *sukiya*-style freestanding tea pavilion was established,[64] and the first of this type was built by him at Daitoku-ji.[65] The typical teahouse was a rustic thatched hut with a single introverted room, reached by a path through a garden. Here tea would be prepared by the host and served to guests in a choreographed, meditative ritual. According to tea master Okakura Kakuzo, "The beverage grew to be an excuse for the worship of purity and refinement, a sacred function at which the host and guest joined to produce for that occasion the utmost beautitude of the mundane."[66]

The teahouse evoked images of a hermitage or a faraway farmhouse and celebrated its rural simplicity and poverty.[67] Its adjacent gardens were called *roji*, or "dewy path," and the entry path approached the teahouse circuitously, with places to pause and a wash basin for ablution. Similar to the scholar's retreat, the teahouse and its path created a setting for a spiritual journey to a sacred place. According to Bring and Wayemberg,

The path represents a psychological transition to the tea room's rarefied atmosphere. One is journeying to the home of a hermit and must enter his frame of mind, putting aside all worldly cares. The spatial sequence of the garden is carefully orchestrated by a series of fences and gateways symbolizing the various internal changes taking place. Along the path, people stop to wash their hands, an echo of the Shinto act of purification, and then enter the tea house through a small door. Bending down to enter through this door is an act of physical humility, and visitors cross the threshold as different people. Once inside they cannot see the garden: it is blocked from view by opaque paper window shades that are kept closed during the ceremony. The pathway is like a set for a psychodrama in which the participants act out a transformation of character in their return to nature for spiritual rejuvenation.[68]

The teahouse as a prototypical hermitage or primordial hut expressed the spirit of *wabi*, which celebrated the virtues of poverty.[69] A court noble of the time is recorded as saying, "I am deeply impressed by this scene. Here in the heart of the city, I have the impression of being in the country. Soji deserves to be called a hermit. . . ."[70] The small, 4½ *tatami* mat size of a typical teahouse expressed simplicity but also symbolized a Buddhist legend popular with the Zen sect about Vimalakirti, a sage who accommodated 84,000 disciples of Buddha in his simple abode.[71]

Humility was encouraged by the architecture of the teahouse, most pointedly by the *nijiri-guchi*, or "wriggling through entrance." This entrance not only forced one to stoop before entering, but required the *samurai* to leave their swords outside. (Often sword racks were placed adjacent to the entrance for this purpose.) The naturalness and spontaneity of the tea ceremony is best described by a story about Sen no Rikyu. His teacher asked him his opinion about a teahouse walkway that had recently been swept clean. Rikyu's answer was to randomly shake some leaves off a nearby tree onto the path.[72] A mystical feeling pervaded the entire setting of the tea ceremony, from walking down the "dewy path," to entering and the ritual of the tea. According to Okakura, the tea master, "wished to create the attitude of a newly-awakened soul still lingering amid shadowy dreams of the past, yet bathing in the sweet unconsciousness of a mellow spiritual light, and yearning for the freedom that lay in the expanse beyond."[73] Similarly, Zen gardens, also influenced by Chinese models, symbolized Zen Buddhist concepts through a variety of forms and methods. Different from the strolling gardens of the Heian era, the Zen gardens were small, enclosed, and principally constructed of only stones, plantings, and raked gravel. Chinese landscape painting was an important influence, and often the garden designers were painters as well.

Typically, today as in the past, the gardens are enclosed physically and visually by walls and planting. As noted at Daisen-in, it is a tightly controlled environment where superfluous elements are scrupulously eliminated. The simple palette of materials, similar to the temple architecture, grew out of an aesthetic of limitations. In the case of the garden, the limitation was of space. Within very small spaces the opposite is achieved; one perceives the garden as a limitless vista, similar to landscape scenes often found painted on screens inside the *hojo*. In opposition to the feeling of compression experienced elsewhere in the temple complex, the garden achieves an effective expansion of space. In fact, the garden, though definitively enclosed, is not limited to its borders but includes distant vistas. The result is a suspension of ordinary scale; a miniaturized world in which one is dynamically involved. Zen gardens were often designed by Zen priests. The design of the garden was a meditative exercise and represented the monk's level of enlightenment. Once completed, it was viewed from the veranda of the *hojo* and used as a meditative tool.

Other Chinese influences, which have design and symbolic significance, appear in the Zen-inspired arts. An important one is the Taoist concept of yin and yang, which in essence suggests a complementary, harmonious relationship between opposites—male and female, light and dark, hard and soft, positive and negative, creative and destructive; opposites that dynamically interact and together form a holistic cosmos. Bring and Wayemberg discuss how the re-creation of the "hermit's retreat" in garden design aimed at a "harmonic ideal," a balance of complementary elements within the total composition. "The buildings and the garden surroundings attempted to re-create this ideal, which reflected the harmony and balance of the universe."[74] Chinese practices of geomancy and the ancient divination system of *feng-shui* were also utilized in the siting of Japanese and Zen Buddhist architecture.[75]

All of the Zen-influenced arts were a synthesis of Chinese practices, Zen Buddhist beliefs, and Japanese culture, and powerfully communicated symbolic meanings. The path and place at Koto-in and other temple sites of its type are didactic also, inculcating Zen Buddhist beliefs and facilitating the spiritual development of the monks.

The Path and the Place at Koto-in

Koto-in was founded in 1601 by Hosokawa Tadaoki. At the time of its founding, a long period of war (called the Age of the Country at War) had just ended, resulting in the establishment of the Tokugawa shogunate (1603–1867). Hosokawa Tadaoki was a powerful and successful military leader during the preceding wars but was also known for his intellect and appreciation of culture. He retained a powerful position after the wars, but in his later life, he devoted himself to the study of Zen under the abbot of Daitoku-ji.[76]

Koto-in is located in the southwestern part of Daitoku-ji and is reached by a section of the monastery's main avenue. Like all of Daitoku-ji's subtemples, it was founded as a self-contained entity but also participated in the communal activities of the monastery at the main temple buildings. The Koto-in complex includes a segmented approach path that leads to the principal building, the *hojo*, or abbot's quarters, which is connected to a secondary building by a covered link. Both the *hojo* and the secondary building contain historically significant tearooms—its founder was a devotee of the tea ceremony—and are surrounded by a series of gardens, the most famous of which is the southern maple-tree garden.

The subtemple path, as in the temple complex, is comprised of a number of walls, edges, and paving patterns. The paths are often constructed of rough stone paving that demands attention to each step, especially for monks who today still habitually wear loose-fitting sandals. Typically, entrance paths of subtemples are marked by a gateway that is smaller but otherwise similar to the entrances to the monastery.

Continuing beyond the subtemple gateway, the volumetric edges of the path expand, while still retaining a feeling of constriction and enclosure. In contrast to the main thoroughfares, however, the alignment of the path is asymmetrical, shifting and turning at right angles as it progresses. Through these shifts, as well as plantings and path enclosure walls, a semienclosed environment is created that offers only partial views of the path just traversed and the path that lies ahead (a device reminiscent of Borobudur). Further accentuating the experience of passage are split paths and additional gateways—thresholds that underline the journey from the outside world to the inner spiritual world. Ultimately the experience is a volumetric one, a passage through a series of spaces culminating in the attainment of the spiritual place, the *hojo*.

Koto-in is typical of Zen subtemples and a poignant example of the path and place in sacred architecture. The path is a spatial sequence with clearly articulated entries, edges, and surfaces that creates a symbolic journey in a relatively small space. The *hojo* is ordered and austere, a clearly delineated entity harmoniously sited in relationship to the surrounding gardens. The *hojo* at Koto-in is a typical *shoin*-style building, a style that displays a high degree of uniformity. In Hosokawa Tadaoki's time, the *hojo* served as both the spiritual center of the subtemple and the official residence of a powerful military leader.

The architectural language of the *shoin*-style *hojo* is characterized by an expressive system of frame and infill and a limited palette of materials used in their natural state. A movable enclosure system allows the interior spaces to be closed off or opened according to use and allows the entire building to be opened up to the surrounding gardens. The constructional system of the *hojo* at Koto-in, typical of traditional Japanese architecture, is comprised of a number of modular elements. These include the foundation and frame superstructure; space-forming systems including roofs, ceilings, floors, and solid walls; infill systems including movable and demountable panels and the *tatami* floor covering; and permanent enclosures such as the *tokonoma* picture recess in the tearoom.

The plan of the Koto-in *hojo* is comprised of two rows of three spaces each, enclosed by a large overhanging roof and surrounded by a veranda (figs. 108 and 109). It is oriented north-south, with the three largest rooms located on the southern edge. The central room is backed by an altar recess, behind which is a storeroom. To the east of the altar area is a small room, possibly a receiving area; to the west, a tearoom. The structural grid at Koto-in is based on the *ken* system of measurement—a system that originated in China—which established the size and placement of the building components. Originally the *ken* only denoted the distance between columns but later came to delineate a system of measure for the entire building, including the modular *tatami* floor covering. At Koto-in, each room size conforms to the number of tatami mats, from the 12½ mat altar room, to the 8-mat tearoom.

The wooden superstructure runs continuously from shallow stone footings to the roof.[77] There is no excavated basement, the floor is attached to the frame, approximately 2 feet (620 mm) from the ground, and the space under the floor is left open. The *hashira*, or columns, are 5½ inches (140 mm) square, connected by a system of joinery and wooden wedges, with few additional attachments. The system is very simple and straightforward, with the limitation of providing little in the way of lateral support. There is rarely if ever any use of diagonal bracing in traditional Japanese architecture, a phenomenon that has been explained by various sources as a result of prudent responses to earthquakes, structural ignorance, or simply tradition.[78] The roof of the *hojo* at Koto-in is a hipped-gable roof, or *iri-moya*, and is constructed from wooden beams and planks with clay tiles placed in a mud setting bed. The roof in Japanese traditional architecture is one of its more distinctive and evocative features, and at Koto-in, its prominent form underlines the *hojo* as a separate entity.

Inside, the ceiling is a modular system of wooden boards called *tenjo-ita*, which rest on a wooden frame suspended from the roof structure. Its height varies according to the size of the room, and the wooden grid and ceiling panels reflect the *tatami* mats below. Perma-

Fig. 108. Site plan, Koto-in Temple (1601), Daitoku-ji Zen Buddhist Monastery, Kyoto.

A. *Hojo*
  1. Tearoom
  2. Tearoom Kitchen
  3. Altar
  4. Veranda
B. Gardens

C. Secondary Entrance
D. Gateway to Secondary Entrance
E. *Gen-kan*
F. *Hojo* Gateway
G. Main Gateway
H. Entry Court

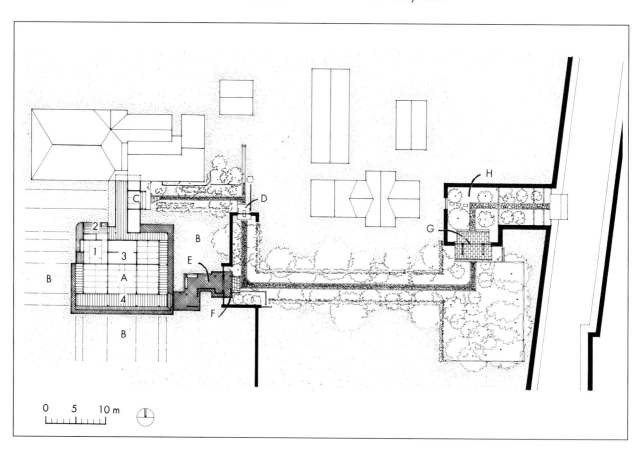

0 5 10 m

Fig. 109. The southern veranda of the *hojo* at Koto-in overlooks the renowned maple tree garden.

nent space divisions in the *hojo* are formed by *komai-kabe,* or "wall with small bamboo laces," a permanent clay wall infilled between columns and also above the tracks of the movable screens.

Movable or demountable panels used at Koto-in, typical of *shoin*-style temples and traditional architecture, serve as modular space-forming systems for the division of interior space and separation from the exterior. The principal screen is the *shoji,* a word that means "interceptor," which is placed between the interior rooms and the veranda and delineates the edge between inside and outside. The *shoji* are constructed of a rectangular framework of wood infilled with a grid of lighter wooden members; white translucent rice paper is attached to one side. At Koto-in, the *shoji* are paired with *amado,* or rain doors, wooden panels used to close the *hojo* at night. The other type of panel is the *fusuma,* a movable screen for the subdivision of interior space which, like the *shoji,* slides on opposing a wooden tracks. The construction of the *fusuma* is the same as *shoji* except that both sides of the frame are covered by opaque paper. In *shoin* temples this surface often serves as a canvas for mural or calligraphic work (such as at Daisen-in), but at the *hojo* at Koto-in all of the extant panels are bare. The size of the *shoji, amado,* and *fusuma* are the same and are derived from the *ken* proportioning system.

The interior of *shoin* architecture, including the *hojo,* is typically open and multifunctional. At Koto-in, however, certain areas were assigned to particular formal functions, one of which was the tearoom and its *tokonoma* (fig. 110). The *tokonoma,* or "picture recess," is a common feature in traditional Japanese architecture and is still found in contemporary Japanese homes. It developed from early Buddhist monastery buildings as an alcove where a statue of the Buddha was placed, flowers arranged, and incense burned. The *tokonoma* also was the formative place for the development of *chanoyu,* the tea ceremony, since originally the monks would gather in front of the altar to ritually drink tea.[79] Later it became a place to hold the *kakejiku,* a single picture scroll, and a single vase and flower. The tearoom of the *hojo* at Koto-in contains a typical example of a *tokonoma*: a single mat recess comprised of a raised platform called a *tokogamachi.*

Fig. 110. The tearoom of the *hojo* at Koto-in Temple.

The entry path at Koto-in is very simple but accomplishes a generous variety of experiences. It is essentially a series of consecutive spaces that are aligned east-west. There are a number of right-angle turns along the path, each occurring at entry gateways. The first segment of the path is an entry court that is adjacent to the monastery avenue. At the far end of this space the path turns 90 degrees to the left and approaches an imposing wooden gateway. Once through this main gateway, the path turns again at a right angle, beginning a long straight section that ends at the *hojo* enclosure wall and gateway. Once through the *hojo* gateway, the path shifts again inside an entry foyer (*gen-kan*) before finally arriving at the southeast corner of the veranda. The southern veranda in essence is the last section of the path, and it leads to the principal spaces of the *hojo*. (There is also a secondary entry path that continues from the *hojo* gateway, passes through a smaller gateway where the path turns left, and continues to the linking portion of the temple buildings. This secondary entrance was most likely used as an informal service entrance.)

The path is created by a simple palette of enclosure and surface-marking elements and is experienced as a series of linked volumes. Each successive space is uniquely proportioned and formed from a limited number of materials. I have identified ten sequential, interrelated

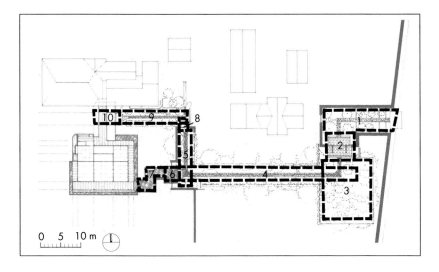

Fig. 111. Site plan noting the volumetric sequence of the entry path.

volumes that comprise the path at Koto-in (fig. 111). The first seven segments take one from the entrance to the *hojo*: the last three comprise the secondary or service entrance to the subtemple. In each of the volumes a specific scale and sense of place is created, eliciting an emotional response and setting up a reference point for the next volume. The path surface is marked by a variety of stone paving patterns and materials which change in each space. The entire path, a continuation of the monastery avenues, unfolds like a story, a symbolic pilgrimage that journeys from the outside to the inside, from the secular to the sacred.

The first volume is the entry court and is entered directly off the monastery avenue (fig. 112). It is inscribed by high clay walls, plantings, and low bamboo railings, all of which provide layers of enclosure. These walls, the top of which are above eye level, establish at their top the upper plane of an inscribed volume. This is further delineated by their tile caps that clearly articulate this edge through line and shadow. All the walls are at the same height, and the space is approximately 19½ feet × 56 feet (6m × 17 m) in plan.[80] The walls afford views beyond to a bamboo grove on the right as one enters, and a deciduous grove on the left and straight ahead. These trees inscribe a larger volume and provide visual relief and an indication of what lies beyond, similar to the practice of *shakkei*, or "borrowed landscape," in Zen temple gardens. Inside this space the path is set within a moss garden and another layer of space inscribed by conifer trees planted on either side. A final smaller volume at the edge of the path itself is created by a bamboo rail that runs alongside it.[81]

At the end of the first section the path turns 90 degrees to the left and approaches the main gateway, which had been partially visible at the beginning of the path (fig. 113). Here a second volume is inscribed by the depth of the gateway and the line and shadow of the roof overhang. This volume begins at the wall recess within the first space and continues to the far side of the gateway. The gateway itself is approximately twice the height of the enclosure walls and contains a monumental set of doors, with two flanking smaller doors. The size of this second volume is approximately 26 feet × 16-1/2 feet (8 m × 5 m) in

Fig. 112. The entry court forms the first volume of the path sequence. A number of elements form the edges of the path. To the left is the main gateway.

Fig. 113. The view through main gateway includes the second and third volumes of the path sequence.

Fig. 114. The path to *hojo* gateway is the fourth volume of the path sequence.

Fig. 115. The *hojo* gateway is set within a recess in the wall. Beyond the entrance doors is the entry foyer, or *gen-kan*.

Fig. 116. The *gen-kan* is a diminutive, circumscribed space, which allows only partial views of the *hojo* beyond.

Fig. 117. The last segment of the entry sequence leads to the southern veranda of the *hojo*.

plan. As one passes through the main gateway, a space of somewhat indefinite size is encountered. As opposed to the preceding two spaces, this space offers relatively unobscured views straight ahead to a grove of trees. It is defined by the surrounding trees and the gateway just passed through. The size of this space is approximately 42½ feet × 52½ feet (13 m × 16 m) in plan.

Inside this third space the path turns 90 degrees to the right and enters the fourth space (fig. 114). This volume is approximately 13 feet × 151 feet (4 m × 46 m) in plan, a long narrow space defined by manicured plantings and bamboo railings. The compressed, linear space offers a view at its terminus of the *hojo* gateway. This gateway is significantly smaller than the main gateway, but one's first reaction is to assume that it is the same size as the main gateway. Thus by comparison to the first gateway, a scale shift is accomplished, creating the impression of a much longer pathway.

At the end of this section of the path, directly opposite the *hojo* gateway, a fifth space is entered. This space is formed by walls on two sides, plantings on another, and by a third gateway and is approximately 13 feet × 49 feet (4 m × 15 m) in plan. Here the path splits— one section continues straight ahead through the *hojo* gateway, the other turns 90 degrees to the third gateway and the service entrance.

In the former section the gateway is set within a recess in a wall that partially encloses the *hojo* (fig. 115). This creates a threshold to the entry foyer *(gen-kan)* and the sixth and seventh spaces inside. Upon entering the sixth space, one experiences a constricted, circumscribed space formed by walls on all sides and a roof. The space is approximately 10 feet × 26 feet (3 m × 8 m) in plan. The constricted space of the entry foyer offers only limited views of the *hojo*, obliquely viewed through openings and a small window (fig. 116). Its experience of constriction and enclosure is in direct contrast to the more open linear path previously traversed. Turning left, then right again, one enters the seventh space which leads to the southern veranda of the *hojo*. It offers the first unobscured view of the *hojo* itself, but because one is so close to the temple, this view is partial (fig. 117).

If instead of entering the *hojo* gateway one continued toward the service entrance, a series of three volumes would be passed. The first is created by the third gateway. This is the smallest of all the inscribed volumes, approximately 10 feet × 10 feet (3 m × 3 m) in plan, indicating its lesser importance. Passing through this gateway, the ninth volume is entered, approximately 10 feet × 56 feet (3 m × 17 m) in plan, and enclosed by plantings. At the end of the path, one enters the tenth volume circumscribed by the entry to the linking portion of the subtemple buildings. This volume is approximately 10 feet × 13 feet (3 m × 4 m) in plan and provides access to the two principal buildings of Koto-in.

The path is marked throughout by a variety of elements. Similar to the monastery avenues, there are a number of edges, and the path is marked by a variety of paving patterns. At the initial entry space, for example, the stone paved path is symmetrically disposed between the surrounding walls and a moss garden. The paving of the path is typical: long, narrow granite strips placed on either side of the path, accentuating its linearity, with irregular granite pavers inside. Additionally, a series of four slabs of granite are placed within the moss garden, perpendicular to the path. These occur at intervals at the beginning of the path, inscribing a number of subtle "gates."

At the gateways the path surface changes, thus reinforcing their threshold qualities. At the main gate, for example, one steps up to a wide stone platform. Also, at each of the path volumes there is a change in paving pattern, accentuating the sense of place at each of them. This is not only visual but textural as well. Some of the paths are smooth, and some take a deliberate effort to find a stable step. In contrast, the entry foyer is paved with a grid of smooth tiles.

The path at Koto-in possesses many of the characteristics of the sacred path and place. "Sacred ground" is clearly marked by a walled enclosure, a fundamental element of sacred sites. The enclosure consecrates the ground and describes a sacred precinct where, as Eliade says, it is "possible to communicate with the sacred." The subtemple is established as a place apart, demarking public from private and secular from sacred. The main entrance exaggerates the sense of enclosure and threshold by its monumental scale and depth. The path is a series of discrete volumes but is also a cohesive whole. The uniqueness of each segment of the path is created in part by each segment allowing limited views of what lies ahead and behind. The unity of experience is engendered by the consistent palette of space-making and path-marking elements. The subtemple served not only sacred but secular functions as well, and its separation from the outside world had practical as well as religious reasons. Koto-in, the residence of a retired military leader still active in political affairs, expressed Tadaoki's importance.

The spatial sequence at Koto-in is analogous to the hero's journey; it is this universal myth incarnate. The entry path at Koto-in is a controlled environment and, similar to Zen gardens, engenders a variety of experiences and emotional responses. Within a relatively small space and with limited means, a symbolic world is created. The linked spaces of the path become increasingly sacred (or private in its political aspect) as the path progresses to the *hojo*. Consequently, it symbolizes a spiritual journey, the experience of which is accomplished by a number of means. First there is the volumetric manipulation of the path, a rhythm of open and closed spaces—the experience of compression and expansion. There is also a manipulation of scale that has the effect of making the path appear longer than it actually is. Additionally, the gateways function as what Kevin Lynch called "strategic foci," further underlining the identity of each path segment.

The marking of the path also is instrumental in establishing the identity of each segment. There is a clarity and legibility of the path through the marking of the edges and surfaces of each section. Its changing texture provides a complex kinesthetic experience, an ever-changing environment experienced through the sensual act of walking. However, even though each path section exists separately, it also possesses strong directionality. Lastly, the "fourth dimension" of its temporal and spatial narrative further establishes the path as a journey.

When a novice priest decides to become a Zen monk, he journeys to the monastery to ask permission to join. First he must gain entrance to the main gateway, proceed along the path, gain entrance to the subtemple, and ring a bell announcing his arrival. Traditionally the novice will be refused admission at first and will wait outside the sub-

Fig. 118. A novice monk traditionally demonstrates his resolve to enter the monastery by assuming a position of supplication outside the temple, often for a period of several days.

temple, sometimes for as long as three days, before temporary permission to enter is given[82] (fig. 118). Thus the physical presence of the path and the separate nature of the place symbolize the process of entrance, journey, and growing spiritual commitment and the attainment of the sacred place.

The "hero's journey" at Koto-in begins with the "finding of the path" within the relatively large, open space of the main gateway courtyard. This space anticipates the attainment of the spiritual place through the "borrowed landscape" of the trees beyond. The gateway serves as the guardian of the sacred ground, separating it from the profane and protecting the uninitiated from entering. Following the entrance, the symbolic story of initiation, the trials and choices along the path, are created through enclosure and marking. The expansion and compression of the path symbolizes the emotional trials of the spiritual path, the psychological tension of the spiritual search followed by the emotional release of transcendence. This aspect is particularly evident when one passes from the constricted space of the entry foyer to the relative openness of the *hojo* veranda and the idealized world of its surrounding gardens. Everyone who entered Koto-in took the journey from the outside avenue to the *hojo*—a shared ritual, similar perhaps to the "cottage pathway" that emotionally prepared guests for the tea ceremony.

The *hojo*, associated buildings, and entry sequence of Koto-in symbolized the prototypical hermitage celebrated in Chinese and Japanese landscape paintings. This is created in part through its internalized world of dwellings set in a bucolic landscape. A harmonious relationship with nature is communicated through the form and materials of the temple, and a blurring of the edge between habitation and nature. Reminiscent of hermitage pavilions, the *hojo* is able to be opened up to its surroundings. The path is an integral component of this created image. The scale, texture, and kinesthetic experience of the path sequence affect an expansion of time and re-create the pilgrimage to the hermit/scholar's mountainside hermitage. Contained within a relatively small space, a symbolic pilgrimage to a site analogous to the seven thousand steps of Mount Tai-shen is re-created. Or perhaps the *hojo* itself represented Daito-kokushi's first hut at Daitoku-ji, re-enacting, as Eliade has described, a primordial event that occurred *in illotempore*. Or, one might say that each person who walked the path took the symbolic journey to Bodhidharma, to the Zen master sitting in meditation in his remote retreat.

The hermit-scholar's retreat is also symbolized by the *hojo*'s materials and construction. As previously stated, Zen transformed the limitations of poverty into a spiritualized aesthetic. It should be clear by now that the *shoin*-style and traditional Japanese architecture demonstrate a striking economy of materials, space, and construction, attributes that profoundly distinguish it from the other examples of sacred architecture. First of all, the size is diminutive, scaled to the individual or small groups. This is explained in part because it was the residence of the abbot, not the hall for a deity, typical at other sacred sites. The materials are simple, common, and limited; the means of construction, sparse and structurally precarious.

There are additional characteristics of the *hojo* that establish it as a sacred place, attributes that are present in other examples of sacred architecture. The clarity and concentration of its form and the spatial definition and hierarchy of the internal spaces create a place for gathering and shared ritual. The repeating space-forming and constructive elements and their interrelationship through proportion and geometry constitute another characteristic that the architecture shares with other sacred sites. The architecture of the abbot's quarters, with its proportioned modularity, communicates a sense of order that, though it is not limited to religious architecture, is central to the creation of the sacred place. Its otherworldliness is incarnate in the interrelationship of the elements, through the plan characteristics, the *ken* measure, and the constructional elements and infill systems. Lastly, the form and language of the *hojo* possesses a rich symbolic content.

The architecture of the *hojo* and its surroundings are didactic, expressing Zen Buddhist beliefs and reflecting influences from the Zen teahouses and Zen-style gardens. For example, the Zen concept of simplicity and the celebration of the ordinary is strongly expressed by the architecture. The materials and construction of the *hojo* describe a spiritual longing for the humbleness and purity of the rural farmhouse, expressing the spirit of *wabi* and influences from the "abode of fancy" of the tea cult. Like the characteristic teahouse, the simplicity of the *hojo* speaks of generosity from limitations. The word *hojo* means "one jo *(tatami)* square," a reference to the 4½ mat room where the legendary Buddhist sage mentioned earlier accommodated thousands. It symbolized that physical and material austerities were no impediment to spiritual riches and spoke about the Zen path to enlightenment by means of imposed limitations.[83]

The path at Koto-in is also didactic, inculcating Zen Buddhist principals and beliefs. For example, nondualism is present throughout the subtemple complex, in the consistent attempt to integrate all elements of the architecture and grounds. The path exhibits many of these same attributes; the creation of edges along the path both reinforces the path and serves to join it with its surroundings. There is a consistent integration of the natural and the human-made along the path that suggests the holistic view of the cosmos held by Taoist and Buddhist philosophy. The balancing of the natural and the human-made, the forest and the path, the dark with the light, the compressed with the open, suggests the harmony that geomancy sought to attain. The path to the subtemple also describes a journey from yin to yang, the Taoist principle so influential in Zen. The dark, earthy path through the forest yielding to the light, human-made environment of the *hojo*. Both elements were balanced, creating a harmonious environment—earth balanced with sky.

In the dynamic interplay of the built and the natural, of the path and the forest, the Taoist and Buddhist conception of the world as self-forming and constantly evolving is expressed. The path is never static (such as one finds at Versailles or other examples of Western state architecture) but is constantly changing as it approaches the *hojo*. The changing, evolving environment of the path, which offers only partial views ahead as well as behind, seems to speak of impermanence, inculcating the lesson of the Second Noble Truth and the nature of attachment and suffering. The segmented path and the articulation of each spatial unit suggests the ephemeral nature of reality stressed by Zen. It was Dogen who said, "Think only of this day and this hour, for tomorrow is an uncertain thing; and no one knows what the future will bring."[84]

The path is humanly scaled, echoing the Zen Buddhist emphasis on individual effort. This is in direct contrast to the path at Karnak, for example, where the path is a communal, processional way. This is consistent with Zen Buddhist beliefs that deny the existence of a central authority and emphasize individual effort. The spiritual path, in essence, has to be walked alone. Edward Hall said the following about Japanese gardens but could just as well have been speaking about the subtemple path sequence: "The study of Japanese spaces illustrates their habit of leading the individual to a spot where he can discover something for himself."

The path as journey also symbolizes the process of spiritual evolution as opposed to any particular goal. In Zen, preoccupation with spiritual goals is discouraged; one is urged "just to sit" in meditation, without preconceived notions of what benefits might result. As Shunryu Suzuki said, "Our effort in our practice should be directed from achievement to non-achievement."[85]

A central goal of meditation and the monastic life was to emulate the Buddha and strive to be aware and mindful at every instant. The path encouraged this mindfulness by offering a variety of paths, volumes, textures, and views. Each step reveals a little more, nothing is immediately seen, thus one's interest and attention is demanded. The paving stones themselves, in places rough and irregularly placed, demand that each step be placed with attention.

Zen is a very pragmatic religion, striving to overcome the limitations of the intellect through direct experience. The natural and physical setting of the path expresses the "here and now" of Zen Buddhist belief, echoing its emphasis that the universe is the ultimate reality. The experience is not of the supranormal, but of ordinary experience and appreciation. It is "nothing special,"[86] and thus the idea of "everyday Zen" is reinforced.

It is difficult to state categorically what the intentions and use of the subtemple and its gardens were for the Zen monks and retired military leaders turned Zen acolytes that built them. One can, how-ever, experience the place as it appears today and synthesize that experience with an understanding of Zen Buddhist influences, monastic practices, and philosophy. When one visits Daitoku-ji and its subtemples, the presence of the sacred place and the path to attain it is clearly discernible. The entry sequence and *hojo* at Koto-in create a place of pilgrimage analogous to the universal myth of the "hero's journey." For the religious aspirant it is also a [mimesis] of the Buddha's spiritual trials—recapitulating the path to the original Zen master in a powerful unity of form and meaning. How powerful the experience must have been, and perhaps still is, for one immersed in the rigors of Zen practice, challenged by encounters with their teacher, affected by lack of sleep, and separated from everyday life, can only be suggested.

The Cathedral of Sainte-Madeleine

The Romanesque pilgrimage church of Sainte-Madeleine is located in the Burgundian village of Vézelay, an area that has long been held as sacred. Nearby is the site of a Gallo-Roman sanctuary, located at a mineral spring on the river Cure. Close to this early site, a monastery was first established in 877 CE.[87]

The present-day cathedral was first begun during the Carolingian era when the monastery was moved to a fortified acropolis for protection. Europe at this time, following the dissolution of the Roman Empire, had periods of great social upheaval and violence. According to Raymond Oursel. "In these disturbed times every inhabited area had first to be a defence and a refuge."[88] The consequences of the fall of the Roman Empire were enormous and were felt for centuries. By 500 CE, Rome had been sacked twice, its population fell from one million to fifty thousand, its institutions were destroyed, and its citizens dispersed. During the following centuries, often referred to as the Dark Ages, Latin was lost as a common language, Roman law was abandoned, and until the modicum of stability offered by Charlemagne during the Carolingian era, very little monumental architecture was built. Urban life and its social institutions were abandoned, and the

Enter by the narrow gate; for the gate is wide and the way is easy, that leads to destruction, and those who enter it are many. For the gate is narrow, and the way is hard, that leads to life, and those who find it are few.

—MATT. 7.13–14

213

population lived in disparate villages spread throughout the country-side. However, Rome may have been destroyed, but its influence was still present through the Holy Roman church and its eventual frame-work of monasteries, which came to replace the social and political structure of the former Roman empire. The Benedictines were founded in 520 CE by Saint Benedict under the austere vows of "pov-erty, chastity, and obedience." Stable and protected communities were necessary to accomplish these vows, and eventually a vast network of Benedictine monasteries was established throughout Europe, centered on the monastery at Cluny in Burgundy. The shared values and liturgy of the Christian faith, and its institutions and architecture, provided a stable social structure during the Middle Ages. The architecture ex-pressed these shared spiritual values, and even though there were many variations of Christian architecture during this time, common ele-ments of Carolingian and Romanesque architecture can be identified. After Charlemagne was ordained in 800 CE at Saint Peter's in Rome as the ecclesiastical heir to the former Roman emperors, the building of Christian architecture accelerated, and over the following years many of the monuments of Romanesque architecture were built, one of which was Vézelay.

The first structure to be built at the newly consecrated church at Vézelay was a crypt that was reputed to contain the relics of Mary Magdalene. This early reliquary, plus its geographic location, estab-lished Vézelay as an important pilgrimage church. It was located at the head of the Limoges-Périgueux Road, one of four pilgrimage routes that led to Santiago de Compostela. Vézelay was also part of a notable network of religious sites in Burgundy, including Cluny, Autun, and Nevers, and was the site of the launching of the Second Crusade by Saint Bernard. His exclamation "God wants it so!" was said to have converted many to the cause who had gathered outside the church to hear him speak.

Starting around the fifth century, Christianity expanded its reli-gious practices to include the worship of saints. Churches were founded on the relics of saints often interred in elaborate cases that were placed in a subterranean crypt. In the expanding social atmosphere of post-Charlemagne Europe, pilgrimages to various sites became popular, and as we observed in chapter 2, routes led from northern Europe to Jerusalem, Rome, and Santiago de Compostela. The route to the latter destination passed by numerous important churches and monasteries and their venerated relics. Stopping places generally were placed every twenty miles, and there was at least one known guide, the *Pilgrim's Guide*, written by Aymery Picaud (who was a monk at Vézelay). The phenomenon of pilgrimage and its shared customs and intercommunication was another stabilizing and synthesizing element during the Middle Ages. This peripatetic act culminated with passage through the portals and spaces of the pilgrimage churches.

Vézelay was a religious and monastic center; its community of monks at one time numbered five hundred. (Today, little remains of the monastic buildings outside of the church itself.) The town at its height had a population of over ten thousand. As an obligatory pilgrimage destination, as well as an important political and economic hub, it became very prosperous. The result was a series of ambitious building programs that built and rebuilt the church over a number of years, most of which occurred during the early twelfth century. Following the French Revolution, the church was abandoned and fell into disrepair. Its early restoration is credited to Viollet-le-Duc in the nineteenth century.

As a pilgrimage site, an active monastery, and a significant economic and political center, Vézelay had many functions. However, among the plethora of functions it served, its symbolic content was of primary importance. For the largely illiterate populace of the Middle Ages, religious architecture performed the role of communicating shared meaningful ideas and concepts. The pilgrimage road that led to the west front, and the axial path that attained the sanctuary, communicated the journey of trial and redemption through numerous symbolic and iconographic means. Jesus says in the Gospel of Saint John, "I am the way, and the truth, and the life; no one comes to the Father but by me." At Vézelay the architecture expressed and facilitated this journey to God, beginning with the distant view of the church looming on the peak of the hill, and concluding with passage through the internalized world of the church itself. The enclosed hermetic space of the church symbolized the *civitas dei,* or "Heavenly Jerusalem," an *imago mundi* similar to other examples we have discussed. Its massive stone walls and towers made it an "impregnable stronghold," only to be entered by means of the "Gate of Heaven."[89]

It was the Romans, through changing social conceptions and engineering advances, who first realized significant public interior spaces. Early Christian architecture evolved from this tradition, which had important ramifications in its development. We have observed how many rituals at Greek sacred sites took place in the open areas fronting the temples. In contrast, early Christianity in imperial Rome, because its followers were persecuted, evolved as an interior religion. Early "churches" were founded in private homes, where the ceremony of the Eucharist would be performed, a ritual sharing of food and drink. One root of the word *mass* means a "course at table" and symbolized the partaking of "spiritual food" and the reciprocity of life and death.[90] After Constantine issued the Edict of Milan in 313 CE and Christianity's adoption as the state religion in 323 CE, it was no longer an underground religion but continued its practice as an essentially interior religion. The first Christian churches evolved from the Roman Basilica and gradually transformed its form in response to the evolution of the Christian liturgy. The word *basilica* is derived from the Greek *basileus,* or "king," and its original meaning was the "king's throne room." In Roman times it was a hall of justice.[91] In the early Christian church, the apse of the basilica, formerly the place for the Roman Tribunal, became the seat of authority of Jesus Christ. In Roman times, sacrifices were made on an altar in front of the apse; in the Christian church this was transformed into the ritual of imbibing the symbolic blood and body of Christ. Just as the young Christian faith subsumed pagan rituals and practices, it also took over its architectural forms. It has been well documented that as the faith spread, many Christian churches were built at sites that were originally places of pagan worship.

Many aspects of the new religion of Christianity were revolutionary. One of the most outstanding aspects of its belief system was the concept of a personal relationship between humans and God through Jesus Christ. This was to have profound architectural implications because now the architecture was not only for the deity but for its worshipers as well,[92] a striking contrast to sacred spaces like the inner sanctum at Karnak or the *cella* and *adytum* at Delphi, which were reserved only for the gods and the priesthood. This demanded particular spatial and symbolic responses in the Christian church which, in part, included a symbolic pilgrimage path from the secular to the sacred, from sin to salvation, from death to life. The basilican model, as it came to be developed by the Western church after the Great Schism of 1054, proved especially fertile for the creation of a symbolic path sequence. It richly and dramatically utilized the basic spatial components of the axial path and its destination.[93] The path passed through a sequence of portals and spaces along the way to the goal of the sanctuary. The altar was the place of meeting between humans and God, and according to Davies, "Many early writers referred to Christ himself as the altar and so the basilican path leads to him and proclaims that the path of life too finds its end in Jesus Christ."[94]

Vézelay was a pilgrimage church, but its plan does not correspond to the typology of pilgrimage churches like those found at Tours, Limoges, Conques, Toulouse, and Santiago de Compostela (as noted by Conant). All of these examples, among other distinctions, contain significant transepts, an evolution attributed to the need for increased capacity for the crowds of pilgrims. There is no transept at Vézelay, which is typical of Burgundian churches, and its plan type is closer to the basilica model than the pilgrimage churches. In fact, it is often referred to as the Madeleine Basilica (fig. 119).

The plan of Sainte-Madeleine is bilaterally symmetrical and is aligned east-west along the nave. At the west end there is a large narthex, a distinguishing feature of Romanesque architecture. Moving eastward, one next enters the nave, flanked by a single aisle on either side. Beyond the nave is the choir and sanctuary placed over the crypt. The sanctuary is surrounded by the ambulatory with five chapels, a development attributed to the pilgrimage church. Similar to pilgrimage churches, the ambulatory and the side aisles are generously sized

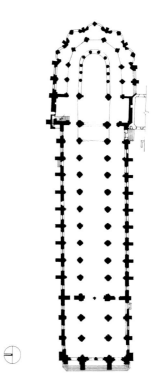

Fig. 119. Floor plan, the Cathedral of Sainte-Madeleine, Vézelay, France (twelfth century).

to allow for the numbers of pilgrims that important churches needed to accommodate.[95] The axial path travels from the west to the east, from the more public foyer of the narthex to the sacred center of the crypt and sanctuary. The ambulatory,[96] along with the side aisles, establishes a clear circulation route that serves to integrate the architecture as a whole.[97]

The form and organization of the cathedral of Sainte-Madeleine utilizes a complex spatial composition and surface and sculptural motifs to create its sacred setting. Over time, its space, articulation and iconography were synthesized to form a highly symbolic place. We will look at each of these components in turn, concentrating on their implications concerning the path and place.

The pilgrimage path led through the crowded main street of the medieval city to a forecourt fronting the church's imposing western facade. One can still walk it today to arrive at the three sets of doors, one capped with a sculptural tympanum, inside of which is the narthex (figs. 120 and 121). Inside the dark constricted space of the narthex, doors lead to the nave and side aisles (fig. 122), all articulated by notable tympana. The nave, volumetrically the most significant space, is principally formed by a repeating bay system of composite columns, spanned by cross vaulting (fig. 123). Flanking the nave are the side aisles, formed at their outside edge by solid exterior walls which are lit only by small openings (fig. 124). The nave space is rectangular, proportioned in a way that accentuates its longitudinal axis.[98] Like the other basilican church types, such as Santa Sabina in Rome and San Zeno in Verona, there is no triforium. Instead, the edges of the volume are defined simply by the aisles and clerestory.

The segments of the columns thrust uninterrupted to the cross vaulting, which accentuates the repeating unit of the bay. Additionally there is the distinctive red-and-white banding on the nave vault arches and incised chevrons, which appear at the aisle arches. Therefore the bays appear, at least at one level, as separate repeating volumes. A marching rhythm of A–B–A–B is established by the vaults and the columns and arches, accentuating the spatial orientation of the nave. The repetition and cadence of the arcading relates the longitudinal axis to

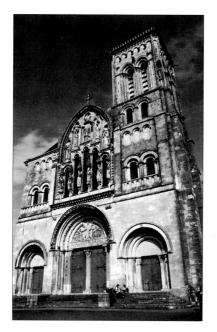

Fig. 120. A view of the west front of the Cathedral of Sainte-Madeleine.

Fig. 121. The west front tympanum, showing Christ in Judgment.

Fig. 122. The narthex looking toward the central tympanum, which depicts Christ in Majesty. Beyond the central post of the entrance is the nave.

Fig. 123. The nave looking east; the rhythm of the arcading accentuates its longitudinal axis.

Fig. 124. The north aisle, looking west. Only small openings light the flanking aisles.

movement along it.[99] Further emphasizing the directionality of the space are horizontal bands that appear at the column capitals, and a string-course above the arcade. The flanking side aisles are composed of repeating spatial modules that form two longitudinal arcades and further reinforce the axiality of the nave and orient the path to its goal in the east. Originally, stained glass in the nave made it dark in comparison to the choir beyond, a feature that was elaborated on in the Gothic that followed.[100] It was a journey from dark to light, which, along with the spatial and linear elements mentioned above, served to compel one forward to the chancel beyond.

At the choir, a simple spatial move is made that has multiple implications. The crypt is not fully enclosed but rises up from the floor level of the nave and ambulatory, thus providing openings that light its space below (figs. 125 and 126). This level change accentuates the choir as a place apart, raised above the surrounding spaces and reached by a set of steps, a feature that can be observed in earlier basilican examples. Also, the choir at one time was partially enclosed by screens. All of these served as symbolic and practical devices to separate the monks and priests from the laity.

Surrounding the choir and the sanctuary and its altar is an ambulatory with five chapels. Originally, mass at these chapels was conducted by the many priests active at the monastery; today they contain relief sculptures depicting the stations of the cross. Both of these settings communicate again the passing scenes encountered along the path, an aspect to which I will now turn.

At one time the interior of Sainte-Madeleine was much more colorful and decorated than it is today. It was during the Cistercian reforms that decoration began to be downplayed. According to Oursel,

> Originally the great Romanesque churches glowed with rich materials, gilding, colour and light. Their architecture reigned supreme; decorative sculpture and the statues surrounding their doors were subservient to it. The interiors of some of the churches were entirely covered with paintings.[101]

221

Fig. 125. The ambulatory and choir, with crypt below.

Fig. 126. The crypt of the Cathedral of Sainte-Madeleine.

At Vézelay, however, decoration still remains in the form of sculptural reliefs. The most distinctive and symbolically rich carvings at Vézelay appear at the tympana inside the narthex. At the aisle entrances, tympana show biblical scenes; the southern one is called the Child Jesus tympanum and shows the annunciation and the nativity flanked by guardian angels. The central narthex tympanum is the most notable and shows Christ in Majesty, surrounded by a *mandorla*, passing his teachings on to his twelve disciples (see fig. 122). *Mandorla* is "almond" in Italian, which accurately describes its shape. Its shape is also called *vesica piscis*, and it was a common motif used to show Christ at the Last Judgment. The almond shape represents a sacred seed or womb from which the whole world emanates, and the almond tree itself was associated with the purity of birth. Also, *vesica piscis* is Latin for "bladder of the fish," which describes the redemptive power of water, a ubiquitous Christian symbol.[102] In this context it is interesting to note that above Christ's uplifted hands are shown the "tree of life" and the "waters of baptism." Rays emanate from his figure—another common *mandorla* motif—depicting the breath of his spirit striking his disciples. Surrounding Christ are Biblical scenes, and below him peoples from all over the world are shown coming toward him.[103]

The interior of Sainte-Madeleine exists as a living Bible, and stories from the Old and New Testaments, along with morality scenes, are depicted in sculptural carvings. Each column capital in the nave contains a different scene—pedantic lessons for the throngs of pilgrims. Along the south aisle are two poignant examples. In the first, (fig. 127) the story of David and the Lion from The First Book of Samuel is depicted, where David says to Saul,

> Your servant used to keep sheep for his father; and when there came
> a lion or a bear, and took a lamb from the flock, I went after him and
> smote him and delivered it out of his mouth; and if he arose against
> me, I caught him by his beard, and smote him and killed him.
> —1 Sam. 17.34–35

Fig. 127. A column capital in the Cathedral of Sainte-Madeleine, depicting the story of David and the Lion.

Fig. 128. A column capital depicting the story of the Evil Rich Man.

The lamb was a common iconographic motif that symbolized the "flock" of humanity under the guidance of the "good shepherd." Jesus said, "Go your way; behold, I send you out as lambs in the midst of wolves" (Luke 10.3). He was often referred to as the Lamb of God whose sacrifice was to save all of humankind. As we read from the Gospel of Saint John, "Behold the Lamb of God, who takes away the sin of the world!" (John 1.29).

An adjacent column capital depicts the fate of the "evil rich man," a New Testament story about the death and damnation of a greedy man (fig. 128). In the sculpture he is shown lying over his sacks of gold while devils snatch his soul with hooks to carry it to hell. In the Gospel of Luke, we read how he looks up from the fires of hell and sees in heaven at "Abraham's bosom" Lazarus who "fed with what fell from the rich man's table." He cries out, "Father Abraham, have mercy upon me, and send Lazarus to dip his finger in water and cool my tongue; for I am in anguish in this flame" (Luke 16.24). He is not offered any relief, however, and the moral both in the Bible and at Vézelay is clear. On a nearby column another morality scene warns against pagan music and dancing. Here a musician is shown blowing music into the ear of a grotesque devil, while a woman intoxicated by his playing allows herself to be fondled. When one enters the nave and sees its myriad of symbolic messages, its intentions are unambiguous; repent and submit to God or suffer eternal damnation. As one walks down the nave and aisles, repeating the act of the generations of medieval villagers and pilgrims, a didactic narrative unfolds. Symbolic lessons confront one along the journey, from the gloom of the narthex and nave to the glory of the choir; from sin to salvation.

The path and place of the original Roman and Christian basilica provided a simple and direct route to the powerful and sacred altar. The path and place at Sainte-Madeleine, a product of its time and influenced by the demands of pilgrimage, has more depth and complexity. The exterior mass and scale of the building contribute to its sense of place and were derived from Roman precedents as well. Two towers flank the entry doors to La Madeleine; the southern one, named for Saint Michael, rises to a height of 120 feet. In Roman imperial city gates and palaces, the combination of towers and gateways was common and symbolized an "imperial stronghold." According to E. Baldwin Smith, as a result "the gateway became a kind of architectural ideogram denoting a *sacrum palatium* as the seat of government and the place from which emanated the divine wisdom of the state." Gateways in many ancient cultures expressed the power and omnipotence of their god-rulers. Often palace gateways were the only places where the populace would see their rulers as they emerged in a royal procession or looked down on them from a raised arcade, and consequently, gateways were symbolic of either the departure or return of the god-ruler. For example, the Egyptian gateway of pylon and trabeated entry portal had powerful symbolic meaning related to the pharaonic gods. Here during ceremonial rites the pharaoh would appear in the "golden loggia" or "window of appearances" as a sun god. Subsequently, the "emperor cult" in imperial Rome adopted certain Ptolomaic pharaonic rituals and architectural devices.[104] At La Madeleine the towers and west front were heir to the symbolic content of the "city gate" and depicted both the gravity and security of the entrance to the *civitas dei.*

The entrance tympanum with its guardian figures and scenes from the Bible creates the first threshold to the path. The word *tympanum* is derived from the Greek *tympanon*, or 'kettle-drum,' and the tension of the surface of a drum suggests the opposing forces present at any spiritual decision.[105] The west entrance and its flanking towers underline their importance as the threshold to God. The tympanum of the central door shows Christ in Judgment, a warning and an encouragement to the uninitiated as well as the laity. Its timeless message demands a commitment to die to the ways of the world and submit to God and the salvation promised by Christ. As Joseph Campbell said, one was "reborn spiritually by entering and leaving a church."[106] Inside, the parallel routes of the aisles and nave, formed by repeating volumes and a series of nodes, create a complex and compelling path. The narrative of the sculpture that leads to the articulated sanctuary further enriches and deepens the symbolic journey. Together the architecture symbolizes Christian beliefs and facilitates the enactment of the shared liturgy.

In its medieval setting Sainte-Madeleine had a number of uses: as a fortress; a place of solitary pilgrimage; a religious community of monks; a setting for processional and religious celebrations; and a place for civic and political events. In each of these scenes, the path and place both symbolized shared beliefs and accommodated communal acts. As I have observed at other sacred sites, the architectural setting serves to distinguish the secular from the sacred and provides a symbolic place for ritual. In the Christian church, particularly at Sainte-Madeleine, these needs were satisfied in a number of ways.

The predominant experience facilitated by the architecture was that of journey. For the pilgrim, this journey would have begun miles away, the church first becoming visible from a promontory twelve miles distant. Pausing here, they would shout *Montjoie!* ("Mount of Joy!") as the sacred acropolis came into view. Next there was the passage through the crowded medieval city, a steep ascent up the hill through the secular world of humans. Next the towers and entrance would be visible, the marking of the beginning of the sacred passage. The tympanum, with its iconographic and allegorical figures, marked the threshold, similar to guardian deities common in other religious sites.

The axis of the church aligned east-west established the path as a journey from the west to the east, an orientation that we have observed at other sacred sites. The relationship of the Christian path to the rising and setting sun most likely has pagan roots, as do many of the symbols and rituals of Christianity. Through the main entrance one enters the narthex, a nodal point along the path. Here there was holy water for the common act of purification before entering the sacred space.[107] At the east end of the narthex were the entries to the aisles and nave, each marked, as we have observed, by a carved tympanum. The images of the carvings not only contained religious messages but served to mark a threshold to the space beyond. At the nave entrance a central column further accentuates the sacred threshold.

The solidity of the massing of the church and the compression of the narthex dramatically dissolve as one enters the nave. Here, through proportion, articulation, repetition, rhythm, and light, is a new world,

Fig. 129. The choir looking west.

self-contained and static but also compelling one forward to the goal beyond. The scale of this space is both monumental and personal. The space in its totality dwarfs the individual, an effect heightened by the diaphanous east end. Simultaneously the scale is personal; the message contained within each column capital speaks directly to the individual.

There is no crossing at Sainte-Madeleine; however, there are two sequential cross-axial spaces, each volumetrically distinct, that serve to separate the nave from the choir (fig. 129). As we have noted, the choir originally was enclosed, and its separateness is underlined both by its raised platform above the crypt and by the surrounding ambulatory. Its inner sanctum was for the initiated only—the monks and priests of the monastery. The pilgrims would have shuffled down the aisles, experiencing its iconographic scenes and the activity of the church itself, and then continued around the ambulatory and its many changing scenes.

The symbolism of trial and redemption is a strong Christian concept, one that appears throughout the Old and New Testaments. The architecture expresses this through the elongation and segmentation of the path, and the creation of a clearly defined goal at the end of the path. According to Norberg-Schulz, "The following of Christ does not imply that the centre is reached at once. The way is long, and in architectural terms it was concretized as a longitudinal axis, as a path of salvation leading to the altar, the symbol of communion with Christ."[108] The plan of the Christian church has been equated to the proportions of the human body and as a symbol, in plan, of the cross. This image is symbolized by the path, a journey from the base desires of humans, the feet being the part of the body in contact with the earth. The crossing is at the heart, the point of decision of whether to submit to God or not. Past this gate, one journeys to the *chevet*, the root of which means "head," the place of spiritual enlightenment.[109] Along the path, a panorama of warnings and encouragement concerning the secular and sacred is expressed by the sculpture.

The nave, a word derived from the Latin *navis*, meaning "ship," symbolized a contained vessel, ferrying souls from damnation to redemption. For the medieval mind, the spaces of the church were physical manifestations of images of heaven, the desired state of grace. Otto von Simpson, writing about the Gothic cathedral, states, "Within its walls God himself was mysteriously present. The medieval sanctuary was the image of heaven."[110] Theologians of this time were concerned with questions concerning transubstantiation, alchemists were trying to change one material to another, and the medieval masons aspired to change physical stone to a divine paradise.[111] According to Eliade, "The very ancient conception of the temple as the *imago mundi*, the idea that the sanctuary reproduces the universe in its essence, passed into the religious architecture of Christian Europe: the basilica of the first centuries of our era, like the medieval cathedral, symbolically reproduces the Celestial Jerusalem."[112] The transformation was accomplished by the simultaneous enclosure and separation of the sacred space and its subtle dematerialization.[113] The medieval masons knew well the structural demands of the architecture. Through the structural organization, surface treatment, and a sophisticated control of light, the constructive elements dissolved, re-forming in the image of an ethereal, sacred spiritualized space. It was an internalized world, separate from the secular world, and attained only through the trials of the path. Unlike pagan religions, Christianity did not directly respond to the natural world. Instead its interior spaces created a hermetic, self-referential place, the primary symbol of which was the path to the redemptive sacred place.[114]

Central to the Christian belief system and the buildings built to serve it is a clearly defined place of arrival, a center (in contrast to the Egyptian concept of "eternal wandering" noted earlier). It was at this place that humans and God were joined by the celebration of the Eucharist; a threshold between earth and heaven.[115] The sanctuary in essence was a specific location where God was present. This specificity is a distinguishing characteristic of Christianity, and the Judeo-Christian concept of time played a role in its conception; linear time having a distinct beginning and end, leading humans to their final goal at the end of the path. This time conception is distinctly different from the traditional view of time as cyclical—the "eternal return"—and it has significant religious and architectural implications. It also reflects the dominance of orthodox Christianity over gnosticism and mysticism, whose notions of God as both everywhere and nowhere are close to other mystical traditions.

The cathedral was a place of powerful symbolic content. It was also the center of both the monastic and lay community, and the stage on which the transitions and celebrations of life were enacted. The relatively prosperous twelfth century was when most of the building of the cathedral took place and when its religious life was at its peak. During this time, weddings, funerals, festivals, and a daily and seasonal round of observances all took place both outside and inside its enclosure. For marriage ceremonies the wedding party would arrive at the west front, where they would be greeted by the priest and the ceremony would begin. First the priest would ask them the obligatory questions about proper age, parental consent, and consanguinity, followed by a short talk about the virtues of marriage. He would then bless the wedding ring and hand it to the groom, who would place it on his bride's finger with the words "with this ring I thee wed." Only then would the party enter the church to celebrate the nuptial mass.[116] Funerals took place inside the church, and for a burgher, there would be a processional down the nave where the coffin would be laid before the altar. A priest's funeral rite, however, would take place inside the choir, the sacred center of the cathedral.

The daily church services began with the congregation standing, while a procession of priests, the choir, and clerks marched down the center of the nave singing, sometimes to organ accompaniment. The church was often damp and cold, and there were no pews or stools as are found today. The congregation would spend the service standing, sitting, or kneeling, as directed by the liturgy, on the straw-covered stone floor. The sermon itself would last a half hour, measured by a water clock placed on the altar. It would conclude with the Creed, the Offertory, and the Kiss of Peace (when the priest would kiss the Gospel). Lastly there would be the celebration of communion before the final blessing and dismissal. The word *mass* in fact is derived from an early expression of dismissal, *Ite missa est*, or "Go, the assembly is sent away." This was related to earlier times when only the initiated were allowed to stay; originally, mass was reserved for the church members only inside the confines of the enclosed sanctuary.

The liturgical year had many associated festivals, many of which took place within the church's sacred enclosure. As we have observed, not all were of a solemn nature, but included lighthearted revelry. The cathedral not only represented the Heavenly Jerusalem and depicted symbolic messages of extreme importance to the populace, but it was also the community's public space and at times served functions of a less serious nature. Plays were a popular event and would be staged within the church during Easter, Christmas, and other religious holidays.

The monastic community also had their daily cycle of requirements. The monastic day of work and devotion was centered around the "seven offices," and the Psalms were sung every three hours. The eighth office was *matins*, or *nocturns*, and began the first hour of the day; the last was *compline* ("completion") and took place at nine o'clock the following evening. The monks would spend approximately four hours a day at this task, their voices ringing in the space of the cathedral, and during a single week, all 150 Psalms would be sung. At each of these vigils, the monks would leave their daily tasks, or shuffle from their cells in the gloom of the night, to gather, standing in facing rows in the choir, at times leaning on their "mercy seats."

The architecture at Vézelay exhibits powerful interplays—good and evil, solidity and dematerialization, static and dynamic, heaven and earth. The ambulatory itself contains a strong ambiguity, as a path that defines but never quite reaches the sanctuary. However, dominating the experience, though not solely defining it, is the path with its goal of the sacred place. For the medieval mind the images, symbolism, and experience of the cathedral was not abstractly or intellectually perceived, as they are for the most part today. During tourist season, sites such as La Madeleine are typically crowded with restless vacationers, talking quietly and consulting their guidebooks, though you still find some who come for silent meditation. One can only imagine the different reaction pious Burgundian pilgrims had on passing the west front and the narthex tympana, entering the nave and perceiving the power and enormity of the sacred space and its rich decoration and legible symbolism. It is safe to assume that their first reaction was to immediately fall on their knees in reverence, supplication, and fear. We have lost this "innocence" of belief and are perhaps consequently poorer. As the next and last example demonstrates, however, the modern is not bereft of meaningful cultural and religious symbolism.

The Brion-Vega Cemetery

The Brion-Vega Cemetery is located outside the village of San Vito d'Altivole in the countryside of northern Italy. The enclosed necropolis for the Brion family is comprised of tombs, chapels, gardens, and pathways and was designed by the Venetian architect Carlo Scarpa. The design of the project was begun in 1969 and the complex completed in 1981. Scarpa, who died in 1978, is buried just outside the enclosure wall. He described his influences and motivation in its design as follows:

> I would like to explain the Tomba Brion because it is a rather recent work. It's very odd, or perhaps strange, and it is not easy to get society to commission this sort of thing: I mean to express oneself freely about highly questionable areas which might exclude modern rational thought, because it could be superfluous to this work.
>
> I consider this work, if you permit me, to be rather good and which will get better over time. I have tried to put some poetic imagination into it, though not in order to create poetic architecture but to make a certain kind of architecture that could emanate a sense of formal poetry. I mean an expressed form that can become poetry. . . .
>
> The tomb of the couple Brion is the sunniest place. And it offers the most beautiful view. The deceased had asked to be close to the earth since he was born in this village—so I decided to build a small arch, which I will call *arcosolium*. (*Arcosolium* is a Latin term from the time of the early Christians in the catacombs. Important persons or martyrs were buried in them.) . . . It's nothing more than a simple arch from the Catholic tradition. I thought it a good idea for two

people who had loved each other to be put in such a way as to be able to greet one another, after death. Soldiers stand erect, movements are human.

The *arcosolium* became an arch, a bridge span, an arch of reinforced concrete and would still have looked like a bridge if I hadn't had it decorated. But instead of painting we used mosaics, a Venetian tradition that I interpret in a different way. This is the path lined with cypresses; small Italian cemeteries have always cypresses. So this path—architects love pathways, there are many, many pathways in Italy—is called *propylaeum*, which means gate, entrance. The first impression you get from the cemetery is by looking through these two "eyes." This piece of land was so large it became a lawn—what we call in French *gazon*; and to rationalize this expanse of space we thought it useful to add a small temple for funeral services. Still too large. So the wall, I call it sacred ground because you have a beautiful panorama from inside whereas from outside you cannot look inside.

Coming from the village you pass by the funeral chapel. . . . Here you have a private atmosphere, a small pavilion in a basin: "une pavillion pour la méditation." So this sums up what we did. The place for the dead in a garden. I wanted to show some ways in which you could approach death in a social and civic way; and further what meaning there was in death, in the ephemerality of life.[117]

The Brion-Vega Cemetery joins other timeless examples from the history of architecture as an evocative and meaningful rendition of the spiritual path and place. As one passes along its segmented paths through the grounds to its destinations, symbolic themes of death and life form a coherent narrative. It is a work that both summarizes the *oeuvre* of a significant late modern architect and crystallizes certain aspects of the modern era. Motifs and methods from Scarpa's earlier projects reappear and find full expression in this, one of his last works. The ambiguity and multivalence of the *Tomba Brion* suggest a succinct depiction of its modern historical context. The work of Scarpa consistently addressed the dialectic of the modern and the timeless through such projects as the Gipsoteca Canoviana at Possagno near Treviso

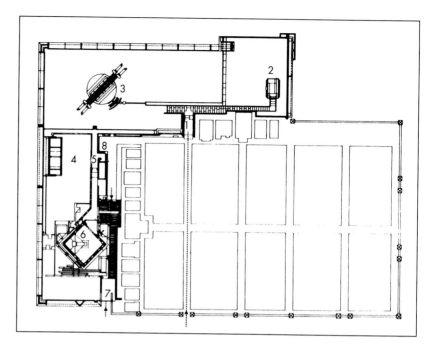

Fig. 130. Site plan, the Brion-Vega Cemetery, San Vito d'Altivole, Italy (1969–1981) Carlo Scarpa.

1. Propylaeum
2. Meditation Platform
3. Tomb of the Brion Couple
4. Tomb of the Brion Family
5. Chapel Passage
6. Chapel
7. Villiage Entrance to the Chapel
8. Carlo Scarpa's Tomb

(1956–1957), and the Galleria Querini Stampala in Venice (1961–1963). Also, there are repeating themes of spatial sequence, detail, and craftsmanship, and juxtaposition of pure materials as seen in the Museo Castelvecchio in Verona (1964).

The overall plan of the family cemetery is "L" shaped and wraps around two sides of an existing village cemetery (fig. 130). Similar to traditional Italian cemeteries, it is enclosed on all sides by a wall and separated from the surrounding farmland. Unlike its predecessors, however, it abandons their gridded organization and citylike layout (with their mausoleums lining the pathways like buildings on a street, often with their occupants' portraits on the front facades). Instead, a mysterious and symbolic journey is created that departs from the familiar and journeys to the unknown. The images are not figurative, but through form, texture, space, and sequence, create a symbolic narrative as powerful as its ancient scenographic and iconographic predecessors.

At the two ends of the L are places of repose, a meditation platform and a chapel, which "float" in the midst of pools of water. Between

Fig. 131. The tomb of the Brion couple is reached by walking down the grass and concrete steps.

Fig. 132. The entrance to the Brion-Vega Cemetery re-creates the spatial characteristics of the adjacent mausoleums, symbolizing a threshold of life and death.

235

them, set at the bend of the L, is the centerpiece of the composition—the tomb of the Brion couple. In plan, the sarcophagi and their enclosure are set at a 45-degree angle to the paths and surrounding walls, which in part establishes their importance. There is a circular depression partially covered by a massive, shallow arch (fig. 131). As one descends into the gloom of this space covered by green tiles on the underside of the arcosolium, it feels like a dark, damp grotto, a threshold to a watery cave. As proposed by Scarpa, it also suggests a Christian catacomb. The two parallel sarcophagi, which are canted toward each other, suggest both solidity and precariousness, richness and simplicity, buried and exhumed, tension and repose, and perhaps a last kiss. Tiles set in the floor serve to join the twin sarcophagi while simultaneously demarking a common threshold. This is one of many symbols of journey apparent at the site; there are four principal destinations: the meditation platform, the Brion couple's tomb, the Brion family tomb, and the chapel. Connecting all is a rich variety of articulated paths and spatial experiences.

The entrance, called the propylaeum, is located inside the village cemetery, adjacent to a group of mausoleums (fig. 132). Instead of where the next *famiglia* would be listed, there is an opening, as wide as its neighbors but higher, and instead of leading to darkness, light is visible at its far end. The entire form erodes at its edges, stepping back to an upper skylight. A brick path surface begins in the village cemetery, and a threshold is established by two courses of lighter-colored bricks. Inside the vertically oriented rectangular propylaeum are a set of steps that demand one's immediate attention. There are actually two sets of stairs; three heroically scaled steps that span from wall to wall, on which rest three smaller steps, asymmetrically placed within the space. It is the latter three steps that are to be ascended, and because of their placement and relatively small size, they immediately awaken one to the task. The process of entry is punctuated by the dynamic interplay of the entry volume and the steps, and the 1–2–3 cadence of one's footfalls on the steel and concrete treads.

Straight ahead, revealing themselves fully as one draws closer, are enigmatic intertwined circles; one red and one blue (the colors are

Fig. 133. Patterns in the floor and walls of the cloister accentuate the linear orientation of the space, and the twinned circles (on the right) and skylight (on the left) mark its threshold. Beyond, looking north, the Brion couple's tomb is viewed.

switched on the outside faces). Their forms appear dark, backlit by the open gardens outside, through which the surrounding wall and fields are partially viewed. The twinned circles serve to introduce the consistent themes of the funerary gardens, that of ambiguity, multiplicity, reciprocity, and nonduality. Their rich and shifting symbolism suggest a unity of opposites: life and death, together and apart, male and female. Here Scarpa, who was influenced by Japanese architecture and gardens, expressed themes sympathetic to the Buddhist belief in nonduality, as found in the *Lankavatara Sutra*.

> False imagination teaches that such things as light and shade, long and short, black and white are different and are to be discriminated; but they are not independent of each other; they are only aspects of the same thing, they are terms of relation, not of reality. Conditions of existence are not of a mutually exclusive character; in essence things are not two but one.

When the path reaches the twinned circles, a threshold is formed in part by a light-filled roof opening that penetrates into the next space. The next path segment runs perpendicular to the propylaeum and is called the "cloister." Here a choice is demanded whether to turn right to the meditation pavilion or left toward the Brion tombs and the chapel. The plan of the entire entry sequence is in the form of a "T" and is a tight, directional series of volumes, inscribed by a variety of patterns and materials on the walls, floor, and ceiling (fig. 133). For example, at the twinned circles, two recessed lines appear on the floor, symmetrically disposed around the center line formed by their intersection, but not corresponding to the centers of each circle. Through both tension and resolution, a threshold inscription is formed. Also, in the floor of the cloister there are two parallel inlaid steel bars that span between alternate panels of the board-formed concrete floor, a pattern that is reflected in the ceiling, and all of which create a clearly directional cadence to the path. Inside the cloister space the rough concrete surfaces are juxtaposed with a smooth applied plaster, a type of finish that Scarpa revived from traditional methods.

Heading south, the path narrows by a shift of the western wall (further inscribed by incremental shifts in the steel strips in the floor). Just beyond this point is a glass door—which opens by recessing into the concrete floor—evocatively counterweighted on the wall outside. When the door is fully recessed, it still must be stepped over, one of many threshold markers. Further marking this point of transition is a change in the ceiling and floor patterns; white plaster on the western wall, and the erosion of the eastern wall (which is delineated by green tiles at its edge). As is apparent here and throughout the complex, the path sequence creates a series of thresholds and way stations. After passing through this particular one, the path, once solid, now appears to float on the surface of the pool. Turning left, one enters the meditation pavilion, which "floats" on the surface of the pool (fig. 134).

The meditation platform, as was mentioned, is one of four destinations inside the cemetery. It is a simply executed place, but like other places in the compound, it contains a multitude of experiences and meanings. The space is formed by a concrete platform and a steel-and-wood enclosure that appear to hover above the water. To enter this space one needs to duck under the enclosure, a humbling experience

Fig. 134. The meditation platform appears to hover on the surface of the water. One needs to duck down to get inside its enclosure.

not unlike the traditional entrance to *sukiya*-style Japanese teahouses. Once inside, the spatial experience also has similarities to the teahouse; the view is limited to the immediate environment, focused on the surrounding water and walls. When one sits down, a larger vista is offered; the contemplative area is now bounded by walls on all sides, its horizontal orientation delineated by a band of multicolored tiles. An additional edge is formed at the northern edge of the pool by a mysterious cluster of steel cables. These stretch from the cloister to an opposite wall, and align with the southern edge of the propylaeum.

The edge of the meditation platform recedes into the water, eroded through the typical means of a series of board-formed crenellations in the concrete. Gazing north at the surrounding shallow pool of water, partially submerged and half-hidden enigmatic images become apparent (fig. 135). Adjacent to the cloister and just under the surface of the water are four concrete cylinders. Aligned with one of these is a concrete-and-tile quaternity form resting just above the surface of the water. Plants grow below and above the surface of the water, and the composition as a whole creates a powerful interplay between the two realms. As Jung has argued, water is an archetypal symbol of the unconscious and the unknown, and Eliade states that "the symbolism of the waters implies both death and rebirth." The interrelationship of all of the elements, which straddle the realm between the water and the air, symbolize transcendence and new understanding that exists just beneath the surface of reality. The ephemeral reflections suggest parallel worlds and complementary dualities; death coexisting with life, a hidden reality that complements and completes our consciousness.

The symbol of completion similarly appears in the counterweighted works of the cloister door. The door itself, as it descends into its hidden recess, suggests another reality that exists just below the surface. Outside, the two-dimensional pattern of the door-works fragments when the door is in the open position, but when the door slides upward to close, the works gradually reassemble and form a vaguely anthropomorphic form reminiscent of a crucifix. As is found throughout the cemetery, the messages are rich, complex, and even at times, conflicting.

Fig. 135. Ancient symbols appear at the pool surrounding the meditation platform.

Fig. 136. The cloister viewed from the garden.

Fig. 137. Located next to the Brion couple's tomb are two cylinders. From one of the cylinders water flows to the pool at the meditation platform—the other is dry.

The path has a very different character where it turns left from the intertwined circles. Instead of the enclosing volume constricting, it opens up, the walls dissolving into the open space beyond (fig. 136). Again the edges of the eroded walls are marked by tiles, this time yellow. There is also bright white plaster applied to the concrete walls on one side, a material that is used at a number of threshold spaces and achieves a brightness that further marks the border. Leaving the enclosure of the cloister, the path, now on grass, follows the water channel that feeds the pool of the meditation platform. The source of this "spring" is a concrete cylinder set in the ground and located close to the second destination along the journey—the Brion couple's tomb. Next to the water source is another concrete cylinder, only this one is dry; and from here a dry channel leads down a grassy slope to the tombs (fig. 137). The spring, a symbol of resurrection and eternal life, is set against a dry and lifeless vessel. They are joined by a thin section of concrete but are equally separate. Perhaps this symbolizes the husk of the body, juxtaposed with the life of the spirit. The channel of water runs from this source, past the edge of the cloister, and feeds the pool at the meditation platform. The dry channel travels in the opposite direction, then turns to lead one into the dark cavity of the couple's tomb.

Leaving the tombs, one walks across the grass and down a set a staggered steps (fig. 138). Here again the path demands a choice. To the right lies the Brion family tomb: straight ahead, the path leads to the chapel. The family tomb is the third destination and shares spatial characteristics of the preceding two places. Like the previous tomb, it is set into the ground and has a grottolike feeling to it: similar to the meditation platform, one has to duck to get inside its constricted space. The path to this tomb is narrow, with a tight 90-degree turn to gain entry. The enclosure on one side is a continuation of the canted temenos wall. Inside, its surfaces at the top are colored black, further increasing the feeling of enclosure. Within the constricted interior space, one is placed uncomfortably close to the grave markers, relief from which is only offered by the opening above.

The path to the chapel is more open and offers a number of spatial and symbolic experiences along the route. It is a long linear passageway

Fig. 138. The steps from the Brion couple's tomb.

first open on one side, then enclosed in a colonnade of sorts, formed by a caretaker's room on the left and a perforated wall on the right (fig. 139). Two steps mark the passage from the open portion of the path to the more enclosed. Just before entering the chapel, the path terminates at a large door within which is set a smaller one. The wall on the left at this point opens up and serves as an entrance from a secondary path used for village funeral services.

The chapel, like the Brion couple's tomb, is rotated 45 degrees off the orthogonal alignment of the paths, which creates a triangular anteroom to the chapel (fig. 140). Passing through this transitional volume, one enters the proportional volume of the chapel itself. Geometry is employed in this space to give focus and directionality. A square, one quarter the area of the chapel, is inscribed and raised up from the roof in the northern corner where a pyramidal skylight is created, casting light at certain hours on the altar below (fig. 141). Corner openings, paving patterns and floor inlays, and the pattern of the ceiling all reinforce the diagonal orientation of the chapel. A pool of water surrounds the chapel on three sides, underlining it as a place apart. At the western corner of the chapel there is a secondary door that leads to a path across the surrounding pool to a grassy area called the Priests' Cemetery (fig. 142). Here concrete slabs create a series of "stepping stones" that appear both above and below the surface of the water. From one step to the next, one straddles two worlds, and the sense of passage is reinforced (fig. 143).

The siting and orientation of the chapel has cosmogonic implications that recall earlier examples of sacred architecture. At the base of the northern corner of the chapel, behind the altar, there are two steel doors that open to the surrounding pool. At the equinoxes, the sun slanting into the chapel through the skylight streams through the open doors to the water beyond. This is a timeless and powerful response to the environment that recalls passage graves found in Ireland and that one finds throughout sacred architecture.

Throughout the experience of the Brion-Vega Cemetery the criteria for the spiritual path and place are met; there is a clearly defined enclosure, a temenos created by the canted concrete wall, the main

Fig. 139. The path to the chapel.

Fig. 140. A triangular anteroom leading to the chapel.

Fig. 141. The altar is located in the northwest corner of the chapel. The corners of the square skylight above are aligned with the cardinal points.

Fig. 142. The west corner of the chapel.

Fig. 143. Enigmatic steps lead across the water from the chapel to the priest's cemetery.

entrance is clearly formed, and a sequence of defined spaces of increasing sacredness is created along the path. There are also choices offered along the path, way stations en route to the four destinations. It is a small site, surprisingly small when first visited, but the manipulation of the path creates an experiential depth far beyond its size. The path itself is clearly marked; there are a variety of edges formed and a plethora of paving patterns (fig. 144). These patterns change as one walks along the path and at places are either with or against "the grain" of the path, which in turn either accelerates or retards the unfolding of the narrative. The places along the path are clearly defined in terms of entry and enclosure; each has a distinct presence, separate yet related to the experience as a whole. Proportion, geometry, orientation, constructive elements, and materials all lend themselves to creating each destination as a "place apart." The richness of detail and texture creates a complexity to the surfaces of the architecture, which is expressed through light and shadow. The message, however, is at times obscured when the layers of detail and meaning are too dense. Toward the latter part of his career, Scarpa's details seemed to approach an almost mannerist phase, especially apparent at the Banco de Populare in Verona. In this garden for the dead and the living, perhaps the simple theme of

Fig. 144. A rich variety of paving patterns enrich the path sequence.

duality-unity would have been more powerful at places if it had been stated more simply.

As one walks the path at the Brion-Vega Cemetery, a symbolic story unfolds. The other modern examples have shown how ambiguity plays a significant role in the message of the architecture. Here the layers of meaning, the "multiple reads," serve to address questions of duality and unity. In essence, the powerful message of Scarpa's work is the blurring of distinctions between these two realms. Thus one experiences many elements that seem to inhabit both worlds, from the just-submerged cylinders in the meditation platform pool to the half-submerged steps to the priests' cemetery. This theme is presupposed by the introduction of the twinned circles at the beginning of the journey; separate yet joined, they not only seem to speak about life and death but about the complex relationship of marriage as well.

The surrounding walls of the cemetery are also eloquently ambiguous. They are solid, massive, canted, and at points buttressed, with a "dry-moat" located inside them. They are also fragmented and eroded. For example, at the corners, the wall transforms into an open lace work, and at the entry, the wall parts and is interrupted, as if to state that the cemetery is both separate from and joined with the outside world. This relationship is particularly powerful at Scarpa's grave, which is placed in a "no-man's-land" (as described by Scarpa), just outside the wall near the main entrance. His marker is an austere, canted metal pipe (a commemorative tablet was added later by his son). Standing next to his grave, one can peer obliquely into the garden through the crenellated, parted wall. The architect hovers between the outside and the inside, and his placement and marker express a profound humility.

The Brion-Vega Cemetery is distinctly modern in its use and symbolic content. It is not a place of communal worship, but a private cemetery for a family and a small village's burial grounds. The cemetery was the personal expression of the architect and the commemoration of a single family, and yet when one enters its sacred precinct, images and feelings arise that suggest a transcendent symbolic content. It is a difficult place to leave, especially in the warm sun of spring when the grass is green and the surrounding countryside is exploding with fecundity and renewal. Its symbolic messages are rich, textured, eclectic, and at times conflicting and ambiguous. Overall it is a composition of multiplicity, or as Aldo van Eyck might say, "It is not one nor the other, but both." The chapel itself, entered from the outside as well as the inside, is both a destination and a beginning.

The path could be described as circular, a symbolic return to beginnings, in contrast to the linear path of traditional Christianity. This suggests the reciprocity of life and death, and of the overall unity of existence. In this way it recalls shared psychic symbols, archetypal meanings that resonate in our "collective unconscious." Its theme is ultimately concerned with life and death, and its message is simultaneously tragic and heroic. Like other examples of the sacred path and place, it is a symbolic narrative of a journey from the profane to the sacred, from the known to the unknown. Moreover, similar to ancient examples of sacred architecture, this monument serves to express the beliefs and conditions of its age. In its pluralism this is not simply a Christian monument but, characteristic of the modern age, indicates sources from many faiths and belief systems. Quaternity symbols, numerology implicit in the twinned circles, the three destinations, and the four submerged cylinders, the use of primary colors—all suggest fundamental sources.

The couple's sarcophagi, set at the apex of this sacred site, appear like gondolas passing under a Venetian bridge, gently rocking ships on a journey to the unknown.[118] In this aspect they join a host of ancient symbols related to the sacred journey, to the death of our lives as we know them, and spiritual transformation. We are reminded of Gilgamesh punting his way across the waters to the land of death, of the sacred barge of Amun-Re disappearing into the gloom of the inner sanctum of Luxor Temple, or the boat guided by Charon that ferries souls across the waters to the Elysian Fields. The symbolism of the couple's tomb also resonates with the image of the *hojo* afloat in the sea of its gardens, like one of the Isles of the Immortals from Taoist mythology, and the shiplike nave of the cathedral which carried one from damnation to salvation. As we see, many others have taken this path. Joseph Campbell said about the spiritual path, "we have not to risk the adventure alone; for the heroes of all time have gone before us; the labyrinth is thoroughly known; we have only to follow the thread of the hero-path."[119] Scarpa at the Brion-Vega Cemetery has created a monument that in its complexity and ambiguity reflects the modern age but also offers a guided path of meaningful symbolic messages to a sacred place.

CHAPTER 7

▪ *Arrival*

The preceding chapters have provided numerous examples of the path and place in sacred architecture from a wide range of historical, cultural, and religious settings. Each site revealed its unique manifestation of religious beliefs in architectural form, and we have observed how the architecture often has served as the setting for the enactment of specific religious rituals. The variety of interpretations of religious motifs is astonishing, but the similarity of fundamental themes is equally remarkable. In other words, the path and place in sacred architecture is comprised of both general and specific forms, elements and symbolic content. In our journey around the world and through the world's religions, fundamental place-forming elements of the path and place at each of the sites have been identified and correspondences established between the form and experience of each example and the religion it served. Consequently, characteristics common to all the sites have become apparent, what might be called shared elements of the sacred path and place.

The following are descriptions of repeating elements common to many of the referenced religious sites. Not all of the shared elements are present at every site; they can take many forms, and they do not hold consistent values from example to example. However, I believe that the path and place in sacred architecture can be described, at least in part, archetypally, in terms of shared elements. Moreover, the argument for repeating patterns is cited primarily to further validate the interrelationship of symbolism, ritual, and meaning in sacred architecture documented in this book.

The entry sequence at sacred sites, as we have observed, appears in many forms and organizations. First, the entry point of the path is clearly marked and thereby establishes a point of decision as to whether or not to begin the journey. This typically is in the form of a clearly defined entry and serves to separate the sacred ground from the surrounding profane territory. Entry rituals, which are often enacted, serve to shed the outside world and purify oneself for the journey ahead, as in ritual ablution. The entry threshold gains access to a subsequent path sequence or to an entire enclosed sacred precinct.

Following the entry, there is typically a sequence of defined spaces, places, or events along a path that grows increasingly more sacred; there are points along the path to pause, change direction, or turn back. Commonly, the path sequence symbolically, spatially, and temporally expresses the mythology and religion for which it was built. The "symbolic story" serves to underline the difficulty and heighten the anticipation of the attainment of the sacred place to be afforded at the journey's end. Often, as we have observed, there is a manipulation of scale, distance, and time along the path, which creates the impression that the journey is longer and thereby more eventful than it actually is.

Many of the paths that lead to the sacred place display a remarkable "clarity and legibility," a clear marking of the path surface and edges. Moreover, the path to the sacred place often possesses a clear directionality and continuity, with "strategic foci" further marking the path sequence. In other words, it is not only comprised of a progression of discrete spatial links, but it also possesses an overall unity. Lastly, the path typically evidences a consistent ordering of constructive and space-forming elements and materials, and overall it is characterized by a legible architectural language.

Similar to the entry path, the goal or place of ultimate destination assumes numerous forms. It also utilizes specific shared elements and organizations related to the path. Typically, one enters the sacred place through a clearly defined entry or threshold at the point where the path attains the sacred place. The sacred place is delineated by enclosure or separation from its surroundings, which establishes it as a "place apart." In many examples the place represents a center point and provides a setting where God, or some spiritual ideal, and humans meet. Consequently, the sacred place is characterized by a form and language that has symbolic content.

Within the sacred place there is typically a clear delineation and hierarchical ordering of space to accommodate specific rituals. Furthermore, there is an interrelationship of constructive elements through proportion and geometry. Lastly, the architecture often makes use of a limited and consistent palette of materials.

In all of the examples, both ancient and modern, some if not all of the above elements are present. Each example presents variations and interpretations of the path and place created by means of particular symbolic space forming and surface marking. The modern examples that have appeared throughout this study also, for the most part, exhibit the overall characteristics of the sacred path and place. However, at times their interpretations of the path and place provide an interesting and distinguishing departure from the ancient examples. For example, modern sacred architecture often relies considerably on the individual expression of the architect for its design and form. Consequently, the symbolic language is no longer limited to shared religious and cultural beliefs but includes the personal interpretation of the architect. They attempt to symbolize certain aspects of shared beliefs but abstract the symbolic and formal language to do so. In the plan of the path and place, for instance, certain characteristics of the archetypal path and place are retained, but otherwise the models are transformed. The new form is generally attributed to the invention of the architect.

Modern and contemporary sacred architecture (as well as secular in many cases) typically evidences a certain degree of ambiguity in its symbolic language. The "built myth" offers various and often conflicting interpretations of cultural and religious themes. This, at least in part, reflects a loss of the power of mythology and religion and its universal interpretations. Consequently, the modern era's "loss of belief" has produced varied, pluralistic, and individualized interpretations of religious themes, and in particular, the path and place.

Contemporary human culture, as exemplified by the dominant Western world, has cut itself off from its past, its roots. In essence it has lost its "memory." Eliade, in his writings, consistently refers to the "desacralization" of the modern world, and he strikingly refers to the amputation of the past as the "second fall" of humans. In other words, using Christian symbolism as a reference, in the first fall, humans became separated from God but were conscious of this split. The apprehension of the division between existence and spirit was retained in the consciousness of our ancestors but now has descended to the unconscious and has been "forgotten."[1] This is a chilling assessment of our common, contemporary condition and reminds me of Joseph Campbell's statement that "it is a grim thing to be a modern human being."[2]

Furthermore, according to Eliade, the modern "nonreligious man refuses transcendence, accepts the relativity of 'reality,' and may even come to doubt the meaning of existence." As Norberg-Schulz has pointed out, this propensity to conceive of the world only "as it is" has reduced the built environment, at least in the most strident examples of modern architecture, to simply a generic providing of "needs." Le Corbusier's statement in *Vers une Architecture* that "the house is a machine for living in" in some ways has come to epitomize an emphasis on functional utilitarian needs over meaningful and symbolic aspects. For example, Hannes Meyer in his 1928 manifesto took this statement out of context to argue that "the new dwelling becomes not only a 'machine for living,' but also a biological apparatus serving the needs of body and mind." According to Meyer, "all things in this world are a product of the formula: (function–times–economy)," and that therefore "all life is function and therefore unartistic."[3] Admittedly, Meyer is an extreme example of the functionalist argument, and it should be noted that he omitted Le Corbusier's attendant statement that "architecture goes beyond utilitarian needs." Le Corbusier and his contemporaries who formulated the polemic of the modern movement often were contradictory in their descriptions of what the "new architecture" should be, and the later career of this influential builder and theoretician is notable for its emphasis on the emotional and the spiritual. Even Walter Gropius, whose works crystallized much of the imagery of the International Style, passionately stated that architecture is the "crystalline expression of man's noblest thoughts, his ardor, his humanity, his faith, his religion!"[4]

The early modernists, while separating the "artistic" from the "functional," still retained a "memory" of the totality of architectural expression and experience. The interrelationship of these components became more abstract and confused during the following years. As humans have more and more accepted a "profane existence," their separation from the spiritual has grown proportionally. Eliade defined profane space and existence as "homogeneous and neutral; no break qualitatively differentiates the various parts of its mass." In the 1960s, Superstudio, the Italian theoretical group, critiqued functionalist planning in a project entitled "il Monumento Continuo," which proposed a uniform planning grid for the entire earth's surface. Their statement that in the future "there will be no further reason for roads or squares," has in part proved prophetic. Our architecture and built environment, dominated by functional and economic concerns, is remarkably lacking in spiritually imbued places and meaningful paths of entry. Much has been said about the lack of "place" in a significant portion of our contemporary built environment, and there are few counterarguments to this observation. The rational-scientific world view dominates our time, and is clearly reflected by our architecture.

It is a strange setting in which we find ourselves. There is a perverse emphasis on individuality in our culture, further supported by an environment that maroons each of us in isolation. There is also pervasive confusion regarding individuality and artistic expression in the creation of architecture—art and the creative process are commonly seen as strictly personal, not the articulation of shared beliefs or the revelation of deep meanings. Thus contemporary architecture is often characterized by a lack of depth and an emphasis on egocentric expression. We are all separated from the rich tapestry of our past and our human interdependence, and we have lost the ability to see that individuality is not how one is "different," but the unique way in which each of us "fits in."

Our built environment expresses the double emphasis of our contemporary tableaux, the placeless monotony of the economically driven functionalism, and the chaos of the cult of the individual.[5] Much architectural theorizing of recent years reflects an increasing separation of humans from themselves and their environment, an estrangement analogous to the mind-body split characteristic of our "head heavy" culture. Moreover, contemporary criticism falls into the same snare of emphasizing how our time is different from previous ages, instead of recognizing the many similarities. We live in a transitional time, much like other eras during which a collapse of shared values resulted in a loss of faith and a plurality of artistic expression.[6] To see our time as unique and untethered to the past is to fall into the same conceit of early modernism. More dangerous are stated objectives to "be honest" and express the chaos and uncertainty of our times, a particularly unreflective, immature, and self-centered attitude.

It leads me to reflect on the historical setting of Koto-in. When it was founded, you may recall, the prolonged Age of the Country at War had just ended, over one hundred years of internecine wars that ultimately engulfed every province in Japan. Daitoku-ji was destroyed twice during the medieval era, and yet during this same time Zen monasteries throughout Japan built some of the most enduring and meaningful architecture and gardens in the history of Japanese culture. I would suggest that the call of our turbulent, chaotic, dislocated, and often meaningless time is to transcend our era, find refuge, and perhaps similarly create timeless and meaningful architecture.

Though our current era may be characterized by a remarkable imbalance in its orientation, Eliade has aptly pointed out that "a purely rational man is an abstraction." Even though we may have enclosed ourselves in a hard shell of rationality, just below the surface exist all the myriad needs and expressions that make us uniquely human. This "inner life" is revealed in many ways, from dreams to contemporary rituals. Joseph Campbell suggests that dreams commonly express mythological themes and that "the logic, the heroes, and the deeds of myth survive into modern times."[7] Eliade writes about the "crypto-religious" behavior found in contemporary society. "Man," he states, "is an inheritor. He cannot utterly abolish his past, since he is himself the product of his past."[8] We may see ourselves as "modern man" distinguished from our ancient ancestors, but our needs remain basically the same. Proof of the unchanging characteristics of our humanity can be readily found in our physiology and our often unconscious social gestures and interactions.[9] Humans, above all definitions, are principally social animals, and no amount of abstraction will obviate our need for a sense of place and community, our unique orientation in the environment. We still need architectural settings so that we can gather for communal and religious purposes. Our time has particular needs that should be rigorously addressed, and it is incumbent on us to synthesize the specific exigencies of our time with the timeless aspects of human existence and its architecture. We need to sincerely walk a "middle path."

Through the analysis of the spiritual path and place, I have identified shared architectural elements and patterns and examined how they are interpreted in a particular time and place. Part of the background to building the case for the existence of architectural paradigms of this type is Jungian psychology and the concept of archetypes of human psychology. Similarly, Mircea Eliade documents repeating patterns in religion, sacred sites, and ritual. Mythology, in particular the universal myth of the hero's journey, has demonstrated that discrete cultures share certain fundamental beliefs. All of these concepts suggest that symbolic and religious themes appear transhistorically and pan-culturally. A principal premise of this book is that the path and place in sacred architecture is "built myth," which symbolizes the belief system and accommodates the enactment of shared rituals. Consequently, if there is a direct relationship between specific mythological and religious beliefs and architectural form, and a pan-cultural relationship between various religions, it is possible that elements and patterns are shared between various sacred paths and places.

I believe that the limited examples of the spiritual path and place examined have revealed particular architectural paradigms. Through the characteristics, articulation, and meaning of the sacred path and place, I have documented shared elements and themes, including similar means of enclosing and entering sacred ground, the symbolic expression of journey and spiritual transformation, and consistent means of forming and ordering the sacred place. Even in the modern examples, with all their differences, similar archetypes have been apparent; Carlo Scarpa's Brion-Vega Cemetery perhaps provides the most notable example. All of the foregoing serve to emphasize the essential importance of symbolism, meaning, and intimate human interaction in the built environment. It is my hope that the examples and focus of this book will offer inspirational models for aspects of the path and place in contemporary sacred as well as secular architecture.

A synthetic approach appropriate to today utilizes both the general and the specific, the timeless and the contemporary, the universal and the particular. This is analogous to what Herman Hertzberger refers to as "structure and interpretation," the interrelationship of the "collective given and individual interpretation."[10] In this way our rich common heritage can rejoin our present setting and needs, and the archetypal can find its unique contemporary expression. This is a far more difficult task than it might at first appear, and I do not minimize its complexity. But all times in their unique settings have been impelled to perform this task. We, as in other eras, are charged to do the same, perhaps more so because of our remarkable separation from our inner needs and cultural roots.

The general, the timeless, the archetypal should not be construed as applicable answers, only as generous sources. Many examples of modern and contemporary architecture demonstrate how a misunderstanding and misappropriation of fundamentals can produce tragic results. Equally myopic is the popular search for a static universal order, the "sacred geometry" that provides easy answers to complex phenomena. All approaches are laudable in their intent but are lacking in content.

However, given the often confusing range of approaches, I argue for an emphasis on a homologic approach. At times it appears that we are all busy inventing the game when the rules, in their elegant simplicity, are already present.[11] In this way, the architectural act is one of discovery as well as creation; a process of uncovering a common, generous source that all share and find meaningful.

Thus finally I am led to questions regarding the meaning of the architecture, what Christian Norberg-Schulz has called "the concretization of existential space," and the lessons that perhaps the examples offer us today. At each of the sacred sites, overtly or implicitly, the universal myth of the hero's journey was expressed by the sequence, form, and symbolic content of the path and place, and a relationship between form and meaning was established. The architecture has been didactic, inculcating spiritual lessons to those who walked its paths and entered its sanctuaries. In this way sacred architecture performed the role of a hierophant; it revealed the mysterious unknown and guided the spiritual pilgrim toward enlightenment. In light of this historical precedent, it is essential to recognize the myths and beliefs of our present age, an age that in many ways has lost its "memory" of the past and its rich mythology. According to Joseph Campbell, myths, being spontaneous products of the psyche, do not die, but simply reappear in different forms, and these forms, not surprisingly, are typically based on universal models. Certainly, the particularly American penchant for "road movies" and the appeal of heroic quests in popular culture attest to the contemporary endurance of the myth of the hero's journey.

In our present age, with its emphasis on the individual and contemporary issues, it is easy to lose sight of all that has come before us. Bernard of Chartres in the twelfth century said, "We are like dwarfs seated on the shoulders of giants; we see more things than the ancients and things more distant, but this is due neither to the sharpness of our sight, nor to the greatness of our stature, but because we are borne aloft on that giant mass."[12] Certainly we are different than our predecessors, but in many ways our needs are the same. One of these unchanging needs is the desire to ask questions about our very existence. These questions have been asked since the beginning of history and to date have remained unanswered, except perhaps in part through the symbolic language of myth and religion. We need myths in one important aspect to provide security in the midst of the enormity of the unknown; that is a role I believe they have always played.

Myths and religious beliefs can be expressed in many ways, one of which is through sacred architecture. In this book, I have illustrated the depth and intrinsic importance of symbolism and ritual in architecture and to support that argument I have established the existence of archetypal patterns shared pan-culturally and transhistorically. The history of architecture provides a rich source of fundamentals that are as appropriate and meaningful to today as they were in earlier ages. These fundamentals are analogous perhaps to what Eliade has described as the belief in a fecund source that is returned to during rites of repetition and renewal, analogously described by the architect Louis Kahn as, "What shall be has always been." The archetypal patterns not only establish the relationship between form and meaning but also provide frameworks for the creation of legible environments. Similar to religion and mythology, legible and meaningful environments provide for the basic human need for emotional security and social interaction.

The path and place in sacred architecture speak about a unity of form and meaning and thus offer valuable lessons for contemporary architecture that often relies too much on image over content. Architecture that conquers this uniquely modern impediment can still speak about a meaningful sense of place and an articulated path to attain it. And this is one of the primary goals of architecture—to provide legible and meaningful environments, paths and places that perhaps lead us to a better understanding of who we are.

Notes

■ **CHAPTER** *1*   *Departure*

1. A. T. Mann, *Sacred Architecture* (Shaftsbury, Dorset: Element Books, 1993), pp. 185–186.

2. Violet Staub de Laszlo, ed., *Psyche and Symbol: A Selection of the Writings of C. G. Jung* (New York: Doubleday Anchor Books, 1958), pp. xiii–xiv.

3. Mircea Eliade, *The Sacred and the Profane: The Nature of Religion* (New York: Harcourt Brace Jovanovich, 1959), p. 204.

4. Ibid., p. 213.

5. For example, little evidence remains of ancient Egyptian settlements, which were generally constructed from perishable mud bricks, whereas Egyptian monumental architecture was constructed from laboriously transported stone.

■ **CHAPTER** *2*   *Symbols, Structures, and Rituals*

1. C. G. Jung, ed., *Man and His Symbols* (New York: Dell Publishing, 1968), pp. 3–4.

2. Ken Wilber, *No Boundary* (Boston: Shambhala Publications, 1981), pp. 31–43.

3. Rollo May, ed., *Symbolism in Religion and Literature* (New York: George Braziller, 1960), p. 19.

4. Jung, *Man and His Symbols*, p. 147.

5. Jung notes that only eighty generations separate the present with the Golden Age of Greece. Violet Staub de Laszlo, ed., *The Basic Writings of C. G. Jung* (New York: Modern Library, 1959), p. 31.

6. May, *Symbolism in Religion*, p. 28.

7. Ibid., p. 12.

8. Ibid., p. 76.

9. Jung, *Man and His Symbols*, p. 41.

10. N. K. Sanders, trans., *The Epic of Gilgamesh* (London: Penguin Books, 1960), pp. 77–78.

11. Eliade, *Sacred and the Profane*, p. 146.

12. See Aniela Jaffe in Jung, *Man and His Symbols*, pp. 257–322.

13. Ibid., pp. 257–322.

14. de Laszlo, *Basic Writings of C. G. Jung*, p. 287.

15. Ibid., p. 288.

16. See Claude Lévi-Strauss, *Structural Anthropology* (New York: Basic Books, 1963), pp. 206–231.

17. Ibid., p. 229.

18. Ibid., p. 210.

19. Joseph Campbell, *The Hero with a Thousand Faces* (Princeton: Princeton University Press, 1949), p. 4.

20. Campbell, *The Hero*, p. 4.

21. Herman Hertzberger, *Lessons for Students in Architecture* (Rotterdam: Uitgeverij 010 Publishers, 1991), p. 93.

22. Christopher Alexander, *The Timeless Way of Building* (New York: Oxford University Press, 1979), p. 407.

23. A term created by Joseph Campbell.

24. Joseph Campbell with Bill Moyers, *The Power of Myth*, (New York: Doubleday, 1988), p. 123.

25. See Campbell, *The Hero.*

26. de Laszlo, *Psyche and Symbol*, p. xx.

27. Campbell, The Hero, pp. 17, 20.

28. Ibid., p. 30.

29. Eliade, *Sacred and the Profane*, p. 201.

30. Campbell, pp. 10–11. Campbell writes about the circumcision rites of Australian aborigines.

31. See Eliade, *Sacred and the Profane*, pp. 188–92.

32. These stations are marked on the Via Dolorosa in Jerusalem and are ritually traversed by pilgrims. They are also found in paintings and sculpture in churches for the same ritual purposes. The stations are as follows (as summarized by Herbert Whone):

1. he is condemned to death
2. he is forced to carry his own cross
3. he falls under the cross
4. he meets his mother
5. Simon the Cyrenian helps him carry his cross
6. Veronica wipes his face
7. he falls under the cross again
8. he speaks to the daughters of Jerusalem
9. he falls a third time under the cross
10. he is stripped of his garments
11. he is nailed to the cross
12. he yields up the Holy Ghost
13. he is taken down from the cross
14. he is placed in the sepulchre

33. Quoted by Campbell with Moyers, in *Power of Myth*, p. 126.

34. Edward Conze, ed., *Buddhist Scriptures* (London: Penguin Books, 1959), pp. 38–40.

35. Campbell with Moyers, *Power of Myth*, p. 13.

36. John G. Neihardt, *Black Elk Speaks: Being the Life Story of a Holy Man of the Oglala Sioux* (New York: Pocket Books, 1932), pp. 152–58.

37. Quoted by Georgio de Santillana and Hertha von Dechend in *Hamlet's Mill: An Essay on Myth and the Frame of Time* (Boston: David R. Godine, 1969), p. 293.

38. Rosemary Harris, *The Lotus and the Grail: Legends from East to West* (London: Faber and Faber, 1974), p. 48.

39. Campbell with Moyers, *Power of Myth*, p. 136.

40. For example, both are subjected to temptations from the devil on their path to spiritual enlightenment. See Campbell with Moyers, *Power of Myth*, p. 137.

41. *Rigveda* 10.14.1–2, quoted by de Santillana and von Dechend, in *Hamlet's Mill*, p. 304.

42. Richard Barber, *Pilgrimages* (Woodbridge, Suffolk, England: Boydell Press, 1991), p. 3.

43. Ibid., p. 2.

44. Scallop shells later came to represent the Cluniac order, which was responsible for the formalization of the major European pilgrimage routes. See Eleanor Munro, *On Glory Roads: A Pilgrim's Book about Pilgrimage* (New York: Thames and Hudson, 1987), p. 92.

45. Barber, *Pilgrimages*, p. 2.

46. Aymery Picaud, *Pilgrim's Guide to Santiago de Compostela*, p. 181. Quoted by Munro, *On Glory Roads*, p. 181.

47. Joseph Gies and Frances Gies, *Life in a Medieval City* (New York: Thomas Y. Crowell, 1973), p. 131.

48. Barber, *Pilgrimages*, p. 120.

49. Munro, *On Glory Roads*, p. 243.

50. See W. R. Lethaby, *Architecture, Mysticism and Myth* (New York: George Braziller, 1975), chapter 7.

51. Barber, *Pilgrimages*, pp. 93–94. Barber describes a particular series of devotions performed by Hindu pilgrims at certain times of the year. There is five-day ritual fasting (*dharrna*) at the temple, worship (*puja*), seeing the deity (*darsana*), partaking of offered food (*prasada*), as well as circling the temple in a clockwise direction (*pradaksina*).

52. Spiro Kostof, *A History of Architecture, Settings and rituals* (Oxford: Oxford University Press, 1985), pp. 227–28.

53. Eliade, *Sacred and the Profane*, p. 182.

54. The New Testament contains numerous examples of miracles performed by Christ, from the turning of water

into wine (John 2.1–10) to the raising of Lazarus (John 11.32–35, 39, 41–44), all of which served to prove Jesus' divinity.

55. Barber, *Pilgrimages*, pp. 54, 59.

56. Though, as was common, the presence of the bones of Saint James was clouded in myth, and at times they were said to be elsewhere. See Barber, p. 54, and Munro, *On Glory Roads*, pp. 178–79.

57. Barber, pp. 75–76.

58. Now there is even a fax service, apparently for those unable to make the journey.

59. Barber, *Pilgrimages*, p. 51.

60. Ibid., pp. 100–101.

61. One of the Five Pillars of Islam.

62. Barber, *Pilgrimages*, p. 32.

63. Ibid., p. 15.

64. Ibid., p. 105.

65. The most well known are Fa-Hsien and his *Records of Buddhist Countries*, and a monk by the name of Tripitaka. See Barber, *Pilgrimages*, pp. 106–108.

66. Munro, *On Glory Roads*, p. 20.

67. Barber, *Pilgrimages*, p. 81.

68. Quoted by Barber, p. 143.

■ CHAPTER *3*   *Elements and Experience*

1. See Kevin Lynch, *The Image of the City* (Cambridge: MIT Press, 1960).

2. J. G. Davies, *Temples, Churches and Mosques: A Guide to the Appreciation of Religious Architecture* (Oxford: Basil Blackwell, 1982), pp. 240–41.

3. Kent C. Bloomer and Charles Moore, *Body, Memory, and Architecture* (New Haven: Yale University Press, 1977), pp. 77–104.

4. Christian Norberg-Schulz, *Existence, Space and Architecture* (New York: Praeger Publishers, 1971), p. 18.

5. Norberg-Schulz, *Architecture: Meaning and Place* (New York: Electa/Rizzoli, 1988), p. 24.

6. However, unlike Davies, I will not consign the examples to mutually exclusive categories of path and place. In-

stead, the examples studied are distinguished because they comprise both path and place. Indeed, I believe that one would be hard-pressed to find an example that is either/or. Davies's otherwise excellent survey of religious architecture is at times limited by overcategorization based on the two types.

7. Geörgy Doczi, *The Power of Limits: Proportional Harmonies in Nature, Art and Architecture.* (Boulder and London: Shambhala Publications, 1981), preface.

8. Hertzberger, *Lessons*, p. 93.

9. See Francis D. K. Ching, *Architecture: Space, Form and Order* (New York: Van Nostrand Reinhold, 1979).

10. See Thomas Thiis-Evensen, *Archetypes in Architecture* (Oxford: Oxford University Press, 1987).

11. See Steen Eiler Rasmussen, *Experiencing Architecture* (Cambridge: MIT Press, 1964), p. 48.

12. As Alberti said, "Colonnades are nothing (but) a perforated wall" (from the *Ten Books of Architecture*). Quoted by Pierre von Meiss, *Elements of Architecture: From Form to Place* (Van Nostrand Reinhold, 1990), p. 102.

13. Diane Ackerman, *A Natural History of the Senses* (New York: Vintage Books, 1991), p. 229.

14. Ibid., p. 230.

15. Edward T. Hall, *The Hidden Dimension* (Garden City, N.Y.: Anchor Books, 1969), p. 93.

16. Bruno Zevi, *Architecture As Space* (New York: Horizon Press, 1957), pp. 22–32.

17. Sigfried Giedion, *Architecture and the Phenomena of Transition* (Cambridge: Harvard University Press, 1971), pp. 2–6.

18. See Hall, *Hidden Dimension*, p. 153.

19. Rasmussen, *Experiencing Architecture*, p. 46.

20. Pierre von Meiss uses the terms *implicit* and *explicit*. *Elements of Architecture*, pp. 101–102.

21. Rasmussen, *Experiencing Architecture*, p. 33.

22. Zevi, *Architecture As Space*, p. 27.

23. von Meiss, *Elements of Architecture*, p. 15.

24. Quoted by Rudolf Arnheim, *The Dynamics of Architectural Form* (Berkeley and Los Angeles: University of California Press, 1977), p. 152.

25. Ibid., p. 20.

26. See Rasmussen, *Experiencing Architecture*, p. 36.

27. See Arnheim, *Dynamics of Architectural Form*, pp. 211–12.

28. See Rudolf Arnheim, *Toward a Psychology of Art* (Berkeley, Calif.: University of California Press, 1966).

29. Rasmussen, *Experiencing Architecture*, p. 35.

30. Children, as Piaget has documented, make use of comparison of the known with unknown to structure their perception of the environment.

31. These terms are described succinctly by Dorothy Singer and Tracey Revenson in *A Piaget Primer* (New York: International Universities Press, 1985).

32. Hall, *Hidden Dimension*, p. 66.

33. Rasmussen, *Experiencing Architecture*, p. 36.

34. In young children, however, this may also be the result of their developmental stage.

35. J. B. Priestley, *Man and Time* (New York: Dell Publishing, 1964), pp. 44–45.

36. Ibid., p. 95.

■ **CHAPTER 4**   *The Sacred Path and Place*

1. T. C. McLuhan, *Touch the Earth: A Self-Portrait of Indian Existence* (New York: Simon and Schuster, 1971), p. 28.

2. Norberg-Schulz, *Existence, Space and Architecture*, p. 12.

3. Eliade, *Sacred and the Profane*, p. 27.

4. Kostof, *Settings and Rituals*, p. 139.

5. Eliade, *Sacred and the Profane*, p. 32.

6. McLuhan, *Touch the Earth*, pp. 170–71.

7. Eliade, *Sacred and the Profane*, p. 58.

8. Campbell, *The Hero*, p. 383.

9. Mircea Eliade, *Patterns in Comparative Religion* (London: Sheed and Ward, 1958), pp. 370–71.

10. The island was one of the earliest seats of Christianity on the British Isles. Saint Cuthbert was the sixth bishop of Lindisfarne Priory, a position he assumed in 685 CE after spending nine years in solitude and prayer on the even more remote Inner Farne Island. The Lindisfarne Gospels were produced at the priory between 698 and 721 in honor of Cuthbert.

11. Eliade, *Sacred and the Profane*, p. 25.

12. Term used by Eliade.

13. Campbell, *The Hero*, p. 43.

14. Eliade, *Patterns in Comparative Religion*, p. 384.

15. Quoted in de Santillana and von Dechend, *Hamlet's Mill*, p. 293.

16. Eliade, *Patterns in Comparative Religion*, pp. 368–69.

17. Mitchell Bring and Josse Wayembergh, *Japanese Gardens: Design and Meaning* (New York: McGraw Hill, 1981), p. 145.

18. Eliade, *Patterns in Comparative Religion*, p. 368.

19. Quoted by Barber, *Pilgrimages*, p. 85.

20. Ibid., p. 75.

21. Quoted by John M. Lundquist, *The Temple: Meeting Place of Heaven and Earth* (London: Thames and Hudson, 1993), p. 7.

22. Eliade, *Sacred and the Profane*, p. 41, and Munro, *On Glory Roads*, pp. 78–85.

23. Janet Bord and Colin Bord, *Mysterious Britain: Ancient Secrets of the United Kingdom and Ireland* (London: Paladin, 1974), p. 77.

24. Quoted by Kostof, *Settings and Rituals*, p. 78.

25. Munro, *On Glory Roads*, p. 59.

26. Mircea Eliade, *The Myth of the Eternal Return: Cosmos and History* (London: Arkana, 1954), p. 10.

27. Eliade, *Sacred and the Profane*, p. 61.

28. Kostof, *Settings and Rituals*, p. 227.

29. Eliade, *Patterns in Comparative Religion*, p. 383.

30. Joseph Rykwert, *On Adam's House in Paradise* (New York: Museum of Modern Art, 1972), pp. 43–44.

31. Quoted by Robert Lawlor in *Sacred Geometry* (London: Thames and Hudson, 1982), p. 10.

32. See Mann, *Sacred Architecture*, p. 115.

33. Kostof, *Settings and Rituals*, p. 227.

34. Ibid., p. 327.

35. Ibid., p. 323.

36. Campbell with Moyers, *The Power of Myth*, p. 82.

37. Kostof, *Settings and Rituals*, p. 41.

38. Lundquist, *The Temple*, pp. 22–23.

39. See Gies and Gies, *Medieval City*, pp. 183–184.

40. Vincent Scully, *The Earth, the Temple, and the Gods: Greek Sacred Architecture* (New Haven: Yale University Press, 1962), p. 76.

41. See Campbell with Moyers, *The Power of Myth*, p. 81.

■ CHAPTER 5 *Many Paths, Many Places*

1. Bring and Wayembergh, *Japanese Gardens*, p. 145.

2. As Japanese culture progressed, Shinto evolved and performed other functions. In the sixth century, Shinto became associated with the deification of the emperor and the royal family. During the Heian period (795–1185 CE), with the advent of Buddhism, the faith became more formalized, and in the medieval period, shrines grew up around trade unions. Shinto as a state religion existed from 1868–1911, during which time most Buddhist influences were eliminated. Following the Second World War the shrines became independent religious organizations.

3. Eliade, *The Sacred and the Profane*, pp. 155–56.

4. The adjacent site, Geku, is dedicated to Toyouke-no-Omikami, the goddess of the necessities of life. Most Japanese feel compelled to make a pilgrimage to Naiku and Geku at some time in their life.

5. See Arnheim, *Dynamics of Architectural Form*, pp. 57–58.

6. Kostof, *Settings and Rituals*, p. 79.

7. Lucie Lamy, *Egyptian Mysteries: New Light on Ancient Knowledge* (London: Thames and Hudson, 1981), pp. 80–81.

8. See Kostof, *Settings and Rituals*, p. 105.

9. Scully, *Greek Sacred Architecture*, pp. 208–10. See also Kostof, *Settings and Rituals*, pp. 171–72.

10. *Landscape Architecture* (March/April, 1986), pp. 44–49.

11. *Lotus International*, no. 11 (1976)

12. Described by van Eyck in these terms.

13. *Lotus International*, no. 11 (1976)

14. As described by van Eyck.

15. *Lotus International*, no. 11 (1976)

16. Kostof, *Settings and Rituals*, p. 58.

17. Christian Norberg-Schulz, *Meaning in Western Architecture* (London: Studio Vista, 1974), pp. 48–50.

18. Quoted in *The Architectural Forum* (January 1938), p. 35.

19. Caroline Malone, *The English Heritage Book of Avebury* (London: B. T. Batsford/English Heritage, 1989), p. 41.

20. Aubrey Burl, *Rings of Stone: The Prehistoric Stone Circles of Britain and Ireland* (London: Frances Lincoln Publishers Ltd., 1979), p. 41.

21. See Rodney Castleden, *Neolithic Britain: New Stone Age Sites of England, Scotland and Wales* (London: Routledge, 1992), pp. 198–205.

22. Burl, *Rings of Stone*, p. 242.

23. However, there was a central aisle that was slightly wider than its surrounding aisles and was axially oriented to the center recess of the *qibla* wall.

24. Kostof, *Settings and Rituals*, p. 252.

25. Norberg-Schulz, *Meaning in Western Architecture*, pp. 65–66.

26. Typical Buddhist meditative mandalas were two-dimensional geometric compositions divided into twelve squares and aligned with the four quadrants. An imaginary path circumambulated through its different sections and passed through a number of thresholds which were guarded by gods or demons. The practitioner would mentally journey along this spiritual path to gain increasingly sacred domains and, eventually, enlightenment.

27. Lundquist, *The Temple*, p. 18.

28. Other Javanese temples dating from after 800 CE, such as Candi Sewu in the Prambanan Plain also display mandala planning. However, though the form of Borobudur suggests a mandala, it does not correspond to any of the 3,500 known patterns.

29. Lundquist, *The Temple*, p. 18.

30. *Mudras* are specific meditation positions based on the placement of the hands and are used for certain purposes.

31. For an in-depth examination of Borobudur, see John Miksic, *Borobudur: Golden Tales of the Buddhas* (Boston: Shambhala Publications, 1990), for which this section is indebted.

32. Eliade, *Sacred and the Profane*, p. 41.

33. Kostof has suggested that by beginning at this location, the ancestors of the *polis* were included as well.

34. The particular type of garden that grew out of the Zen tradition is called *kare-sansui*, or "dry landscape style."

35. Other buildings in the subtemple include the *kuri*, or monk's kitchen; the *zendo*, a dormitory and meditation hall; and the *sodo*, or instruction hall.

36. Called *kato-mado*.

37. A *koan* is a spiritual practice favored by the Rinzai sect. It is a story or riddle of a paradoxical and illogical nature, which is designed to put the mind in a state of turmoil; the only escape from it is transcendence. Probably the most famous of all the *koans* is: "We are all familiar with the sound of two hands clapping. What is the sound of one hand?"

38. Jean Petit, *Texts and Sketches for Ronchamp* (Association Oeuvre de Notre Dame du Haut, 1965).

39. William J. R. Curtis, *Modern Architecture Since 1900* (London: Phaidon Press, 1982), p. 273.

40. The use of only small wooden members for the construction of the chapel was dictated in part by the desire not to cut down many of the trees on the site. All the materials used were carried in by hand.

41. Nominal dimensions are 1.5 in. × 3.5 in. (37.5 mm × 87.5 mm), 1.5 in. × 5.5 in. (37.5 mm × 137.5 mm), and 1.5 in. × 11.5 in. (37.5 mm × 287.5 mm).

42. Unfortunately, the space between the outside space and this wall, so enigmatic from the distance, houses the air-handling equipment for the building.

43. Mary M. Innes, trans., *The Metamorphoses of Ovid* (Middlesex: Penguin Books, 1955), p. 199.

44. This type of approach also had defensive uses, as evidenced by the narrow, segmented entry sequence at the Citadel of Mycenae.

45. See both Scully, *Greek Sacred Architecture*, p. 12–14, and Kostof, *Settings and Rituals*, p. 111–112.

■ CHAPTER *6* *A Journey to Selected Sites*

1. Lamy, *Egyptian Mysteries*, p. 11.

2. Müller Lloyd and Martin Lloyd, *Ancient Architecture: Mesopotamia, Egypt, Crete, Greece* (New York: Harry N. Abrams, 1974), p. 130.

3. Geoffrey Parrinder, ed., *World Religions: From Ancient History to the Present* (New York: Facts on File Publications, 1984), p. 142. See also Mircea Eliade, *A History of Religious Ideas*, Vol. I. (Chicago: The University of Chicago Press, 1978), p. 93.

4. Eliade, *A History of Religious Ideas*, p. 112.

5. Kostof, *Settings and Rituals* (Oxford: Oxford University Press, 1985), p. 86.

6. Marvin Trachtenberg and Isabelle Hyman, *Architecture: From Prehistory to Post-Modernism/The Western Tradition* (New York: Harry N. Abrams, 1986), p. 63. Also, a later typical example is the Temple of Horus at Edfu, which dates from the Ptolemaic era.

7. Kostof, *Settings and Rituals*, p. 79.

8. The hypostyle hall in the New Kingdom was also called the Hall of Two Crowns because this is where the pharaonic investiture took place.

9. A similar "basilican space" was also found at the Ramesseum in West Thebes.

10. Scenes depicting the Festival of Opet are found incised on walls at this temple. See Kostof, *Settings and Rituals*, p. 87.

11. Norberg-Schulz, *Meaning in Western Architecture*, p. 8.

12. Eliade, *Myth of the Eternal Return*, p. xii.

13. Eliade's term.

14. Eliade, *Sacred and the Profane*, p. 157.

15. Norberg-Schulz, *Meaning in Western Architecture*, p. 9.

16. E. Baldwin Smith, *Egyptian Architecture and Cultural Expression* (New York: D. Appleton-Century, 1938), p. 246.

17. Rykwert, *House in Paradise*, p. 166.

18. Eliade, *History of Religious Ideas*, p. 99.

19. Isis and Osiris were both the twins born of the goddess Mut, and husband and wife. Seth and Nephthys were twins of Nut, born at a later date. One night Osiris by mistake slept with Seth's wife Nephthys, and when Seth discovered this, he plotted to kill him in revenge. Through trickery he lured Osiris into an empty sarcophagus which was then sealed shut and thrown into the Nile. Osiris floated down the river and washed ashore in Syria. A tree grew up where he lay, entwining the sarcophagus in its trunk. A local king found the fragrant tree and had it cut down and installed as a column in his palace. It was here that the heartbroken Isis found Osiris, freed him, and brought him back to Egypt, where she lay with her dead husband and conceived. Out of death comes life, and Horus was born in a papyrus grove. He avenged his father's murder by killing Seth.

In another version of the myth, after the body is returned to Egypt, Seth finds it and cuts it into fourteen pieces which are then scattered around the country. Isis finds all the pieces, puts them back together and begets Horus. There were temples located throughout Egypt that were associated with the different parts of Osiris's body and his regeneration, and the Nile is said to have emerged from his lower leg. Horus is credited with bringing Osiris back to life, when after killing Seth he journeys to the underworld. "Osiris! thou wert gone, but thou hast returned; thou didst sleep, but thou hast been awakened; thou didst die, but thou livest again!" he says, and Osiris is reanimated. See Eliade, *History of Religious Ideas*, p. 98.

20. Campbell, *The Hero*, pp. 175–76.

21. Often there were elaborate rituals performed when temple foundations were laid, which included the placing of magic amulets and animal sacrifices in the pit to insure its purity.

22. Davies, *Temples, Churches and Mosques*, p. 12.

23. Sometimes the ceiling depicted mythological themes. For example, on the ceiling of the outer hypostyle hall at Dendara, Nut, the goddess of the sky, is shown swallowing the sun in the evening and giving birth to it in the morning, a theme again of death and resurrection.

24. Cults, such as the cult of the Virgin Mary in fourteenth-century Europe, are an example of this type of transformation.

25. Petrus G. Themelius, *Delphi: The Archaeological Site and the Museum* (Athens: Ekdotike Athenon, 1984), p. 5.

26. Norberg-Schulz terms this a "longitudinal oasis."

27. Edith Hamilton, *The Greek Way* (New York: W. W. Norton and Co., 1930), p. 30.

28. Quoted by Scully, *Greek Sacred Architecture*, p. 109.

29. Themelius, *Delphi*, p. 6.

30. Scully, *Greek Sacred Architecture*, p. 3.

31. Christian Norberg-Schulz, *Genius Loci: Towards a Phenomenology of Architecture* (New York: Rizzoli International Publications, 1980), p. 28, 31.

32. Scully, *Greek Sacred Architecture*, p. 109.

33. Themelius, *Delphi*, pp. 6–7.

34. Aubrey de Selincourt, trans., *Herodotus: The Histories* (Middlesex: Penguin Books, 1954), p. 60.

35. In this myth King Laius of Thebes consulted the oracle, who prophesied that he would die at the hands of his son, and so when a son was born to the king, he had him bound and set on a mountainside, there presumably to die. However, the boy was found by King Polybus, named Oedipus, and raised as his son. Then Oedipus consulted the oracle, who told him that he would kill his father, which prompted him to leave the house of the man he thought was his father and journey far away. In the end the prophecies all come true: Oedipus meets his true father on a distant road and, when challenged by him, fights and kills him. The rest of the story is familiar to all: He meets and marries his mother, and they have children, until one day the terrible truth becomes known to them.

36. Originally there were a number of entrances from the village that at one time surrounded the precinct.

37. Scully, *Greek Sacred Architecture*, p. 111.

38. Norberg-Schulz, *Meaning in Western Architecture*, pp. 21, 24.

39. Scully, *Greek Sacred Architecture*, p. 112.

40. Ibid., p. 5.

41. Ibid., p. 115.

42. See Scully, pp. 109–110.

43. See Themelius, *Delphi*, p. 8.

44. The myth of the slaying of the snake (or the dragon as in the case of Saint George) is repeated in many cultures. See Nigel Pennick, *Earth Harmony* (London: Century Hutchinson, 1987), pp. 83–85.

45. Scully, *Greek Sacred Architecture*, p. 112.

46. Norberg-Schulz, *Meaning in Western Architecture*, p. 32.

47. Kostof, *Settings and Rituals*, p. 127.

48. There are two principal schools of Zen Buddhism in Japan—Rinzai and Soto. Rinzai was introduced in 1191 by the monk Eisai (1141–1215). Soto arrived in 1227 via the monk Dogen (1200–1253). Daito-kokushi (1282–1337) traced his line of succession to Eisai. The Soto school of Zen relies primarily on meditation (*zazen*) as a route toward enlightenment. Rinzai emphasizes *zazen* but also employs other practices such as the *koan*. Part of Rinzai training includes passing through a series of *koans*, for which "correct" answers are needed to progress. In the Rinzai school there is typically a daily *sangen*, or meeting with the *roshi*, for questions, instruction on practice, or to give answers to a particular *koan*. In both schools of Zen, the abbot also gives *dharma* talks to the assembled monks, and as in other religions, there is a yearly schedule of ritual observances.

49. The *honbo* is the monastery's *hojo*, the administrative center of the monastery.

50. The basic world view of Buddhism, as articulated by the Buddha, is laid out by the Four Noble Truths. The Eightfold Path is the Fourth Noble Truth, a spiritual "map" to guide one toward enlightenment. The first truth states that life is suffering; the second that suffering is caused by desire; and the third that the overcoming of desire leads to an end to suffering.

51. See Bring and Wayembergh. *Japanese Gardens*, p. 153.

52. Zen Buddhism is a member of the Mahayana branch of Buddhism and is a result of numerous influences as Buddhism traveled from its native India to China before arriving in Japan. Around 600 CE Buddhism came to Japan, where the native religion of Shinto was practiced. There followed a period of assimilation and a melding of the two faiths.

53. The Kamakura period lasted from 1192 to 1333. The other major periods of Japanese history are as follows:

710–794	Nara-Nagaoka
795–1185	Heian
1336–1392	Namboku-cho
1392–1573	Muromachi (Ashikaga)
1573–1603	Momoyama
1603–1867	Tokugawa
1868–1926	Meiji-Taisho
1926–present	Showa

54. See H. Mack Horton, trans., *Architecture in the Shoin Style: Japanese Feudal Residences by Fumio Hashimoto* (New York: Kodansha International, 1981), p. 13.

55. For a more general discussion, see Heinrich Engel, *The Japanese House: A Tradition for Contemporary Architecture* (Rutland, Vt.: Charles E. Tuttle, 1964), p. 372. Engel discusses the relationship between Zen Buddhist philosophy and its architecture, and among others, makes the following three points: First, the architecture is a celebration of simplicity. Zen, he states, did not establish this aesthetic, but adopted it from traditional architecture which initially resulted from genuine poverty. The development of the architecture was a "continuous elimination of the superfluous," a "reduction of form, space, motif, construction, function and material to comply with the purpose of existence." Second, he sees in the architecture a "unity of form and meaning." In its bare simplicity the essence of the architecture is revealed, and one's emotional response is immediate and profound. Lastly, Engel cites the Zen concept of the transitory nature of life; the architecture, with its simple, minimal materials precariously constructed, speaks of the fragility of life.

56. The regimen of the monastic life, today as in the past, aims at creating an environment that facilitates spiritual practice. Similar to early Christian monastic life, it is demanding and all consuming. The daily schedule consists of little sleep and a pattern of religious practice and work. Central to Zen monastic life is the practice of meditation. In essence, *zazen*, sitting in meditation, is a mimesis of the

Buddha's meditation under the Bo Tree, the setting for his enlightenment.

57. Norman F. Carver, Jr., *Japanese Folkhouses* (Kalamazoo, Mich.: Documan Press, 1987), p. 7.

58. *Direct experience* is a fundamental Zen concept that is related to its mistrust of language and a reluctance to set out specific descriptions of its beliefs and goals. Instead, as in Buddhism itself, it stresses the experience of reality as opposed to theoretical inquiry. For example, some Zen stories recount instances in which the *roshi* slaps the student or twists his nose to drive home the point of the present moment. *Freedom from attachment* is a concept that is related to *direct experience* and the Second Noble Truth. This is freedom from attachments such as preconceptions, desire for pleasure, reliance on certain amounts of food or sleep, or concepts about oneself. Zen reinforces the experience of the moment by the abandonment of all preconceptions and a dropping away of attachments to thoughts about the past or worrying about the future. Similarly, Zen passionately embraces the Buddhist concept of *impermanence* or the inevitability of change and *acceptance* of one's situation at each moment. For example, when one is not discriminating, judging the world in relative terms, then acceptance can take its place. Thus we find the seventeenth-century Zen poet Hokushi saying:

My house is burned,
But the cherry tree in my garden
Scatters its blossoms
As if nothing had happened.

—from **Nobuyuki Matsuo Yuasa**, trans., Basho, *The Narrow Road To The Deep North and Other Travel Sketches* (New York: Penguin Books, 1966), p. 166.

Openness best describes the giving up of theories and preconceived notions—an emptying of the mind. The aim of meditation is to attain emptiness of mind, a state of receptivity to one's "true self" or "original face" (from a Zen koan). *Celebration of the ordinary* forms another underlying thread. With its Mahayana belief in the possibility of enlightenment for all, Zen stresses that *satori* is possible at any moment. Zen, as in other Japanese faiths, does not make definitive distinctions between religion and everyday life; it emphasizes a unity of existence and spirituality. Daily work is seen as an essential part of a monk's training. This idea is wonderfully expressed in the famous saying by P'ang Yun, an eighth-century Buddhist layman:

My daily activities are not different,
Only I am naturally in harmony with them.
Taking nothing, renouncing nothing,
In every circumstance no hindrance, no conflict . . .
Drawing water, carrying firewood,
This is supernatural power, this is marvellous activity.

Simplicity is an attribute that is expressed by the value placed on the austere, essential life, unencumbered by the weight of the secular world. The Zen monastic life, similar to other religious traditions, eschews material possessions, embraces poverty, and emphasizes the spiritual over the material (not dissimilar to the Benedictine credo of "poverty, chastity and obedience"). The *process* of the act of approaching perfection in Zen practice is more important than the goal of perfection itself: not having goals, but simply living life as an ongoing process of enlightenment. Simply put, the practice of *zazen*, at least in the Soto tradition, is seen as enlightenment in itself. As Zen master Dogen says in his *Eihei Koroku*: "This is very clear. Zazen itself is already the ultimate posture of satori. In other words, satori is just doing zazen." Related to Taoism and its emphasis on a unity with everyday life is the concept of *nonduality* or nonseparation. Humans are seen as part of the flux of the universe. They are not egocentric and willful, as we find in some other traditions, but indistinct and passive; the distinction between self and not-self is blurred. Also, judgment—which appears in the familiar forms of good versus bad, or enough versus too little—is discouraged. As the Chinese Zen teacher Seng Ts'an said, "Do not like, do not dislike; all will then be clear."

Spiritual austerities and the device of *tension and release* are part of Zen practice, as they are in many religious traditions. Analogous to the Buddha's experience under the Bo Tree, through rigorous spiritual trials and practices, the aspirant is placed in emotional turmoil, the escape from which is transcendence. Zen, as especially evidenced by the *koan*, aims to turn the world "upside down." By illogical and supralogical methods the mind is put into turmoil, demanding an alternative view of reality. *Naturalness*, or an emphasis on spontaneity, is another Zen concept. Instead of thinking before acting, one instead acts before the mind has clouded the moment with thoughts, memories, and fears. Also, throughout Zen there is a delight in and *reverence for the natural world*. This emphasis, in part, is related to Shinto and its view of nature as a revealer of the "world of reality."

Lastly, there is a consistent effort of *mindfulness*, which in essence is to remain in the present, experiencing each moment in its fullness. The practice of meditation, along with other meditative practices, is the ultimate path to attain a state of mindfulness. However, mindful activity is encouraged in all aspects of monastic life, from eating to raking the stones of the Zen gardens.

59. Bring and Wayembergh, *Japanese Gardens*, p. 153.

60. Nancy Wilson Ross, *The World of Zen* (New York: Vintage Books, 1960), p. 20.

61. A Buddha associated with the Pure Land sect of Buddhism.

62. Donald Keene, *Anthology of Japanese Literature: From the Earliest Era to the Mid-Nineteenth Century* (New York: Grove Press, 1955), pp. 206–207.

63. The drinking of tea in China has a long history. Early Buddhist monks drank tea to combat drowsiness during long periods of meditation. It was during the Tang dynasty that the methods of preparing and serving tea were formalized. During the Sung dynasty the use of powdered tea whipped into a green froth with a bamboo whisk was developed, a method later favored in Japan. Sung tea aficionados also emphasized the mystical and spiritual aspects of tea and used it as a meditative exercise. Zen monks would gather together in front of an altar and ritualistically share a common bowl of tea. It was this communal practice that formed the roots of the tea ceremony in Japan. Tea parties were a popular pastime with the aristocracy during the Heian period in Japan. Often these gatherings were ostentatious displays of art and precious tea equipment imported from China. Zen monks later reformed the tea ceremony and established the form that we know today. See Okakura Kakuzo, *The Book of Tea* (Rutland, Vt.: Charles E. Tuttle, 1956), pp. 22–30.

64. A style of architecture that was influenced by the teahouse and the *shoin* style was also known as *sukiya*.

65. Tatsusaburo Hayashiya et al., *Japanese Arts and the Tea Ceremony* (New York: Weatherhill, 1974), p. 37.

66. Okakura, *The Book of Tea*, p. 33.

67. Bring and Wayembergh, *Japanese Gardens*, p. 174.

68. Bring and Wayembergh, *Japanese Gardens*, p. 174.

69. Another name for the teahouse was *Soan* or "grass cottage." See Nishi and Hozumi, *What Is Japanese Architecture?*, p. 106.

70. Tatsusaburo Hayashiya, *Japanese Arts*, p. 29.

71. Engel, *Measure and Conservation of the Japanese House*, p. 61.

72. Tatsusaburo Hayashiya, *Japanese Arts*, p. 29.

73. Okakura, *The Book of Tea*, p. 62.

74. Bring and Wayembergh, *Japanese Gardens*, p. 154.

75. According to the geomantic tradition, there are certain attributes afforded to compass points that dictate the layout of cities and buildings. *Ch'i* is a term used to describe "energy" present in the environment, with which buildings need to be placed in harmony. The siting and orientation of Zen temples were often based on geomantic principles, with a southern orientation being particularly auspicious. See Bring and Wayembergh, *Japanese Gardens*, p. 157.

76. Koto-in was built by Hosokawa Tadaoki's son for his father's retirement. The monastic use of Koto-in following Hosokawa's death is unclear, though typically temples founded by military rulers became monasteries or subtemples. Today it is a museum.

77. Edward S. Morse, *Japanese Homes and Their Surroundings* (New York: Dover Publications, 1961), p. 15.

78. Carver, *Japanese Folkhouses*, p. 140.

79. Okakura, *The Book of Tea*, p. 59.

80. All dimensions are derived from drawings prepared by Kohichiro Shiomi and Junichi Nabeshima, Kyoto University, and the author's site observations and measurements.

81. At the end of the first space, just off axis from the path, is a small doorway. This was possibly a private entrance to a residence on the other side.

82. Koji Sato, *The Zen Life* (New York/Tokyo: Weatherhill/Tankosha, 1972), pp. 18–21.

83. Horton, *Japanese Feudal Residences*, p. 45.

84. Reiho Masunaga, trans., *A Primer of Soto Zen: A Translation of Dogen's Shobogenzo Zuimonki* (Honolulu: University of Hawaii Press, 1971), p. 24.

85. Shunryu Suzuki, *Zen Mind, Beginner's Mind.* (New York: John Weatherhill, 1970), p. 59.

86. Suzuki, *Zen Mind*, pp. 46–49.

87. Damien Vorreux, *The Story of Vézelay* (France: Ouest, 1988), p. 6.

88. Raymond Oursel, *Living Architecture: Romanesque* (Oldbourne/London: Oldbourne Book Co., 1967), p. 173.

89. E. Baldwin Smith, *Architectural Symbolism of Imperial Rome and the Middle Ages* (Princeton: Princeton University Press, 1956), p. 4.

90. Herbert Whone, *Church, Monastery, Cathedral: An Illustrated Guide to Christian Symbolism* (Dorset, England: Element Books, 1977), p. 120.

91. Ibid., p. 20.

92. Davies, *Temples, Churches and Mosques*, p. 91.

93. Norberg-Schulz, *Meaning in Western Architecture*, p. 119.

94. Davies, *Temples, Churches and Mosques*, p. 98.

95. Apparently there would be concurrent services in the chapels of the ambulatory to serve the great numbers of pilgrims.

96. A word derived from the Latin *ambulare*, "to walk."

97. Davies, *Temples, Churches and Mosques*, p. 145.

98. Ibid., p. 92.

99. See Norberg-Schulz, *Meaning in Western Architecture*, p. 88, and Davies, *Temples, Churches and Mosques*, p. 152.

100. The loss of the original stained glass windows, as well as paintings and tapestries, makes the interior considerably lighter today. However, the chancel is still significantly brighter than the nave.

101. Oursel, *Living Architecture*, p. 61.

102. Whone, *Church, Monastery, Cathedral*, p. 118.

103. Vorreux, *The Story of Vézelay*, p. 15.

104. Smith, *Architectural Symbolism of Imperial Rome and the Middle Ages*, pp. 10–11.

105. Whone, *Church, Monastery, Cathedral*, p. 193.

106. Campbell with Moyers, *The Power of Myth*, p. 179.

107. At Roman triumphal arches, for example, there were often places of ablution for the returning leaders. See Smith, *Architectural Symbolism of Imperial Rome and the Middle Ages*, p. 20.

108. Norberg-Schulz, *Meaning in Western Architecture*, p. 74.

109. Whone, *Church, Monastery, Cathedral*, p. 45.

110. Otto von Simpson, *The Gothic Cathedral* (Princeton: Princeton University Press, 1956), p. vii.

111. Oursel, *Living Architecture*, p. 50.

112. Eliade, *Myth of the Eternal Return*, p. 17.

113. See Norberg-Schulz, *Meaning in Western Architecture*.

114. Ibid., p. 120.

115. von Simpson, *The Gothic Cathedral*, p. xv.

116. Gies and Gies, *Life in a Medieval City*, p. 70.

117. Philippe Duboy, Regina Haslinger, Peter Noever, Johannes Wieninger, eds., *The Other City Carlo Scarpa: The Architect's Working Method as Shown by the Brion Cemetery in San Vito d'Altivole.* (Berlin: Ernst and Sohn, 1989), pp. 17–18.

118. Peter Buchanan, *The Architectural Review* 178 (September 1985): pp. 54–59.

119. Campbell, *The Hero*, p. 25.

■ **CHAPTER 7**   *Arrival*

1. Eliade, *The Sacred and the Profane*, p. 213.

2. Campbell, *The Hero*, p. 131.

3. Ulrich Conrads, *Programs and Manifestos on 20th-Century Architecture* (Cambridge: MIT Press, 1986), p. 117.

4. Ibid., p. 46.

5. Norberg-Schulz, *Architecture: Meaning and Place*, p. 187.

6. See Eliade, *History of Religious Ideas*, pp. 102–103.

7. Campbell, *The Hero*, p. 4.

8. Eliade, *The Sacred and the Profane*, p. 204.

9. A smile, for example, dates from our primate ances-

tors and was initially a sign of appeasement by means of displaying one's primary weapon, the teeth.

10. Hertzberger, *Lessons for Students*, p. 92.

11. As Joseph Rykwert said in his discussion of the fundamental "primitive hut": "It seems to have been displayed by practically all peoples at all times, and the meaning given to this elaborate figure does not appear to have shifted much from place to place, from time to time. I should like to suggest that this meaning will persist into the future. . . . (Rykwert, *House in Paradise*, p. 183). Christopher Alexander, perhaps the most eloquent and strident spokesman for a timeless approach to architecture, states that, "To seek the timeless way, we must first know the quality without a name." He defines this source as "alive," "whole," "comfortable," "free," "exact," "egoless," and "eternal," but, similar to Taoism and other mystical spiritual approaches, he in the end calls it "unnameable" (see Alexander, *Timeless Way of Building*, pp. 19–40).

12. Quoted in Anne Fremantle, *The Age of Belief: The Medieval Philosophers* (New York: Mentor Books, 1955), p. ix.

Bibliography

Ackerman, Diane. *A Natural History of the Senses*. New York: Vintage Books, 1991.

Alexander, Christopher. *The Timeless Way of Building*. New York: Oxford University Press, 1979.

Arnheim, Rudolf. *The Dynamics of Architectural Form*. Berkeley and Los Angeles: University of California Press, 1977.

———. *Toward a Psychology of Art*. Berkeley, Calif.: University of California Press, 1966.

Barber, Richard. *Pilgrimages*. Woodbridge, Suffolk, England: Boydell Press, 1991.

Basho, Matsuo. *The Narrow Road to the Deep North and Other Travel Sketches*. Nobuyuki Yuasa, trans. New York: Penguin Books, 1966.

Bayrd, Edwin. *Kyoto*. London: Reader's Digest Association, 1974.

Bloomer, Kent C., and Charles Moore. *Body, Memory, and Architecture*. New Haven: Yale University Press, 1977.

Bord, Janet, and Colin Bord. *Mysterious Britain: Ancient Secrets of the United Kingdom and Ireland*. London: Paladin, 1974.

Borràs, Maria Lluïsa. *Daitoku-ji, Katsura*. Barcelona: Ediciones Poligrafa, n.d.

Bring, Mitchell and Josse Wayembergh. *Japanese Gardens: Design and Meaning*. New York: McGraw Hill, 1981.

Bunyan, John. *The Pilgrim's Progress*. Sharrock, Roger, ed. New York: Penguin Books, 1965.

Burl, Aubrey. *Rings of Stone: The Prehistoric Stone Circles of Britain and Ireland*. London: Frances Lincoln Publishers, 1979.

Campbell, Joseph. *The Hero with a Thousand Faces*. Princeton: Princeton University Press, 1949.

Campbell, Joseph, with Bill Moyers. *The Power of Myth*. New York: Doubleday, 1988.

Carlo Scarpa. Tokyo: A + U Publishing Company, 1985.

Carver, Norman F., Jr. *Japanese Folkhouses*. Kalamazoo, Mich.: Documan Press, 1987.

Castleden, Rodney. *Neolithic Britain: Stone Age Sites of England, Scotland and Wales*. London: Routledge, 1992.

Chang, Amos Ih Tiao. *The Tao of Architecture*. Princeton: Princeton University Press, 1956.

Ching, Francis D. K. *Architecture: Space, Form and Order*. New York: Van Nostrand Reinhold, 1979.

Clifton-Taylor, Alec. *The Cathedrals of England*. London: Thames and Hudson, 1967.

Cohn, William. *Chinese Painting*. London: Phaidon Press, 1948.

Conant, Kenneth John. *Carolingian and Romanesque Architecture 800–1200*. New Haven: Yale University Press, 1992.

Conrads, Ulrich. *Programs and Manifestos on 20th-Century Architecture*. Cambridge: MIT Press, 1986.

Conze, Edward, ed. *Buddhist Scriptures*. New York: Penguin Books, 1959.

Crippa, Maria Antonietta. *Carlo Scarpa: Theory, Design, Projects*. Cambridge: MIT Press, 1986.

Curtis, William J. R. *Modern Architecture Since 1900*. London: Phaidon Press, 1982.

Davies, J. G. *Temples, Churches and Mosques: A Guide to the Appreciation of Religious Architecture*. Oxford: Basil Blackwell, 1982.

Davis, F. Hadland. *Myths and Legends of Japan*. New York: Dover Publications, 1992.

de Santillana, Georgio, and Hertha von Dechend, *Hamlet's Mill: An Essay on Myth and the Frame of Time*. Boston: David R. Godine, 1969.

de Selincourt, Aubrey, trans. *Herodotus: The Histories*. New York: Penguin Books, 1954.

Doczi, Geörgy. *The Power of Limits: Proportional Harmonies in Nature, Art and Architecture*. Boston: Shambhala Publications, 1981.

Doxiadis, C. A. *Architectural Space in Ancient Greece*. Cambridge: MIT Press, 1972.

Eliade, Mircea. *A History of Religious Ideas*. Vol. 1. Chicago: University of Chicago Press, 1978.

———. *The Myth of the Eternal Return: Cosmos and History*. New York: Arcana, 1954.

———. *Patterns in Comparative Religion*. London: Sheed and Ward, 1958.

———. *The Sacred and the Profane: The Nature of Religion*. New York: Harcourt Brace Jovanovich, 1959.

———. *Symbolism, the Sacred and the Arts*. Edited by Diane Apostolas-Cappadona. New York: Crossroad Publishing, 1990.

Engel, Heino. *Measure and Construction of the Japanese House*. Rutland, Vt.: Charles E. Tuttle, 1985.

Engel, Heinrich. *The Japanese House: A Tradition for Contemporary Architecture*. Rutland, Vt.: Charles E. Tuttle, 1964.

Feng, Gia-fu, and Jane English, trs. *Lao Tsu: Tao Te Ching*. New York: Vintage, 1972.

Fletcher, Sir Bannister. *A History of Architecture on the Comparative Method*. London: B. T. Batsford, 1950.

Fremantle, Anne. *The Age of Belief: The Medieval Philosophers*. New York: Mentor Books, 1955.

Giedion, Sigfried. *Architecture and the Phenomena of Transition*. Cambridge: Harvard University Press, 1971.

Gies, Joseph, and Frances Gies. *Life in a Medieval City*. New York: Thomas Y. Crowell, 1973.

Hall, Edward, T. *The Hidden Dimension*. Garden City, N.Y.: Anchor Books, 1969.

Hamilton, Edith. *The Greek Way*. New York: W. W. Norton and Co., 1930.

———. *Mythology*. Boston: Little, Brown and Co., 1942.

Harris, Rosemary. *The Lotus and the Grail: Legends from East to West*. London: Faber and Faber, 1974.

Haruzo, Ohashi. *The Japanese Garden: Islands of Serenity*. New York: Kodansha International, 1986.

Hashimoto, Fumio. *Architecture in the Shoin Style: Japanese Feudal Residences*. Translated by H. Mack Horton. New York: Kodansha International, 1981.

Hayashiya, Tatsusaburo, Masao Nakamura, and Seizo Hayashiya. *Japanese Arts and the Tea Ceremony*. Translated by Joseph P. Macadam. New York/Tokyo: Weatherhill/Hiebonsha, 1974.

Heinz, Thomas A. *Frank Lloyd Wright*, Architectural Monographs, no. 18. London and New York: Academy Editions/St. Martin's Press, 1992.

Hertzberger, Herman. *Lessons for Students in Architecture*. Rotterdam: Uitgeverij 010 Publishers, 1991.

Holborn, Mark. *The Ocean in the Sand, Japan: From Landscape to Garden*. Boston: Shambhala Publications, 1978.

Innes, Mary M., trans. *The Metamorphoses of Ovid*. New York: Penguin Books, 1955.

Inoue, Mitsuo. *Space in Japanese Architecture*. New York: Weatherhill, 1985.

Johnson, Norris Brock. "The Garden in Zuisen Temple, Kamakura, Japan: Design Form and Phylogenetic Meaning." *Journal of Garden History* 10, no. 4 (1990): 214–236.

———. "Geomancy, Sacred Geometry, and the Idea of a Garden: Tenryu-ji Temple: Kyoto, Japan." *Journal of Garden History* 9, no. 1 (1989): 1–19.

———. "Temple Architecture as Construction of Consciousness: A Japanese Temple and Garden." *Architecture and Behavior* 4, no. 3 (1988): 229–249.

Jung, C. G. *The Basic Writings of C. G. Jung*. Edited by Violet Staub de Laszlo. New York: Modern Library, 1959.

———. *Man and His Symbols*. New York: Dell Publishing, 1968.

———. *Psyche and Symbol. A Selection from the Writings of C. G. Jung*. New York: Anchor Books, 1958.

Kaltenmark, Max. *Lao Tzu and Taoism*. Stanford, Calif.: Stanford University Press, 1969.

Keene, Donald. *Anthology of Japanese Literature: From the Earliest Era to the Mid-Nineteenth Century*. New York: Grove Press, 1955.

Kostof, Spiro. *A History of Architecture: Settings and Rituals*. Oxford: Oxford University Press, 1985.

Kuck, Loraine E. *The World of the Japanese Garden: From Chinese Origins to Modern Landscape Art*. New York: Walker/Weatherhill, 1968.

Lamy, Lucie. *Egyptian Mysteries: New Light on Ancient Knowledge*. London: Thames and Hudson, 1981.

Lawlor, Robert. *Sacred Geometry*. London: Thames and Hudson, 1982.

Lethaby, W. R. *Architecture, Mysticism and Myth*. New York: George Braziller, 1975.

Lévi-Strauss, Claude. *Structural Anthropology*. New York: Basic Books, 1963.

Lloyd, Müller, and Martin Lloyd. *Ancient Architecture: Mesopotamia, Egypt, Crete, Greece*. New York: Harry N. Abrams, 1974.

Lotus International, no. 11 (1976). "Pastoor van Ars-kerk, Den Haag."

Lundquist, John M. *The Temple: Meeting Place of Heaven and Earth*. London: Thames and Hudson, 1993.

Lynch, Kevin. *The Image of the City*. Cambridge: MIT Press, 1960.

Malone, Caroline. *English Heritage Book of Avebury*. London: B.T. Batsford/English Heritage, 1989.

Mann, A. T. *Sacred Architecture*. Shaftsbury, Dorset: Element Books, 1993.

Masunaga, Reiho, trans. *A Primer of Soto Zen: A Translation of Dogen's Shobogenzo Zuimonki*. Honolulu: University of Hawaii Press, 1971.

May, Rollo, ed. *Symbolism in Religion and Literature*. New York: George Braziller, 1960.

McLuhan, T. C. *Touch the Earth: A Self-Portrait of Indian Existence*. New York: Simon and Schuster, 1971.

Miksic, John. *Borobudur: Golden Tales of the Buddhas*. Boston: Shambhala Publications, 1990.

Mirsky, Jeannette. *Houses of God*. Chicago: University of Chicago Press, 1965.

Morse, Edward S. *Japanese Homes and Their Surroundings*. New York: Dover Publications, 1961.

Munro, Eleanor. *On Glory Roads: A Pilgrim's Book about Pilgrimage*. New York: Thames and Hudson, 1987.

Neihardt, John G. *Black Elk Speaks: Being the Life Story of a Holy Man of the Oglala Sioux*. New York: Pocket Books, 1932.

Nishi, Kazuo, and Kazuo Hozumi. *What Is Japanese Architecture?*. Translated, adapted, and with an introduction by H. Mack Horton. Tokyo: Kodansha International, 1985.

Nitschke, Gunter. " 'Ma' the Japanese Sense of 'Place' in Old and New Architecture and Planning." *Architectural Design* 36 (March 1966).

Norberg-Schulz, Christian. *Architecture: Meaning and Place*. New York: Electa/Rizzoli, 1988.

———. *Existence, Space and Architecture*. New York: Praeger Publishers, 1971.

———. *Genius Loci: Towards a Phenomenology of Architecture*. New York: Rizzoli International Publications, 1980.

———. *Meaning in Western Architecture*. London: Studio Vista, 1974.

Nuttgens, Patrick. *The Story of Architecture*. Oxford: Phaidon, 1983.

Okakura Kakuzo. *The Book of Tea*. Rutland, Vt.: Charles E. Tuttle, 1956.

Oursel, Raymond. *Living Architecture: Romanesque*. London: Oldbourne Book Co., 1967.

Paine, Robert Treat, and Alexander Soper. *The Art and Architecture of Japan*. New York: Penguin Books, 1955.

Palnes, James, trans. *Le Corbusier: My Work*. London: Architectural Press, 1960.

Parrinder, Geoffrey, ed. *World Religions: From Ancient History to the Present*. New York: Facts on File Publications, 1984.

Pennick, Nigel. *Earth Harmony*. London: Century Hutchinson, 1987.

Petit, Jean. *Texts and Sketches for Ronchamp*. Association Oeuvre de Notre Dame du Haut, 1965.

Priestley, J. B. *Man and Time*. New York: Dell Publishing, 1964.

Rasmussen, Steen Eiler, *Experiencing Architecture*. Cambridge: MIT Press, 1959.

Reps, Paul, ed. *Zen Flesh, Zen Bones: A Collection of Zen and Pre-Zen Writings*. Rutland, Vt.: Charles E. Tuttle, 1957.

Ross, Nancy Wilson. *The World of Zen*. New York: Vintage Books, 1960.

Rykwert, Joseph. *On Adam's House in Paradise*. New York: Museum of Modern Art, 1972.

Sanders, N. K., trans. *The Epic of Gilgamesh*. London: Penguin Books, 1960.

Sato, Koji. *The Zen Life*. New York/Tokyo: Weatherhill, 1972.

Scully, Vincent. *The Earth, the Temple, and the Gods: Greek Sacred Architecture*. New Haven: Yale University Press, 1962.

Singer, Dorothy, and Tracey Revenson. *A Piaget Primer*. New York: International Universities Press, 1985.

Smith, E. Baldwin. *Architectural Symbolism of Imperial Rome and the Middle Ages*. Princeton: Princeton University Press, 1956.

———. *Egyptian Architecture and Cultural Expression*. New York: D. Appleton-Century, 1938.

Smith, Huston. *The Religions of Man*. New York: Harper and Row, 1958.

Sullivan, Michael. *The Arts of China*. Berkeley: University of California Press, 1967.

Suzuki, Daisetz Teitaro. *An Introduction to Zen Buddhism*. New York: Grove Press, 1964.

Suzuki, Shunryu. *Zen Mind, Beginner's Mind*. New York: John Weatherhill, 1970.

The World's Religions. Herts, England: Lion Publishing, 1982.

Themelius, Petrus G. *Delphi: The Archaeological Site and the Museum*. Athens: Ekdotike Athenon, 1984.

Thiis-Evensen, Thomas. *Archetypes in Architecture*. Oxford: Oxford University Press, 1987.

Trachtenberg, Marvin, and Isabelle Hyman. *Architecture: From Prehistory to Post-Modernism/The Western Tradition*. New York: Harry N. Abrams, 1986.

von Meiss, Pierre. *Elements of Architecture: From Form to Place*. New York: Van Nostrand Reinhold, 1990.

von Simpson, Otto. *The Gothic Cathedral*. Princeton: Princeton University Press, 1956.

Vorreux, Damien. *The Story of Vézelay*. France: Ouest, 1988.

Watts, Alan W. *The Way of Zen*. New York: Vintage Books, 1957.

Whone, Herbert. *Church, Monastery, Cathedral: An Illustrated Guide to Christian Symbolism*. Dorset, England: Element Books, 1990.

Wilber, Ken. *No Boundary*. Boston: Shambhala Publications, 1981.

Wood, Michael. *In Search of the Trojan War*. New York: Dutton, 1989.

Zevi, Bruno. *Architecture As Space*. New York: Horizon Press, 1957.

Illustration Credits

Fig. 2: "Christ Bearing the Cross," after Giovanni Bellini, (ca. 1505). Isabella Stewart Gardner Museum, Boston; **Fig. 3:** Photograph by Bruno Balestrini, courtesy of Electa, Milano; **Fig. 14:** From *The Power of Limits: Proportional Harmonies in Nature, Art, and Architecture* by György Doczi. © 1981 by György Doczi. Reprinted by arrangement with Shambhala Publications, Inc., P. O. Box 308, Boston, MA 02117; **Fig. 15:** Photograph by Bruno Balestrini, courtesy of Electa, Milano; **Fig. 19:** Reconstruction drawing, courtesy of Electa, Milano; **Fig. 24:** Drawing by Kazuo Hozumi, from *What Is Japanese Architecture?* by K. Nishi and K. Hozumi (Tokyo: Kodansha International, 1983, by permission of the authors; **Fig. 25:** Reconstruction drawing by E. Baldwin Smith; **Fig. 30:** Reconstruction drawing from *A History of Architecture: Settings and Rituals* by Spiro Kostof. Original drawings by Richard Tobias. Copyright © 1985 by Oxford University Press, Inc. Reprinted by permission. **Fig. 31:** Reconstruction drawing from *Askepieion* by P. Schazmann, Berlin, 1932; **Fig. 33:** From *Romanesque Architecture in Western Europe* by A. W. Clapham. Copyright © 1936 by the University Press, Oxford. Reprinted by permission; **Fig. 35:** Courtesy of Canadian Centre for Architecture, Montréal; **Fig. 36:** Gelatin silver print with gouache, 1938, courtesy of Canadian Centre for Architecture, Montréal; **Figs. 37, 39, 40:** Courtesy of A. & H. van Eyck Architects, Amsterdam; **Fig. 42:** Drawing of the Ziggurat of Ur Nammu at Ur, after Sir Leonard Woolley's theory, from *The Power of Limits: Proportional Harmonies in Nature, Art, and Architecture* by György Doczi. © 1981 by György Doczi. Reprinted by arrangement with Shambhala Publications, Inc., P. O. Box 308, Boston, MA 02117; **Fig. 43:** Restored axonometric view courtesy of Electa, Milano; **Fig. 44:** Plan from Conant, J. K. *Carolingian and Romanesque Architecture, 800–1200.* Reprinted by arrangement with Yale University Press; **Fig. 45:** Photograph by Charles MacKeith; **Fig. 46:** From *Precedents in Architecture* by Roger H. Clarke and Michael Pause (New York: Van Nostrand Reinhold Company, 1985), courtesy of the authors; **Fig. 51:** Reconstruction drawing by Alan Sorrell courtesy of English Heritage; **Fig. 56:** Courtesy of Electa, Milano; **Fig. 58:** Photograph by Bruno Balestrini, courtesy of Electa, Milano; **Figs. 60, 61:** From *The Power of Limits: Proportional Harmonies in Nature, Art, and Architecture* by György Doczi. © 1981 by György Doczi. Reprinted by arrangement with Shambhala Publications, Inc. P. O. Box 308, Boston, MA 02117; **Fig. 62:** Photograph by Marcello Trancini; **Fig. 64:** Courtesy of Electa, Milano; **Fig. 65:** Redrawn after Bring and Wayembergh and Kochichiro Shiomi (Kyoto University); **Fig. 73:** From *Precedents in Architecture* by Roger H. Clark and Michael Pause (New York: Van Nostrand Reinhold Company, 1985), courtesy of the authors; **Fig. 75:** Courtesy of Fay Jones and Associates Architects; **Fig. 79:** From *A History of Architecture: Settings and Rituals* by Spiro Kostof. Original drawings by Richard Tobias. Copyright © 1985 by Oxford University Press, Inc. Reprinted by permission; **Fig. 80:** Reconstruction drawing by E. Baldwin Smith; **Figs. 81, 90:** From *A History of Architecture: Settings and Rituals* by Spiro Kostof. Original drawings by Richard Tobias. Copyright © 1985 by Oxford University Press, Inc. Reprinted by permission; **Fig. 91:** Courtesy of the Metropolitan Museum of Art, New York; **Fig. 99:** Redrawn after Kohichiro Shiomi, Kyoto University; **Fig. 106:** Okada Beisanjin (1744–1818), *Going to Meet the Noble Hermit*, courtesy the Gitter Collection, New Orleans; **Fig. 107:** Bunsai (active mid-15th century) *Landscape*, (detail), courtesy of the Museum of Fine Arts, Boston, Chinese and Japanese Special Fund. **Fig. 108:** Redrawn after Kohichiro Shiomi and Junichi Nabeshima, Kyoto University; **Fig. 118:** From *The Zen Life* by Koji Sato and Sosei Kuzunishi, © 1972 by John Weatherhill, Inc. Reprinted by permission; **Fig. 119:** Redrawn after Damien Vorreux, *The Story of Vézelay* by Damien Vorreux, (France: Ouest, 1988); **Fig. 130:** Drawing from Maria Antonietta Crippa, *Carlo Scarpa: Theory, Design, Projects.* © 1986 The MIT Press, Cambridge. Reprinted by permission; **Figs. 131, 137, 138:** Photos by Eric Anderson.

Index

ablution, 74–75, 81, 116, 170
Abu Simbal (Egypt), 60
Abydos (Egypt), 76
Acropolis (Athens, Greece), 58, 68, 125–127
Ajanta (India), 30, 60, 66
Alexander, Christopher, 19
Alhambra, Court of the Lions (Granada, Spain), 116
ambulatory, 118–119
Amiens (France), 30
Amun-Re, Temple of (Karnak, Egypt), 30, 87, 149–165, 217
Angkor Thom (Cambodia), 122
Angkor Wat (Cambodia), 119, 122
Apollo, 167, 169, 178, 179; Temple of (Delphi, Greece), 28, 93, 125–126, 166–180
archetypes, 16–20, 40–41, 55–56, 64; 125 (*see also* Jung, Carl G.)
architecture, Byzantine, 66, 118; Christian, 34, 70, 93–94; Cistercian, 70–72, 221; Gothic, 71, 94; Romanesque, 16, 213–232
architecture, sacred, 1–2, 5, 20, 62, 67–78, 84–85, 251–255
Ark of the Covenant, 62, 64
art, 15–16, 191–195, 255
articulation, 6, 148
Asklepios, 28, 31; Temple of (Kos, Greece), 92–93
Asplund, Gunnar, 94
Athena, 126, 167–169
Athena Nike, Temple of (Athens, Greece), 127
Athens, Greece, 53, 58, 126–127
Augustine, Saint, 70–71

Autun (Burgundy, France), 214
Avebury (Wiltshire, England), 74, 111–115
axis mundi, 30–31, 53, 61–64

baptistry, 119
Basho, Matsuo, 1, 26
basilica, 93–94, 118–119, 216–217
Benares, India, 35
Benedictines, 32, 214
Bernard, Saint, 70–72, 214, 259
Bernini, 106–107
Bible: Exodus, 22, 33, 56, 64; Ezekiel, 64; Genesis, 15, 22, 53, 64; John, 22, 26, 224; I Kings, 67; Luke, 26, 224; Matthew, 213; Revelations, 64–66; I Samuel, 223
Black Elk, 23–25
Bodh Gaya, India, 35
Borobudur, Java, 30, 62, 119–125
Bourges Cathedral (France), 60
Bramante, 116
bridge, 12, 29, 57–58
Brion-Vega Cemetery (San Vito d'Altivole, Italy), 232–249
Brunelleschi, Filippo, 58, 68–70
Buddha, Buddhism, 22–27, 32, 35–36, 46, 57, 64–66, 74, 79–84, 122–125, 127–135, 180–213

Campbell, Joseph, 18–19, 29, 55
Canterbury Cathedral (England), 94
Carnak, France, 15
catacombs (Rome, Italy), 31, 33

cathedral, Christian, 64–66, 230–231 (*see also specific cathedrals*)
cave sites, 30, 66, 77
celestial city, 54, 64–66
center, of the world, 53, 61–64
characteristics, 148
Charlemagne, 213–214
Chartres Cathedral (France), 30, 71
Cheops, Pyramid of (Giza, Egypt), 56, 67–68
Chephren, Pyramid of (Giza, Egypt), 63
Chichén Itzá, Mexico, 60
Ching, Francis D. K., 41–42
Christianity. *See individual topics*
circumambulation, 30
civitas die, 64, 216, 225
cloister, 119
Cluny, France, 32, 214
columns, sacred, 63–64 (*see also specific sites*)
comparison, act of, 48–49
Constantine, Emperor, 93, 216
cosmos, image of the, 54, 64–66
creation, and place, 60–61
Croesus, King of Lydia, 169
Crusades, Christian, 31, 34

Daisen-in, Daitoku-ji Temple (Kyoto, Japan), 127–135
Daito-kokushi, 181, 188
Daitoku-ji Zen Buddhist Monastery (Kyoto, Japan), 180–213, 256
Davies, J. G., 38–39, 217
Delphi, Greece, 74, 76, 217; The Sacred Way and Temple of Apollo, 125, 166–180
Demeter, 167
Doczi, György, 41
Dogen, 212
dome, 30, 94, 118 (*see also specific sites*)
Dome of the Rock (Jerusalem, Israel), 34, 119–122
Doxiadis, C. A., 173
drama, 76–77, 231
dreams, 14–15
Duomo (Florence, Italy), 38
Dyplion Gate (Athens, Greece), 77, 126

edge, 37–39, 87
Egypt. *See specific topics*
Egyptian Book of the Dead, 150

Eightfold Path, Buddhist, 188–189
El-Aqsa Mosque (Jerusalem, Israel), 58–59
elements, architectural, 6, 40–46, 74, 251–260
Eleusis, Greece, 77
Eliade, Mircea, 3–4, 164
enclosure, 56–60 (*see also specific sites*)
Engel, Heinrich, 190
entrance, 55, 59, 81–82 (*see also specific sites*)
environment, 37–38, 49, 56, 256
Erechtheion (Athens, Greece), 127
experience, 47–50
Eyck, Aldo van, 40 (*see also* Pastoor van Ars-kerk)

Fatima, 28
festivals, 33, 66, 74, 76, 87, 94, 140, 149–165, 169
folktales, 14–15, 20–27
Fontenay Abbey (France), 71–72, 119, 121
Forbidden City (China), 94, 118
forms, 11–16
Fortuna Primigenia, Sanctuary of (Palestrina, Italy), 104–105
Fortuna Virilis, Temple of (Rome, Italy), 93
Frey, Dagoburt, 39
Fushimi Inari Shrine (Kyoto, Japan), 80
Futami-ga-ura, Japan, 15, 80

Gaia, 167
Gandavyuha, 124
Ganges (India), 35, 61
gardens, Zen Buddhist, 57, 129–135, 193–194
geometry, 15, 67–72
Giedion, Sigfried, 46
Gilgamesh, Epic of, 14, 25, 27, 60
Giza, Pyramids at (Egypt), 56, 63, 67–68
gods, the, and place, 60–61
Goethe, Johann Wolfgang, 47
Golden Temple of Vishwanath (Khajuraho, India), 35, 94
Golgotha, 62
Great Mosque of Cordoba (Spain), 116–118
Great Mosque (Mecca, Saudi Arabia), 30, 34; *see also* hajj
Great Stupa (Sanchi, India), 30, 64
Great Temple (Modhera, India), 74
Greece, 53; *see also specific sites*
Gropius, Walter, 255
Grough Patrick, 28
guardian deities, 60, 81, 87

Guide for Obtaining Audience at the Four Famous Mountains, 35
Gyangtse Monastery, Kum Bum Chapel (Tibet), 122

H. Sergios and Bakchos (Constantinople), 119
Hagia Sophia (Istambul, Turkey), 67
hajj, 27–28, 33–34
Hall, Edward, *The Hidden Dimension*, 45, 49, 212
Hathor, Temple of (Dendara, Egypt), 88–91
Hatshepsut, Mortuary Temple of (Deir el-Bahri, Egypt), 85–87, 151
healing sites, 31–32
heaven, 53
Henderson, Joseph, 12–13
hero's journey, 20–27, 54–55, 147–148, 209
Hertzberger, Herman, 19, 41
hierophany, 53, 67
Hinduism, 27, 32, 35, 58, 74
Hippocrates, 92
hojo, 129–135, 195–213
Holy of Holies, 30, 58–60
Holy Land. *See* Jerusalem
Holy Sepulchre, Church of the (Jerusalem, Israel), 34, 118
Hopi, 54
Hosokawa Tadaoki, 195
human figure, and sacred geometry, 70
hut, primitive, 66

Ibn Tulun, Mosque of (Cairo, Egypt), 74, 116
imago mundi, 64–66, 216, 229
India, 61, 66 (*see also* Hinduism)
in illo tempore, 53, 59, 73–74
initiation, 21–22, 28, 77
Ise Jingu, Japan, 51, 80–84
Islam, 22, 27–28, 34, 116
Israel. *See specific sites*

Jainism, 35, 58
Japan, 35 (*see also specific sites*)
Jerusalem, Israel, 7, 32, 34, 61–62 (*see also specific sites*)
Jerusalem, Temple of (Israel), 32–33, 62–64, 67
Jones, E. Fay, 139–145
Joyce, James A. A., *Portrait of the Artist as a Young Man*, 50
Judaism, 27, 33 (*see also* Jerusalem, Temple of)
Jung, Carl G., 3, 11–18
Justinian, 67

Kahn, Louis, 41
kami, 61, 80
Kamo no Chomei, *An Account of My Hut*, 191–192
Kapilovasta, India, 35
Karli, India, 66
Khons, Temple of (Karnak, Egypt), 151–152
Kataragama, Sri Lanka, 29–30
Kempis, Thomas à, *Imitation of Christ*, 27
Knock, 28
Knossos, Royal Palace at (Crete, Greece), 144–148
Kogaku Soko, 128
Kom Ombo, Temple of (Egypt), 157
Komir, Egypt, 88
Kostof, Spiro, 73, 146
Koto-in Zen Temple, Daitoku-ji (Kyoto, Japan), 127, 180–213, 256
Külliye of Süleymann I, 94
Kushinagara, India, 35

labyrinth, 30, 146–148
landmark, 37–38
language, linguistics, 18–19, 41, 55
Lankavatara Sutra, 237
Larkin Building (Buffalo, N.Y.), 107
Lascaux, France, 66, 77
Laugier, Marc-Antoine, *Essai sur l'architecture*, 66
Le Corbusier, 57, 134–139; *Vers une Architecture*, 254–255
Leonardo da Vinci, 70
Lévi-Strauss, Claude, 16–18
Lewerentz, Sigurd, 94
light and shadow, 87 (*see also specific sites*)
Limoges-Perigueux Road, 214
Lindisfarne Priory (England), 56
Louis XIV, 132
Lourdes, 28
Lugash, Temple at (Babylonia), 64
Luxor, Temple at (Egypt), 70, 151, 161
Lynch, Kevin, 6; *The Image of the City*, 37–38, 208

MIT Chapel (Cambridge, Mass.), 57–58
Mahabharata, 35, 61
Maison Carrée (Nimes, France), 93
mandala, 70, 122, 124
mandorla, 223
Masjid-i-shah (Isfahan, Pakistan), 58
May, Rollo, 13

meaning, 5, 51–54, 148
Mecca, Saudi Arabia, 30, 34, 62
Meiss, Pierre von, 42
"men's house" (New Guinea), 64
Mentuhotep, Mortuary Temple of (Deir el-Bahri, Egypt), 85, 87
Meyer, Hannes, 254
Michelangelo, Buonarroti, 107
Midrash Tanhuma, 62
Mildred B. Cooper Chapel (Bella Vista, Ark.), 139
Mohenjo-Daro, Great Bath at (Pakistan), 74
Monasteries, 58, 214
Mont-Saint-Michel (France), 56
Moore, Charles, 39
Morse, Edward, *Japanese Homes and Their Surroundings*, 190
mound, primordial, and place, 61–64
mountains, 15, 58, 61–64; Mount Arafat, 34; Mount Athos, 58; Mount Badon, 112; Mount Girnar, 58; Mount Hira, 26; Mount Kailas, 29, 35; Mount Mashu, 60; Mount Meru, 122; Mount of Olives, 61; Mount Parnassos, 166; Mount Sinai, 58, 60–61; Mount Tai-shen, 35, 60
movement, 47, 102
music, 47–48, 71
Mut, Temple of (Karnak, Egypt), 88
mystery cults, 73, 77
mythology, 6–7, 14–15, 19–22, 54–56, 73, 253–260; Egyptian, 159–165; Greek, 15, 25, 77, 146–148; Japanese, 25–26; Native American, 23–25, 51, 54

nave, 228–229
Nevers (Burgundy, France), 214
node, 37–38
Norberg-Schulz, Christian, 6, 39, 164
Norwich Cathedral (England), 94
Notre Dame du Haut (Ronchamp, France), 134–139
numerology, and sacred geometry, 67

Okakura Kakuzo, 192–194
omphalos, of the world, 61–64, 76 (*see also specific sites*)
orientation, 37–40
Osiris, 26–27, 150, 164
Oursel, Raymond, 213, 221

paintings, 16, 77, 221
Pantheon (Rome, Italy), 64–65, 93
paradise, 66

Parthenon (Athens, Greece), 68, 127
Pastoor van Ars-kerk (The Hague, Netherlands), 97–103
path, 6, 37–40, 55, 156, 247–249; axial, 79–103, 156–157; circumambulating, 118–125; grid, 116–118; linear, 45; and place, 39–40, 55, 58–60, 77–78, 150, 195–213, 224–232, 251–260; radial, 111–116; segmented, 45, 125–148, 169–180, 181–213, 223–249; split, 103–111 (*see also specific sites*)
path, spiritual, 1, 21, 54–56 (*see also specific sites*)
pattern(s), 16–20, 39
Pazzi Chapel (Florence, Italy), 58
perception, 45, 47–50
Peterborough Cathedral (England), 94–95
phenomenology, 6
Piaget, Jean, 48–49
Piazza San Marco (Venice, Italy), 38
Picaud, Aymery, *Pilgrim's Guide*, 35
pilgrim, pilgrimage, 27–36 (*see also specific sites*)
Pisa, Cathedral of (Italy), baptistry, 119
place, architectural, 37–40; sacred, 51–55; spiritual, 22, 26
plan, Latin and Greek cross, 116; typology, 42–45
Plato, *The Republic*, 67
Pollio, Marcus Vitruvius, 70
Pontigny, Abbey Church of (France), 42, 44
Poseidon, Temple of (Sounion, Greece), 68
Potala (Lhasa, Tibet), 58
priesthood, 30, 165
Priestly, J. B., 49
proportion, 69
Protestantism, 27–28
psychology, 16–17, 19–20, 22, 48
Puente-la-Reina, Spain, 32
Puranas, 35
pyramids, 56, 62–64, 67–68
Pyramid Texts, 63

quadrata, Roman, 115–116, 118

Rasmussen, Steen Eiler, 46–49
Reims, France, 30
religion, 7, 15, 19–20
reliquary, 28–31 (*see also specific sites*)
Renaissance (Europe), 68–72
return, 21, 31
Rigveda, 27
Rikyu, Sen no, 192–194

ritual, 5, 15, 29–33, 55, 73–78
rivers, 61 (*see also specific sites*)
Roc Amadour (France), 29
Roman Empire, 93, 105, 125, 213–216, 225
Rome, Italy, 33 (*see also specific sites*)
Rykwert, Joseph, 256

Saarinen, Eero, 57–58
Saint Albans Cathedral (England), 94
Saint Catherine's Monastery (Sinai Penninsula), 58; "Steps of Repentance," 60
Saint Gall, ideal monastery of, 94
Saint George, Convent of (Cairo, Egypt), 74
Saint Peter's Cathedral (Rome, Italy), 33, 106–107, 116
Saint Pierre (Cluny III), Abbey Church of (France), 94
Saint Quentin (France), 30
Sainte Madeleine, Cathedral of (Véselay, France), 60, 213–232
Sainte-Marie-de-la-Tourette, Couvent de (France), 57
saints, 31, 214–215
San Giovanni in Laterano (Rome, Italy), 93
San Lorenzo (Florence, Italy), 68–71
San Spirito (Florence, Italy), 94
San Vitale (Ravenna, Italy), 119
San Zeno, Basilica of (Verona, Italy), 60, 93
Santa Costanza (Rome, Italy), 118–119
Santa Maria (Rome, Italy), 47
Santa Sabina (Rome, Italy), 93
Sant' Andrea (Mantua, Italy), 58, 94
Sant'Angelo, Castel, Pont (Rome, Italy), 106
Santiago de Compostela, Cathedral of (Spain), 29, 32, 94, 105–106
Sarnath, India, 35
Saussure, Ferdinand de, 18
scale, 47, 49 (*see also specific sites*)
Scarpa, Carlo, 232–249
scholar-retreat, 191–192, 210
Scrovegni Chapel (Padua, Italy), 5
Scully, Vincent, 93, 173
separation, 21–22, 28–29
Shakespeare, William, 50
Shimogamo Shrine (Kyoto, Japan), 81–83
Shinto, 15, 32, 79–84 102 (*see also specific sites*)
Shoin style, 190, 196, 200
sight, vision, 45, 47–50
signs, 13

Silbury Hill (England), 62–63
Simpson, Otto von, 229
Smith, E. Balwin, 163, 225
Solomon's Temple (Jerusalem, Israel), 67 (*see also* Jerusalem, Temple of)
space, 6, 40–46, 58, 64, 216
Speyer Cathedral (Germany), 94
spiritual journey, 27–36 (*see also specific sites*)
Sterne, Laurence, *Tristram Shandy*, 50
stone circles and earthworks (British Isles), 112 (*see also specific sites*)
Stonehenge (England), 15, 112–115
Strasbourg Cathedral (France), 60
structure(s), 16–20
stupa, 64
Sultan Hassain, Mosque of (Cairo, Egypt), 74–75
Suger, Abbot, 71, 119
Sun, Temple of the (Teothuacán, Mexico), 62, 118
Superstudio, 255
Suzuki, Shunryu, 212
symbolism, symbols, 11–16

Taj Mahal (Agra, India), 68
Taoism, 27, 58
teahouses, Zen Buddhist, 74, 192–194, 239
Telesterion (Eleusis, Greece), 77
Tell el-Amarna, Egypt, 162
Tell Halaf, Syria, 60
temple, sacred, 67; Buddhist, 57, 61, 64, 66, 74, 94, 119–125, 127–135, 180–213; Egyptian, 63, 67–68, 85–91, 149–165; Greek, 68, 91–93, 125–127, 166–180; Islamic, 30, 34, 58–60, 62, 64, 74–75, 94, 116–122; Mesopotamian, 103, 105; Roman, 93–94, 104–105, 118; Shinto, 79–87; Taoist, 58 (*see also Christian religious sites*)
Thiis-Evensen, Thomas, 41–42
Thorncrown Chapel (Eureka Springs, Ark.), 139–144
threshold, 58–59, 74 (*see also specific sites*)
Tillich, Paul, 13–14
time, 47, 49–50, 73–74; *in illo tempore*, 53, 59, 73–74
Tolstoy, L. N., *War and Peace*, 50
topping-off ceremonies (crypto-religious behavior), 3, 62
Treasury of the Athenians (Delphi, Greece), 170–173
Treasury of Atreus (Mycenae, Greece), 91–92

Unity Temple (Oak Park, Ill.), 107–110, 136, 138
Ur-Nammu, Ziggurat of (Ur, Iraq), 62, 103–105

van Eyck, Aldo, 40, 97–102
Vastu-purusha, 70
Vastuvidya, 66
Vatican (Rome, Italy), 106–107 (*see also* St. Peter's Cathedral)
Versailles, France, 116
Viatuvida, 70
vision. *See* sight, vision
volume. *See* space

water (symbolism of), 74–75 (*see also* ablution, *specific sites*)
Whitby Abbey, 43

Woodland Cemetery (Sweden), 94–97
Wright, Frank Lloyd, 66, 107–111

Zen Buddhism, 189–190 (*see also specific sites*)
Zeus, 15, 167
Zevi, Bruno, 45–46
ziggurats (Mesopotamian). *See* Ur-nammu, Ziggurat of
Zoser, Pyramid of King (Saqqara, Egypt), 63
Zwartnots, Church of (Armenia), 119